Robert Christie

A History of the Late Province of Lower Canada

Parliamentary and Political, from the Commencement...: Vol. II.

Robert Christie

A History of the Late Province of Lower Canada
Parliamentary and Political, from the Commencement...: Vol. II.

ISBN/EAN: 9783337078614

Printed in Europe, USA, Canada, Australia, Japan

Cover: Foto ©ninafisch / pixelio.de

More available books at **www.hansebooks.com**

QUEBEC

A HISTORY

OF THE

LATE PROVINCE

OF

LOWER CANADA

PARLIAMENTARY AND POLITICAL

FROM THE COMMENCEMENT TO THE CLOSE OF ITS
EXISTENCE AS A SEPARATE PROVINCE.

By ROBERT CHRISTIE.

IN SIX VOLUMES.

VOL. II.

MONTREAL:
RICHARD WORTHINGTON,
PUBLISHER AND BOOKSELLER.
1866.

Entered, according to act of the Provincial Legislature, in the year one thousand eight hundred and sixty-five, "for the protection of copy rights in this province," by RICHD. WORTHINGTON, in the office of the Registrar of the province of Canada.

August, 1865.

NOTICE.

This volume, commencing with the administration of sir George Prevost, in 1811, brings the history of the province down to the close of 1822; relating the military and naval operations in the Canadas, during the late war with the United States—parliamentary proceedings, and other important public matters in Lower Canada, with ample notices of the impeachments of chief justices Sewell and Monk, and subsequently of Mr. justice Foucher—and their results—the several administrations of sir Gordon Drummond—Sir John Coape Sherbrooke—the duke of Richmond—Mr. Monk—sir Peregrine Maitland—and the first and second years of lord Dalhousie's administration—containing a variety of statistical and other useful and interesting information relating to the government, and public affairs of the province during that period—the call upon the assembly, in 1818, to make provision for the civil list, pursuant to its offer in 1810 to that effect—the beginning of the so called " financial difficulties" arising from it, between the executive government and the assembly—the misunderstanding with Upper Canada, on matters of finance—introduction of the union bill, in 1822, in the house of commons, in consequence thereof—consternation in Lower Canada by reason of the projected union—petitions for and against it, and the arguments *pro* and *con*, as given at public meetings and embodied in the petitions forwarded to England on the subject.

CHAPTER XIV.

Lieut.-general Sir George Prevost arrives from Halifax—assumes the government—major-general Brock administrator of the government in Upper Canada—parliament meets—proceedings—bill for the better preservation of his Majesty's government lost—alien bill also—militia bill passed—liberal provisions in contemplation of war—finances of 1811—prorogation—finances, &c.—"the *Henry plot*,"—four battalions of militia embodied in contemplation of war—war declared against Great Britain by the United States—legislature convoked—measures adopted—sedentary militia do garrison duty in Quebec and Montreal—riotous assemblage at Lachine—put down—hostilities commence—Michillimackinac taken from the enemy—general Hull invades Upper Canada—driven back upon Detroit—capitulation and surrender of that fort to general Brock—general Hull and his army sent to Montreal prisoners of war—armistice between Sir George Prevost and general Dearborn, commanding the American forces, disallowed by the president of the United States.

AFTER an interregnum of nearly three months, Sir George Prevost, the late lieut.-governor of Nova Scotia, arrived at Quebec, and assumed, on the 14th September, 1811, the government of Lower Canada, as successor to Sir James H. Craig, in command of the british north american provinces. The popularity of his administration in Nova Scotia, afforded a hope that his government in Lower Canada, would prove more auspicious than the preceding. The trying juncture into which the policy of America hurried these provinces, impressed the people with serious apprehensions, and all parties seemed to concur in a desire for unanimity, as essential to the public security.

Soon after his excellency's arrival, major-general Brock was appointed president and administrator of the government in Upper Canada, instead of lieut.-governor Gore, who had recently retired. To obtain a local knowledge of the frontiers of the lower province, which were likely soon to become the theatre of war, his excellency, shortly after his arrival, set out on a tour of inspection, visiting in the district of Montreal, the forts of St. John, Chambly, William Henry, and the military positions in their neighbourhood. From the period of his arrival until the opening of parliament, we meet with no extraordinary occurrence.

The parliament met on the 21st of February, 1812. The governor in his speech informed the legislature that having been appointed by the Prince Regent to the chief command of the british american provinces, he had hastened, in obedience to his orders, to assume the administration of Lower Canada, but that his commission not having arrived, he continued to administer the government under a provisional authority to that effect. He congratulated them on the brilliant achievements which had attended the british arms in the deliverance of Portugal, and for the rescue of Spain from the tyranny of the ruler of France. " Notwithstanding"—said he—" the astonishing changes that mark the age in which we live, the inhabitants of this portion of the empire have witnessed but as remote spectators the awful scenes which desolate Europe; and while Britain, " built by nature for herself against infection and the hand of war," has had her political existence involved in the fate of surrounding nations, you have hitherto, undisturbed in the habitations of your fathers, viewed without alarm the distant storm which now seems bending its course towards this peaceful and happy region." He recommended an increased and unremitting care and vigilance in securing the colony from either open invasion or insidious aggression, and he hoped the parliament would testify its loyalty by an early attention to those acts, which experience had proved essential for the preservation of his Majesty's government, as also by its readiness in supplying government with such aid as should be suitable to the exigence of the times, by enabling the loyal canadian subjects to assist in repelling any sudden attack made by a tumultuary force, and effectually to participate in the defence of their country against a regular invasion at any future period.

The assembly in answer, assured the governor that they would give their attention to those acts which he regarded as essential to his Majesty's government, notwithstanding the repugnance they might feel from an improper use of one of them, and the bad effects which might have resulted therefrom to his Majesty's government, had it not been for the unshaken fidelity of his Majesty's loyal canadian subjects, and their conviction of the goodness of his government, and the transient inconveniences which, from the common fate of human things, were inevitable: assuring him however, that the confidence they placed in his excellency, considerably diminished their fears of the use which might thereafter be made of this act. In reply to this, the governor briefly expressed his regret that they should have thought it expedient to revert to any proceedings which had taken place under any one of those acts, and earnestly recommended to them as the most effectual means of ensuring tranquillity to the province, and of evincing their zeal for the public good, to direct their attention solely to the present situation of affairs.

But they were too deeply concerned in the events of the last administration to leave them at rest, and at an advanced period of the session they came to the resolution :—

"That it is a justice due to the good character of his Majesty's canadian subjects in this province, that some measure should be adopted by this house, to acquaint his Majesty of the events which took place in this province under the administration of *Sir James Henry Craig*, its late governor, and the causes which gave rise to the same ; in order that his Majesty, in his paternal goodness, may take such steps as will prevent the recurrence of a similar administration, which tends to misrepresent the good and faithful people of this province, and to deprive them of the confidence and affection of his Majesty, and from feeling the good effects of his government, in the ample manner that the law has provided."

It was, in addition to this, resolved, on motion of Mr. Lee, seconded by Mr. L. J. Papineau, "that an inquiry be made into the state of the province, and the public events which took place, under the administration of *Sir James Henry Craig*, and into the causes that gave rise thereto."* A committee of five members, was appointed accordingly to proceed upon the inquiry—consisting of Messrs. Lee, L. J. Papineau, P. Bedard, Viger and Papineau, to whom Messrs. Bellet, Roi and Blanchet were subsequently added, and upon motion of Mr. Lee, seconded by Mr. L. J. Papineau, it was resolved, "that the said committee be a secret committee." The result of its labours has never transpired; and it would seem that these resolutions were not carried into effect, owing to the intervention of more urgent concerns. In the mean time a bill, "for the better preservation of his Majesty's government," was passed, and sent down from the legislative council to the lower house. Here several amendments were proposed, the principal one of which was, to transfer the power formerly vested in the executive council, of imprisoning persons suspected of treasonable practices, to the governor or person administering the gov-

---

* The division on this, was as follows:—

Yeas—Messieurs Bruneau, L. J. Papineau, M. Caron, Desbleds, Robitaille, Francois Caron, Louis Roi, Borgia, Bellet, Bernier, Lee, Blanchet, and Pierre Bedard.—(13.)

Nays—Messieurs Mure and Cuthbert.

ernment alone; and a proviso that nothing contained in it " should be construed to extend to give power to imprison or detain any member of either house of the provincial parliament, by virtue of and under the authority of the act." The alien bill had in like manner been passed in the council and sent down to the assembly, who also amended it. The legislative council disapproving of the amendments, a conference ensued; but both branches persevering in their opinions, the bill was lost, much to the satisfaction of the lower house; the alien bill was lost in like manner.

The consideration of appointing an agent in England was resumed by the house, but not determined upon. The expedience of providing a fund for the payment of members of the house of assembly was also discussed, and a bill introduced to that effect, which however failed. On motion, by Mr. L. J. Papineau, that this bill be engrossed, it was moved in amendment by Mr. Lee, to leave out the words "be engrossed," and insert "hath a tendency to increase in this house the number of persons who from want of education, are incapable of judging of the spirit of the constitution in its effects."—This brought upon the mover a shower of invective, and was overruled, by a vote of 14 to 4.* The bill was cast aside in the upper house. The militia bill

---

* Yeas—Messieurs Irvine, Debartzch, Mure and Lee,—(4.)
Nays—Messieurs Bruneau, Louis Roi, Huot, Bellet, L. J. Papineau, Augustin Caron, Viger, Gauvreau, J. B. Bedard, Robitaille, Larue, Bernier, Desbleds, and Blouin.—(14.)

passed after much debate in the lower house. The governor was authorized by it to embody two thousand bachelors between the age of eighteen and twenty-five for three months in the year; and in case of invasion or imminent danger thereof, to retain them for one year, relieving one half of the number embodied, by fresh drafts at the expiration of that period. In the event of war, invasion, insurrection, or imminent danger thereof, he was empowered to embody the whole militia of the province, should it become necessary. No substitutes were to be allowed, nor were commissioned officers permitted to take any militiamen as servants, under a penalty of ten pounds for every offence of that nature. These provisions were however winked at in actual service. It was made penal to enlist any militiaman into the regular forces, and such enlistment was declared null. Twelve thousand pounds were granted by the legislature, one moiety for drilling and training the local militia, the other for other purposes of the militia act. Twenty thousand pounds were granted, to be employed for such services as the safety of the province and the exigence of the times might require, and the further sum of thirty thousand pounds currency, to be at the Governor's disposition in case of war between Great Britain and America. These liberal supplies enabled the government to contemplate the approaching contest with confidence in the patriotism and support of the provincial legislature, and of the whole mass of the canadian population. On the nineteenth of May the governor prorogued the legislature.

In proroguing the session, he thanked the assembly for the labour they had bestowed upon the improvement of the militia system, and for the increased means they had afforded him for the defence of the province. He also expressed his best thanks for the proofs he had received of their confidence in his administration, by the very liberal provision they had made for the exigencies of the public service.

The revenues of the last year (1811) amounted to £75,162, currency,—the civil expenditure to £49,017, sterling. The salaries to officers of the legislature and contingencies amounted to £3,934, sterling, more.— The number of vessels cleared at Quebec, was 532, amounting to 116,687 tons, of which 37 had that year been built at Quebec, containing 12,688 tons.

About this time a ferment existed in the neighbouring republic, excited by the discovery of the "*Henry Plot,*" as it was called, exaggerated by the United States government into an attempt on the part of this government, to bring about a revolution in the eastern states, and to dissolve the union. John Henry, an adventurer, of some talents and address, is said to have been by birth an Irishman, and to have emigrated when a youth to America, where through the interest of friends, he was appointed a captain in the militia, and from thence bore the style of captain Henry. Not succeeding in the States to the extent of his wishes, he migrated to Montreal, where he found means to ingratiate himself with the principal personages of this province, and commenced his studies at law, with a view of qualifying himself for a seat in the judiciary of Upper Canada, to which he was already ambitious enough to aspire. He was recommended by some of those at Montreal who patronised him, to the governor, who from the proceedings of the federal faction in the eastern states, suspected a desire on their part, to form a political connection with Great Britain. In order, therefore, to ascertain the real state of parties and their views, Henry, being acquainted with the country, was selected for the mission, and readily accepted of it, proceeding to Boston, where he sauntered away his time in the public houses, writing from time to time to Canada,* his views of passing events, but conveying no information that the public newspapers of the day did not give. Henry, however, estimated his services much beyond any thing his employer was disposed to admit of, and therefore resorted for a compensation to the government at home. In a memorial to lord Liverpool, stating his services, he suggested that the appointment of judge advocate general of Lower Canada, with the salary of five hundred pounds per annum, or a consulate in the United States, *sine cura*, would

---

* This happened in the course of the winter of 1809.

be considered by him as a liberal discharge of any obligation that the government entertained in relation to his services. The minister, unwilling, it would seem, to recognise him as a british agent, coolly referred him back to the colonial government, then in charge of Sir George Prevost. Chagrined with disappointment, he immediately made his way back to America, where, upon receiving a stipulated sum from the United States government, (fifty thousand dollars it was said) he gave up to it his correspondence with Sir James H. Craig, or rather with his secretary, Mr. Ryland. The traitor, soon after this, left the United States for France.

Sir George Prevost, it was soon observed, cultivated to *souplesse* unbecoming, as some thought, his station, those who had been particularly obnoxious to his predecessor, reinstating them in their military rank, taking them into his confidence, and placing them, as opportunities offered. in situations of honor, trust, and emolument, by that means soothing them, flattering their partisans, and reconciling the mass to unanimity and combined action for the approaching war—a policy, though it gave offence at the time to many, at once equitable, wise, successful.

The governor, by a general order of the 28th May, directed the levy of, and organised four battalions of embodied militia in virtue of the new Act. The alacrity with which they were filled, reflected credit upon the canadians. A regiment of canadian Voltigeurs was raised, and placed under the command of Major De Salaberry, (a gentleman of a respectable french canadian family, patronised by his royal highness the duke of Kent, who procured him and two brothers, both of whom died honorably in the service, commissions in the british army,) of the 60th regiment of foot, which, in the course of the war, distinguished itself.

On the 18th June, Congress declared war against Great Britain, and on the 24th, the event was known at Quebec. The province was, however, now, in some measure, prepared for defence. A notification was immediately made by the police, that all american citizens must leave Quebec by the 1st July, and be out of the limits of that district, on the third of the same month. On the last day of June, the period was extended by the governor's proclamation: fourteen days were allowed to such americans as were in the province, as they were principally persons who had entered it in good faith and in the prosecution of commercial pursuits. On the same day, proclamations issued imposing an embargo upon the shipping in the port, and convoking the legislature for the 16th of July.

At the opening of the session, the governor briefly informing the parliament of the recent declaration of war by America, said, he relied upon the spirit of his Majesty's subjects in the province, their attachment and zeal for the religion of their forefathers, their loyalty to their Sovereign, and their ardent love for the true interests of their country; and that he should depend implicitly under divine providence, upon their best exertions aided by the courage and loyalty of the militia, and by the valour, skill, and discipline of his Majesty's regular forces, for repelling every hostile attempt that might be made upon the colony. He observed with concern that the necessary establishment of the militia forces, together with the various services and operations of the approaching campaign, would be attended with considerable expense, but that he relied upon their wisdom and public spirit, for such supplies as the exigencies of affairs might be found to require: he at the same time expressed his approbation of the embodied militia, and his confidence in their increasing discipline, which encouraged an expectation that they would materially contribute to the defence of their country.

In thanking his excellency for his opening speech, the assembly said,—

" We feel grateful to your excellency for assembling us at a crisis when called upon, by every principle of duty, and every consideration of interest, to exert our united efforts in support of our sovereign's rights, and for the defence of this important portion of his Majesty's dominions, and your excellency may rely on our zealous co-operation in every measure tending thereto.

" We cannot but regret that the determined hostile disposition of the american government, has frustrated the earnest endeavors of our gracious sovereign, for the preservation of amity with the United States, and that it has finally manifested itself in a declaration of war, notwithstanding the convincing proofs so repeatedly afforded by his Majesty, of the justice of his cause, of the moderation of his pretensions, and of his sincere desire for a continuance of peace.

"Your excellency may place full confidence in the spirit of his Majesty's subjects throughout the province; their attachment and zeal for the religion of their forefathers, their loyalty to their sovereign, and their ardent love for the true interests of their country, are such strong incitements, that no threats of the enemy will intimidate them, nor will they be deluded by any insidious efforts they may make.

"Proud of the confidence your excellency is pleased to place in the exertions of his Majesty's canadian subjects, and in the courage and loyalty of the militia, we confidently promise to ourselves a happy and fortunate result to any hostile attempt that may be made on this colony, whilst that courage and loyalty have the aid and support of the tried valor, skill and discipline of his Majesty's regular forces.

* * * * * "We are much gratified by your excellency's expressions of satisfaction at the good conduct and increasing discipline, your excellency has lately witnessed in the incorporated battalions of militia, and we are convinced that they will be found essentially to contribute towards the defence of the province against every hostile attack."

The public coffers were drained, and the governor to obviate the deficiency, resolved to issue army bills payable either in cash, or in government bills of exchange on London, but the concurrence of the legislature in this measure being indispensable, as well to insure their currency, as to provide funds for the payment of the interest that might become due upon them, two private and confidential messages were sent to the house of assembly by the governor; one submitting to its consideration the necessity of immediately strengthening the hands of government, by arming him with authority to suppress any attempt to produce disorder or insubordination, and for the immediate punishment of any offences which might interrupt or endanger the public tranquillity, which he trusted the legislature would have the less hesitation in doing, from its conviction that he could at all times by virtue of his commission avail himself of the power of declaring martial law to its fullest extent: and from the persuasion which he trusted was entertained by the house, that in seeking from them a partial exercise of it, he could have no other object in view than the preservation of the tranquillity and welfare of the province, with the least possible injury to the public convenience. The other represented the want of specie to satisfy the demands of the increasing militia and military establishments, and the impossibility of procuring money to the extent required for government bills of exchange. He at the same time laid before the house, an opinion and advice of the executive council, recommending the issue of army bills under certain conditions to the amount of two hundred and fifty thousand pounds currency. He therefore called upon the house of assembly for such aid as might be deemed expedient for the accomplishment of an object, rendered more peculiarly important by the present extraordinary crisis of public affairs. and strongly recommended to them the adoption of such measures as should give confidence in those bills, and guard both the public and individuals against the possibility of any loss to arise from them.

The house of assembly appears to have declined any measure tending to sanction a recurrence to martial law, or at least, to have left the responsibility with the governor of exercising in the event of need, those powers with which he thought himself vested in virtue of his commission: the same house however in the following session resolved that martial law could not be legally resorted to unless with the authority of the provincial parliament.

A bill to facilitate the circulation of army bills was introduced, and the liberality of the house of assembly surpassed the hopes of the executive. Fifteen thousand pounds annually for five years, were granted to pay the interest that might become due upon army bills, of which two hundred and fifty thousand pounds were authorized to be put in circulation, (large bills of twenty-five dollars, and upwards, bearing interest at the rate of four pence per day for every one hundred pounds.) They were made current in the revenue, and to have the effect of a legal tender, and were redeemable at the army bill office, either in cash, or government bills of exchange on London, at the option of the commander of the forces. Small bills of four dollars were at all times payable in cash at the army bill office. All contracts in which any distinction should be made between army bills and cash, were to be void; and at the expiration of five years, all those who might then be holders of such army bills, were entitled to receive the amount of the same with interest

Chap. XIV. 1812.

due upon them, out of the provincial treasury. To defray the expense of the army bill office in issuing, circulating and cancelling the army bills, the assembly also granted the further sum of two thousand five hundred pounds per annum. On the first day of August 1812, this bill received the royal sanction, and the governor prorogued the parliament, with acknowledgments for the liberal aid they had granted him, to meet the exigencies of the public service. This seasonable provision of the legislature, at once enabled government to meet the demands of the public service, and revived the public spirit.

In the mean time the cities of Quebec and Montreal assumed a military aspect. The sedentary militia regularly attended drill and exercise; and all classes manifested a zeal verging upon enthusiasm for the public service.

On the 5th of July, the regular troops having previously left Quebec for the district of Montreal, the sedentary militia of the city, commenced garrison duty, and the Montreal militia soon followed the example.* On the

---

* The Quebec militia was relieved of garrison duty on the 12th of August, pursuant to the following general order:—

" Militia General Order.

" Head-quarters,—Castle of St. Lewis,
" Quebec, 3d Aug., 1812.

" In consequence of the arrival of a reinforcement of troops for this command, his excellency the governor general is pleased to dispense for the present and after the 12th inst., the battalions of Quebec militia from garrison duty. The very satisfactory report which has been made to his excellency of the zeal and spirit manifested by the officers and men in volunteering in the most patriotic and disinterested manner to share the duty of this garrison with his Majesty's regular forces, has afforded the governor general the most lively gratification.

6th, the whole militia of the province, were, by a general order, commanded to hold themselves in readiness to be embodied, and march to such points as might be requisite for the defence of the province; and the flank companies of the Montreal militia, were formed into a battalion and armed.

A movement that occurred in the neighbourhood of Montreal at this time, the progress of which was, however, promptly checked by the interposition of the military, deserves to be mentioned. Some young men who had been drafted into the embodied militia from the parish of Point Claire, refused to join the battalion into which they were drafted: four of the delinquents were apprehended after some opposition by their adherents, who having rescued one, threatened to assemble and proceed to La-

and confirmed the opinion which he was always disposed to entertain of their determination to defend bravely their country, and in imitation of their veteran fathers, evince by deeds, the loyalty they profess.

" By order of his excellency the commander in chief.

" X. LANAUDIERE, dept. adjt. gen. of militia."

They again resumed garrison duty in October:—

" The three battallions of Quebec militia have revived their garrison duty by weekly rotation, they want only a little more discipline to be complete soldiers. This we expect will be accomplished in a short time. That their hearts beat high in their country's cause, there can be no question. A spirt of emulation appears to actuate one and all. The enemy will do well to keep at a respectful distance.—*Quebec Mercury, October 6, 1812.*

" Office of the adjutant general of militia.

" Quebec, 1st October, 1812.

" His excellency the commander in chief has been pleased to reinstate Pierre Bedard and Joseph Levasseur Borgia, esqrs., in the rank which they formerly held in the 1st. battalion of Quebec militia, with seniority according to the date of their respective commissions.

" By order of his excellency the commander in chief.

" X. LANAUDIERE, dept. adj. gen. of militia."

prairie, and bring away such of their friends as had already joined the embodied militia at that depôt. On the ensuing day, a mob assembled at Lachine, to the number of between three and four hundred (some estimate them at a greater number,) of whom, nearly eighty were armed with fusils and fowling pieces. Deaf to remonstrance, it was deemed expedient to call out the military, and accordingly the light company of the 49th regiment, and a detachment of artillery with two field-pieces, under the command of major Plenderleath, proceeded from Montreal, accompanied by a magistrate; who, upon arriving at Lachine, remonstrated with the assemblage upon their misconduct. They, in answer, gave him to understand, that they were informed the militia bill had not been sanctioned by the governor and legislative council, and that consequently, the militia law was not in force. They, however, with repeated shouts of *vive le roi*, declared they were ready, one and all, to serve the king against the common enemy, should the governor call for their services. The ferment was already too high to hope for any good result from argument. The riot act being therefore read, the magistrate ordered them to disperse, and upon their refusing to comply, a round shot was fired by the artillery, too high to injure, in order to intimidate them. This was instantly returned by the mob, with small arms; a volley was then fired by the troops with grape and small arms, but still purposely too elevated to do any harm : this was also returned. Decision became now absolutely necessary, and the troops were ordered to direct their fire against the multitude, who immediately dispersed, keeping up a straggling fire from the bushes, and concealed by the darkness, which began to set in. One man was found dead, and another dangerously wounded. A few prisoners were taken and sent to Montreal. On the following day a detachment of the Montreal militia, consisting of four hundred and fifty men, marched to Point Claire, and from thence to St. Laurent, in the rear of the Island of Montreal, and brought into town, twenty-four of the culprits, who, with thirteen already in custody, made thirty-seven in all. Many others immediately came into Montreal to crave the governor's pardon, which, after reproving their misconduct and pointing out the danger wherein they had placed themselves, he granted, upon condition of their giving up the deserters of the embodied militia, and and declaring the ringleaders. Several of these deluded men were afterwards brought to trial, and being convicted of rescues and rioting, were punished by fine and imprisonment.

Hostilities had in the mean time commenced in Upper Canada, and the most brilliant success dawned upon the british arms in that quarter. Captain Roberts who was stationed at the small post or block-house of St. Joseph's situated on an island in lake Huron, to the north-west of Mackinac, and at about forty-five miles distance, received, on the eighth of July, from general Brock, commanding in Upper Canada, a notification dated on the 26th June, of the declaration of war, with orders to make an immediate attack upon Mackinac if practicable; or in the event of an attack by the americans upon St. Joseph's, to defend it to the utmost, or retreat upon St. Mary's, a post belonging to the north-west company, at no great distance, and to make the best possible defence. He, however, at once determined upon an attempt against Mackinac, and having communicated his intentions to Mr. Pothier, a gentleman of the south-west company, then at St. Joseph's, he was confirmed in his resolution, by the approbation and zeal with which Mr. P. concurred in the enterprise; who, to facilitate it, patriotically threw open the stores of the company, and laid every thing in them that could contribute to its success, at the disposition of captain Roberts, and at the same time volunteered his personal services upon the expedition, attended by about one hundred and sixty canadian voyageurs, one half of whom were armed with muskets and fowling pieces. On the 15th of July, captain Roberts had prepared his little armament, consisting of thirty regulars, with two artillery-men and a sergeant, one hundred and sixty canadians, and two iron field pieces, neither of which in an emergency could be of much service; and on the following day, he set out with his flotilla of boats and canoes, convoyed by the Caledonia brig belonging to the north west company, loaded with stores and provisions. On the ensuing morning, he effected his landing before Mackinac without opposition, and immediately summoned the garrison to surrender, which after a few minutes was complied with, without the effusion of blood. The american officer had no certain intelligence of the declaration of war previous to the arrival of the british before Mackinac.* A quantity of military stores of every description suitable for the indian trade was found in the fort. Two vessels with furs, not aware of the capture, came shortly after into the harbour, but the property was restored to the proprietors, by order of a board of claims afterwards held at Montreal, at which major general De Rottenburgh presided. This achievement, effected by the promptitude and judicious arrangements of capt. R. not only inspired the country with confidence and gave a turn to the present campaign fatal to the views of America, but by enabling us to maintain our influence among the indian nations of the west, which otherwise must have been lost, essentially contributed to the successful struggle afterwards maintained against the american arms in Upper Canada. General Hull after the capture of his army and the fall of Detroit, in his official despatch, relative to these events, attributes his disasters to the fall of Mackinac; upon the

Chap. XIV.
1812.

---

* The garrison of Mackinac (correctly called Michillimackinac) consisted of a captain's command of about seventy-five men.

surrender of which, as he himself states, almost every tribe and nation of the indians. except a part of the Miamies and Delawares, north from beyond Lake Superior, west from beyond the Mississippi, south from Ohio and the Wabash, and east from every part of Upper Canada, and from all the intermediate country joined in open hostility against the army he commanded.

Previous to the declaration of war, the american government had concentrated a division of their army at Detroit, and in the Michigan Territory, under the command of brigadier general Hull, with the intent of following up their declaration, by an immediate invasion of Upper Canada, and by that means to intercept the british influence over the indians, as well as to maintain co-operating relations with such forces as might be elsewhere engaged against the british provinces.

On the 12th of July, this officer, possessed of discretionary authority from his government, and having as he thought a sufficient force to secure an easy and victorious progress in the upper province, crossed without opposition from Detroit to Sandwich on the british side, with about fifteen hundred men. Here he established his head quarters, and issued a proclamation memorable from the tone in which he anticipates the easy conquest of Canada, and the hostile threat of extermination and indiscriminate slaughter of every white man who should be found fighting by the side of an indian.* General Brock upon receiving this proclamation at Fort George, issued on the 22d July a proclamation as remarkable for solid reason and the dignity of its language, as that

---

" By William Hull, brigadier general and commander of the north-western army of the United States.

" A PROCLAMATION.

" Inhabitants of Canada !

" After thirty years of peace and prosperity the United States have been driven to arms. The injuries and aggressions, the insults and indignities of Great Britain have once more left them no alternative but manly resistance, or unconditional submission.

" The army under my command, has invaded your country, and the standard of UNION now waves over the territory of Canada. To the peaceable unoffending inhabitant, it brings neither danger nor difficulty. I come to *find* enemies, not to *make* them, I come to protect, not to injure you.

" Separated by an immense ocean, and an extensive wilderness from Great Britain, you have no participation in her councils, nor interest in her conduct. You have felt her tyranny, you have seen her injustice, but I do not ask you to avenge the one or redress the other. The United States are sufficiently powerful to afford you every security, consistent with their rights, and your expectations. I tender you the invaluable blessings of civil, political and religious liberty, and their necessary result individual and general prosperity—that liberty which gave decision to our councils and energy to our conduct in our struggle for independence, and which conducted us safely and triumphantly through the stormy period of the revolution. That liberty which has raised us to an elevated rank among the nations of the world, and which has afforded us a greater measure of peace and security, of wealth and improvement, than ever fell to the lot of any people.

" In the name of my country and by the authority of my Government, I promise protection to your persons, property and rights. Remain at your homes—pursue your peaceful and customary avocations—raise not your hands against your brethren—many of your fathers fought for the freedom and independence we now enjoy. Being children, therefore, of the same family with us, and heirs to the same heritage, the arrival of an army of friends must be hailed by you with a cordial welcome. You will be emancipated from tyranny and oppression, and restored to the dignified station of freemen.

" Had I any doubt of eventual success, I might ask your assistance, but I do not. I come prepared for every contingency. I have a force which will look down all opposition, and that force is but the vanguard of a much greater. If contrary to your own interests, and the just expectation of my country, you will be considered and treated as enemies, the horrors and calamities of war will stalk before you.

of the american, for its presumption.* He immediately convoked the provincial parliament which assembled on the 28th at York, the capital of Upper Canada; and in the mean

---

" If the barbarous and savage policy of Great Britain be pursued, and the savages are let loose to murder our citizens, and butcher our women and children, this war, will be a war of extermination.

" The first stroke of the tomahawk, the first attempt with the scalping knife, will be the signal of one indiscriminate scene of desolation. No white man found fighting by the side of an Indian, will be taken prisoner—instant destruction will be his lot. If the dictates of reason, duty, justice and humanity, cannot prevent the employment of a force which respects no rights, and knows no wrong, it will be prevented by a severe and relentless system of retaliation.

" I doubt not your courage and firmness; I will not doubt your attachment to liberty. If you tender your services voluntarily, they will be accepted readily.

" The United States offer you peace, liberty, and security. Your choice lies between these and war, slavery and destruction. Choose then, but choose wisely; and may he who knows the justice of our cause, and who holds in his hands the fate of nations, guide you to a result the most compatible with your rights and interests, your peace and prosperity.

" W. HULL.

" By the General,   " A. F. HULL,
" Capt. 13th regt, U. S. Inf. and aid-de-camp.
Head-quarters, Sandwich, July 12, 1812."

" PROCLAMATION.

* " The unprovoked declaration of war, by the United States of America, against the United Kingdom of Great Britain and Ireland and its dependencies, has been followed by the actual invasion of this province in a remote frontier of the western district, by a detachment of the armed force of the United States. The officer commanding that detachment, has thought proper to invite his Majesty's subjects not merely to a quiet and unresisting submission, but insults them with a call to seek voluntarily the protection of his government.— Without condescending to repeat the illiberal epithets bestowed in this appeal of the american commander to the people of Upper Canada, on the administration of his Majesty, every inhabitant of the province is desired to seek the confutation of such indecent slander, in the review of his own particular circumstances: where is the canadian subject who can truly affirm to himself that he has been injured by the government in his person, his liberty or his property? Where is to be found, in any part of the world, a growth so rapid in wealth and prosperity, as this colony exhibits?—Settled not thirty years, by a band of veterans, exiled from their former possessions on account of their loyalty, not a descendant of these brave people to be found

time despatched colonel Proctor with such reinforcements as could be spared, to assume the command at Amhertsburgh, then in charge of lieut. colonel St. George. General Hull

who under the fostering liberality of their Sovereign, has not acquired a property and means of enjoyment superior to what were possessed by their ancestors. This unequalled prosperity could not have been attained by the utmost liberality of the government, or the persevering industry of the people, had not the maritime power of the mother country secured to its colonies a safe access to every market where the produce of their labour was in demand.

"The unavoidable and immediate consequence of a separation from Great Britain, must be the loss of this inestimable advantage; and what is offered you in exchange? to become a territory of the United States, and share with them that exclusion from the ocean which the policy of their present government enforces—you are not even flattered with a participation of their boasted independence, and it is but too obvious, that once exchanged from the powerful protection of the United Kingdom, you must be re-annexed to the dominion of France, from which the province of Canada was wrested by the arms of Great Britain, at a vast expense of blood and treasure, from no other motive but to *relieve* her ungrateful people from a cruel neighbor: this restitution of Canada to the empire of France was the stipulated reward for the aid afforded to the revolted colonies, now the United States; the debt is still due, and there can be no doubt but the pledge has been renewed as a consideration for commercial advantages, or rather for an expected relaxation in the tyranny of France over the commercial world.—Are you prepared, inhabitants of Upper Canada, to become willing subjects, or rather slaves, to the despot who rules the nations of Europe with a rod of iron?—if not; arise in a body, exert your energies, co-operate cordially with the King's regular forces, to repel the invader, and do not give cause to your children, when groaning under the oppression of a foreign master, to reproach you with having too easily parted with the richest inheritance of this earth.—a participation in the name, character and freedom of Britons.

"The same spirit of justice, which will make every reasonable allowance for the unsuccessful efforts of zeal and loyalty, will not fail to punish the defalcation of principle: every canadian freeholder is, by deliberate choice, bound by the most solemn oaths to defend the monarchy as well as his own property; to shrink from that engagement is a treason not to be forgiven: let no man suppose that if in this unexpected struggle, his Majesty's arms should be compelled to yield to an overwhelming force, that the province will be eventually abandoned; the endeared relation of its first settlers, the intrinsic value of its commerce, and the pretensions of its powerful rival to repossess the Canadas, are pledges that no peace will be established between the United States and Great Britain and Ireland, of which

VOL. II.   C

Chap. XIV. 1812

remained for some time inactive, under pretext of making preparation to prosecute the campaign with vigour; but it was the idle hope of an early insurrection in his favor that lulled him into this supineness fatal to his army. Amherstburgh lay but eighteen miles below him, and the mud and picketed fortification of that post was not in a condition to make resistance against a regular siege. The american, confident of an easy conquest, had not as yet a single cannon or mortar mounted, and to attempt to take it at the point of the bayonet he

---

the restoration of these provinces does not make the most prominent condition.

" Be not dismayed at the unjustifiable threat of the commander of the enemy's forces, to refuse quarter should an indian appear in the ranks.—The brave bands of natives which inhabit this colony, were, like his Majesty's subjects, punished for their zeal and fidelity by the loss of their possessions in the late colonies, and rewarded by his Majesty with lands of superior value in this province; the faith of the british government has never yet been violated, they feel that the soil they inherit is to them and their posterity protected from the base arts so frequently devised to overreach their simplicity. By what new principle are they to be prevented from defending their property? If their warfare, from being different from that of the white people, is more terrific to the enemy, let him retrace his steps—they seek him not—and cannot expect to find women and children in an invading army; but they are men, and have equal rights with all other men to defend themselves and their property when invaded, more especially when they find in the enemy's camp a ferocious and mortal foe using the same warfare which the american commander affects to reprobate.

" This inconsistent and unjustifiable threat of refusing quarter for such a cause as being found in arms with a brother sufferer in defence of invaded rights, must be exercised with the certain assurance of retaliation, not only in the limited operations of war in this part of the King's dominions but in every quarter of the globe, for the national character of Britain is not less distinguished for humanity than strict retributive justice, which will consider the execution of this inhuman threat as deliberate murder, for which every subject of the offending power must make expiation.

" Isaac Brock, maj. gen. and president.

" Head quarters, Fort-George. 22d July, 1812.

" By order of his honor the president, J. B. Glegg, Capt. A. D. C.

" God save the King."

wisely thought inexpedient. During this delay his situation became more and more precarious: three detachments from his army were, on three successive days, beaten back by a handful of the 41st regiment and a few indians, from the bridge over the river Canard, three miles from Amherstburgh, which they endeavoured to seize, in order to open the route to that post. Another detachment, in attempting to ford the river higher up, was put to flight by a small party of eighteen or twenty indians, who lay concealed in the grass. The enemy, panic struck at their sudden and hideous yell, fled with precipitancy, leaving their arms, accoutrements and haversacks. The british sloop of war Queen Charlotte, carrying eighteen twenty-four pounders, lay in the Detroit river, opposite the mouth of the river Canard, so that it was impossible for the americans to convey by water to Amhertsburgh any artillery, of which, after much labour, they had at last mounted two twenty-four pounders. Lieutenant Rolette, a provincial officer, commanding the armed brig Hunter, had, on the 3d of July, at about ten o'clock in the forenoon, by a bold attempt in his barge with only six men, succeeded in capturing the *Cayahoga* packet, bound from Miami river to Detroit, with troops, and loaded with baggage and the hospital stores of the american army, the loss of which was now severely felt. Michilimackinac in his rear, had been taken since the commencement of the invasion, while the Indians from that quarter were flocking in to the british standard. Our naval force being superior on the lake, colonel Proctor pushed over to Brownstown, a village nearly opposite to Amherstburgh, twenty miles below Detroit, a small detachment of the 41st regiment under the command of captain Tallon, with a few indians, who, on the 5th of August, surprised and routed a party of two hundred americans under major Vanhorne, on their way from Detroit to the river Raisin, to meet a detachment of volunteers from Ohio under captain Brush, with a convoy of provisions for the army. In this affair, a quantity of booty and general Hull's despatches to the secretary at war, fell into the hands of the victors, whereby the deplorable state of the american army was disclosed; and colonel Proctor lost no time in sending over a reinforcement of one hundred of the 41st regiment, with some militia and four hundred indians, the whole commanded by major Muir, under protection of the Hunter sloop of war. In the interim, the american general received a despatch from general Hall, on the Niagara frontier, intimating that he could not expect a co-operation in that quarter, which would have created a diversion in his favour. Such was the hopeless state of things when the american general began to be sensible of his danger; his army hemmed in on every side, cut off from its resources, and hourly wasting away with defeat, death, sickness and fatigue, unsupported by any insurrection of the country people in his favour, and unaided by any co-operating army, and above all, dismayed at the report of general Brock's resolution to advance against him, his schemes of conquest vanished, and in the sinking state of his affairs, he saw no other alternative than a retreat to Detroit, under the pretence of there concentrating his main army, and after re-opening his communication with the rivers Raisin and Miami, through which he received the whole of his supplies, to resume offensive operations against Upper Canada. Accordingly, on the evening of the seventh and the morning of the eighth of August, the whole of his army, except a garrison of two hundred and fifty men and a few artillery left in charge of a small fortress they had thrown up on the british side, a little below Detroit, recrossed the river. General Hull now detached a body of six hundred men under lieutenant colonel Miller, to dislodge the british from Brownstown, and open the communication with the rivers Raisin and Miami, upon which the existence of his army depended. On the ninth, this detachment was met by the british and indians, under major Muir, at Maguago, between Brownstown and Detroit, who, after a desperate battle, in which the americans lost seventy-five men, were obliged to retreat, but with inconsiderable loss. On the seventh, lieutenant Rolette, with the boats of the Queen Charlotte and Hunter, under cover of the guns of the latter, attacked and captured a convoy of eleven batteaux and boats of the enemy,

Chap. XIV. 1812.

having on board fifty-six of their wounded, and two english prisoners, on their way from Maguago to Detroit, escorted by two hundred and fifty american troops on shore.

Amidst these reverses of fortune, the american general was startled at a summons to surrender Detroit, by general Brock, who, after having closed the public business at York had prorogued the parliament, and collecting a few regulars and militia, with incredible exertion, had reached Amherstburgh on the 13th of August.* So resolute a demand, struck the american commander with dismay, who at the worst had never contemplated a pursuit into his own territory by the british. He still, however,

---

" HEAD-QUARTERS, Sandwich, Aug. 15, 1812.

" SIR.—The force at my disposal authorizes me to require of you the immediate surrender of Fort Detroit.—It is far from my inclination to join in a war of extermination, but you must be aware, that the numerous body of indians who have attached themselves to my troops, will be beyond my controul the moment the contest commences. You will find me disposed to enter into such conditions as will satisfy the most scrupulous sense of honor. Lieut.-Colonel M'Donnell and Major Glegg are fully authorized to conclude any arrangement that may lead to prevent the unnecessary effusion of blood.

" I have the honour to be,
" Sir, your most obedient servant,
(Signed) " ISAAC BROCK, major-general.
" His excellency brig. general Hull, commanding at Fort Detroit."

" HEAD-QUARTERS, Detroit, Aug. 15, 1812.

" SIR.—I have received your letter of this date. I have no other reply to make, than to inform you, that I am prepared to meet any force which may be at your disposal and any consequences which may result from any exertion of it, you may think proper to make.

" I avail myself of this opportunity to inform you that the flag of truce, under the direction of captain Brown, proceeded contrary to the orders, and without the knowledge of Col. Cass, who commanded the troops which attacked your picket, near the river Canard bridge.

" I likewise take this occasion to inform you that Gowle's house was set on fire, contrary to my orders, and it did not take place until

maintained sufficient presence of mind to return a prompt and positive refusal, upon receipt of which, the british, who now occupied the ground lately in possession of the enemy in front of Detroit, where they threw up a battery under the directions of captain Dixon of the royal engineers, commenced at about four in the afternoon on the fifteenth, a brisk cannonade upon Detroit, from two $5\frac{1}{2}$ inch mortars, one eighteen, and two twelve pounders, under the management of captain Hall, of the provincial navy, with a party of sailors, which was continued for upwards of an hour with great effect. Early on the morning of the sixteenth, the cannonade recommenced, while general Brock with about seven hundred regulars and militia, and six hundred indians, crossed the river without opposition at the spring wells, three miles below Detroit under cover of the Queen Charlotte and Hunter. This small but resolute force, after forming upon the beach, advanced in column, flanked on the left by the indians, with the river of Detroit on their right, and took, at the distance of a mile, a position in line, in front of the american fort, into which the enemy had re-

after the evacuation of the fort.—From the best information I have been able to obtain on the subject, it was set on fire by some of the inhabitants on the other side of the river.

"I am, very respectfully,
"Your excellency's most obedient servant,
(Signed) "W. HULL, brig. gen..
"Commanding the N. W. army of the U. S.

His excellency major general Brock, commanding his britannic Majesty's forces, Sandwich, Upper Canada."

tired. Here every preparation was making for an immediate assault, when to the surprise of both armies a white flag was seen flying upon the walls of the fort, and a messenger advancing with proposals from the american general to capitulate. Lieutenant colonel M'Donnell of the militia, and major Glegg of the 49th regiment, aid-de-camp to general Brock, immediately proceeded by his orders to the tent of the american general, where in a few minutes they dictated the terms of capitulation.* By this, the

---

* "Capitulation of the fort of Detroit, Aug. 16, 1812.

CAMP AT DETROIT, 16th Aug., 1812.

"Capitulation for the surrender of fort Detroit, entered into between major-general Brock, commanding his britannic Majesty's forces on the one part, and brigadier general Hull, commanding the north western army of the United States, on the other part.

"Art. 1st.—Fort Detroit with all the troops, regulars as well as militia will be immediately surrendered to the british forces, under the command of major-general Brock, and will be considered prisoners of war, with the exception of such of the militia of the Michigan territory, who have not joined the army.

"Art. 2.—All public stores, arms, and all public documents, including everything else of a public nature will be immediately given up.

"Art. 3.—Private persons and property of every description will be respected.

"Art. 4.—His excellency brigadier-general Hull having expressed a desire, that a detachment from the state of Ohio on its way to join its army as well as one sent from fort Detroit, under the command of colonel M'Arthur, should be included in the above capitulation; it is accordingly agreed to. It is however to be understood that such part of the Ohio militia as have not joined the army, will be permitted to return to their homes on condition that they will not serve during the war. Their arms however will be delivered up if belonging to the public.

"Art. 5.—The garrison will march out at the hour of 12 o'clock this day, and the british forces will take immediate possession of the fort.

(Signed) "J. M'DONNELL, Lt.-col. militia, P. A. D. C.
"J. B. GLEGG, major, A. D. C.,
"JAMES MILLER, Lt.-col. 5th regt.,
"E. BRUSH, col. U. S. infantry, Com'g 1st regt. Michigan militia.

"Approved W. HULL, brigadier general, commanding the N. W. army.
"Approved, ISAAC BROCK, major general.

whole of the american army, including a detachment of three hundred and fifty men under colonels M'Arthur and Cass, despatched on the 14th for the river Raisin, to escort the pro-

"An article supplemental to the articles of capitulation, concluded at Detroit, 16th August, 1812.

"It is agreed that the officers and soldiers of the Ohio militia and volunteers shall be permitted to proceed to their respective homes, on this condition, that they are not to serve during the present war, unless they are exchanged.

(Signed) "W. HULL, brig. gen. commanding N.W. army, U.S.
"ISAAC BROCK, major general.

"An article in addition to the supplemental article of the capitulation, concluded at Detroit, August 16, 1812.

"It is further agreed that the officers and soldiers of the Michigan militia and volunteers, under the command of major Wetherell, shall be placed on the same principles as the Ohio militia and volunteers are placed by the supplemental article of the 16th instant.

(Signed) "W. HULL, brig. gen., commanding N.W. army U.S.
(Signed) "ISAAC BROCK, major general.

"Return of ordnance taken in the fort and batteries at Detroit, August 16th, 1812.

ORDNANCE.

IRON.		BRASS.	
42 pounders	9	6 pounders	3
12 do.	8	4 do.	2
9 do.	5	3 do.	1
6 do.	3	8 inch howitzer	1
		5½ do.	1
Total	25	Total	8

RECAPITULATION.
Iron pieces of ordnance 25
Brass ditto. 8

(Signed) "FELIX TROUGHTON, lieut. commanding royal art'y.
"Major General BROCK, commanding the forces U. Canada.

"By ISAAC BROCK, Esq., major-general, commanding his Majesty's forces in the province of Upper Canada, &c. &c. &c.

"Whereas the territory of Michigan was this day, by capitulation, ceded to the arms of his britannic Majesty without any other condition than the protection of private property, and wishing to give an early proof of the moderation and justice of the government, I do hereby announce to all the inhabitants of the said territory that the laws heretofore in existence shall continue in force until his Majesty's pleasure be known, or so long as the safety and peace of the said territory will admit thereof. And I do hereby also declare and make known to the

visions in charge of captain Brush, from thence to Detroit, became prisoners of war; and Detroit with the Michigan territory, surrendered to the british arms. The american statements of their own strength, nearly coincide with the british reports, which make it two thousand five hundred men, regulars and militia. The militia were paroled and permitted to return home, on condition of not serving during the present war. The regulars were sent down to Quebec. The british force, including indians, is acknowledged by the enemy to have consisted of only one thousand and thirty men, or thereabout. Our own, no doubt the more correct reports, state it to have consisted of three hundred and thirty regular troops, four hundred militia, and six hundred indians, who, upon the present occasion, are said not to have sullied the glory of the day by any wanton acts of savage barbarity incident to the indian mode of warfare. Twenty-two pieces of iron and eight pieces of brass ord-

---

said inhabitants that they shall be protected in the full enjoyment of their religion, of which all persons both civil and military will take notice and govern themselves accordingly.

"All persons having in their possession or having knowledge of any public property shall forthwith deliver in the same, or give notice thereof to the officer commanding or lieutenant colonel Nichol, who are hereby duly authorized to receive and give proper receipts for the same.

"Officers of the militia will be held responsible that all arms in possession of the militia-men be immediately delivered up, and all individuals whatever who have in their possession arms of any kind will deliver them up without delay.

"Given under my hand at Detroit, this sixteenth day of August, 1812, and in the fifty-second year of his Majesty's reign.

(Signed) "ISAAC BROCK, major-general."

"GOD SAVE THE KING.

nance, the latter chiefly of those taken from us in the revolution, with a quantity of stores of every description, and one armed brig, called the John Adams (afterwards named Detroit,) fell into the hands of the victors.

Chap. XIV. 1812.

Thus ended the first attempt at the conquest of Upper Canada. The loss of Mackinac and Detroit, with the flower of their army at the outset of the war, was a disgrace which filled the american government with consternation and alarm, as their plans of aggrandisement were not only totally defeated, but their whole western frontier was also now laid open to the inroads of hostile indians, and at the mercy of a people indignant at the late invasion.

General Brock having issued a proclamation addressed to the inhabitants of the Michigan Territory, confirming them in the full enjoyment of their property, laws and religion, left colonel Proctor in command of Detroit, and returned to York, where he arrived on the twenty-seventh of August, amidst the heartfelt acclamations of a grateful people, rescued by his promptitude from the ignominy of submitting to a conqueror. In the short space of nineteen days, he had, with the assistance of his parliament, settled the public business of the province, under the most trying circumstances, and having united and prepared his little army, effected a long and fatiguing march of some hundreds of miles: and with means incredibly limited, repelled an invading enemy of double his force, pursued him into his own territory, and finally had compelled him to surrender his whole army; thereby extending the british dominion without bloodshed, over an extent of territory almost equal to Upper Canada. General Hull with the officers and men of his army, were led into Montreal, on the evening of the 6th of September, in a triumphal procession, amidst the shouts of a scornful multitude, indignant at the savage threat of extermination he had breathed in his proclamation at the outset of his invasion. The commander of the forces however, received him with the courtesy and attention due to his rank, and unsolicited, allowed him to return to the states upon his parole; but his officers with few exceptions were sent to Quebec.*

Our miniature navy on lake Erie, and on lake Ontario, though the enemy were making the most active exertions, still maintained a decided ascendancy, and upon it depended the safety of Upper Canada and the future fate of the british provinces. General Brock intended to have followed up his first success by an attempt upon Niagara, a fort nearly opposite to Fort George; which in all probability as well as Oswego, and Sacket's Harbour, the nursery of the enemy's fleet and forces, would have yielded to the terror of his name and the

---

* General Hull was, some months after his return to the United States, and after having been regularly exchanged, tried by a general court martial for his misconduct in this campaign. He was found guilty and sentenced to be shot, but being recommended on account of his services in the revolutionary war, he was pardoned by the president of the United States.

tide of success that attended his arms; but controuled by his instructions, he was prevented from adopting measures, which, probably, might have for ever blasted the hopes of America in the upper province.

Chap. XIV
1812.

The commander of the british forces, conscious of the inferiority of his strength, and uncertain of reinforcements from home, seemed to have adopted a defensive system, rather than incur the risk of wasting his army in hazardous enterprises which in case of failure might lead to disasters ruinous to the provinces entrusted to his charge. Forbearance towards America had long been the known and favorite policy of Great Britain, and there is cause to believe that Sir George Prevost acted, in the present instance, pursuant to directions from his Majesty's government, which, in the hopes of a speedy termination of the differences with America, studied, by temporizing, to avoid measures tending to widen the breach and give cause to the american people to embark heartily in the quarrel of their government.

Major General Dearborn, commander in chief of the forces of the United States, had, soon after the commencement of hostilities, fixed his head quarters at Greenbush, near Albany. which was converted into a military depot, with a view of collecting an army to overawe Lower Canada, and, by preventing succours to the upper province, afford general Hull a facility in his accomplishment of the conquest of that province. Here he received, towards the end of

July or in the commencement of August, despatches from Sir George Prevost, by the adjutant general, colonel Baynes, bearing a flag of truce, notifying the repeal of the orders in council, information whereof had been transmitted his excellency from Halifax, by Mr. Foster, the late minister in America. A proposition accompanying these, of the propriety of suspending hostilities, until the pleasure of the president of the United States should be known, was submitted to the american general, in the hope that this conciliatory measure, removing the alleged principal ground of difference between the two nations, would be met by a corresponding disposition on the part of the american government. General Dearborn readily consented to an armistice, (except as to general Hull, who, he said, acted under the immediate directions of the secretary at war,) and forwarded the despatches to his government, which, misconstruing this friendly proffer into a sense of weakness, and of danger on the part of the british commander, and probably flushed with the prospect of subjugating Upper Canada, refused to ratify the armistice. Messengers had in the meantime been despatched to Upper Canada, to inform general Brock of the provisional armistice agreed upon between the british and american commanders, but the promptitude of that officer luckily had secured Detroit before their arrival.—So much for decision in counsel and promptitude in action, in both of which this excellent soldier was remarkable.

CHAPTER XV.

Montreal threatened by the american forces under general Dearborn—a line of defence formed along the frontier—various incidents—invasion and defeat of the americans at Queenston—fall of general Brock—succeeded by general Sheaffe—american navy in the ascendant, on lake Ontario, and threaten Kingston—Dearborn makes a move towards Montreal—movement of the american forces under general Smyth, on the Niagara frontier, to invade Upper Canada, foiled—legislature meet—proceedings—liberal provision in support of the war—miscellaneous matters--proposal to exclude judges from the legislative council—another attack on the press for pretended breach of privileges—arrivals at Quebec—revenue and expenditure of 1812, &c.

THE american government was humbled by the results of the late invasion, but the capture of H. M. S. Guerrière, by the United States frigate Constitution, a ship superior to the former, in tonnage, weight of metal, and the number of her men, afforded some solace to their wounded pride. The american forces on the confines of Lower Canada, under the immediate command of general Dearborn were increasing rapidly, and threatened Montreal with invasion by St. John's and Odelltown. Their force at Niagara, and on the Niagara frontier under brigadier general Van Ransalaer, was also already formidable, and afforded good grounds of apprehension to general Brock of a speedy irruption from that quarter; while general Harrison was actively employed in collecting an army at the river Raisin near Detroit, from Ohio, and Kentucky. The naval establishment at Sacket's Harbour in the meantime increased with celerity, and the ascendency of their fleet on lake Ontario was by the indefatigable exertions of commodore Chauncey now almost established.

It was, as yet uncertain at what point their main force would be directed; or whether their object was by a combined movement to overwhelm both provinces at the same instant. The shewy, but unsubstantial legions they had assembled, were not, however, dreaded by the british forces, who were supported by a brave and loyal militia.

A cordon was formed along the frontiers of Lower Canada, from Yamaska to St. Regis, where the line of separation between the United States and Lower Canada, touches the St. Lawrence, consisting of canadian Voltigeurs, and part of the embodied militia. A light brigade of the elite of the forces, regular and militia, was formed at Blairfindie, under the command of lietenant colonel Young, of the 8th regiment, consisting of the flank companies of the 8th, 100th, 103d, regiments, with the canadian Fencibles, the flank companies of the 1st battalion of embodied militia, and a small brigade of the royal artillery, with six field pieces.

The road to the United States, from the

camp of Blairfindie (or l' Acadie) through Burtonville and Odelltown, was cut up and rendered impracticable by *abbatis*, and every precaution taken to prevent a sudden irruption from that quarter. The Voltigeurs, with extraordinary perseverance, effected this fatiguing duty in the course of a very short time, under the superintendance of their commanding officer Major De Salaberry.

The slender reinforcements that arrived this summer, were barely sufficient to relieve the citizens of Quebec for a short time from garrison duty. They consisted but of the 103d regiment from England, with a few recruits for other regiments; and a battalion of the 1st (or royal Scots) from the West Indies, and the three battalions of Quebec militia resumed garrison duty in the beginning of October, which they continued throughout the winter, each taking in turn its week.

In September, another battalion of the militia was embodied, principally from the Montreal militia, called the fifth battalion (afterwards canadian Chasseurs). The north west company raised a corps of Voyageurs, which, however, was disbanded in the ensuing spring, while the merchants and tradesmen of the 1st battalion of Montreal sedentary militia, organised themselves into four companies of volunteers for garrison duty, and field service in case of emergency.

A party of one hundred and fifty americans, under captain Forsyth, crossed over in September, from Gravelly point to Gananoque, some miles below Kingston, from whence they dislodged a party of fifty militia, and took possession of a quantity of arms and ammunition, which they carried away after burning the store and a small quantity of provisions. Their conduct is represented to have been disgraceful towards the defenceless inhabitants.

From the frequent interruption of the convoys from Montreal, or rather Lachine, to Kingston in Upper Canada, by the americans at Ogdensburgh, opposite Prescott; colonel Lethbridge commanding the latter, formed the design of dislodging the enemy and possessing himself of Ogdensburgh. With a view to effect this purpose, he assembled a force of seven hundred and fifty men, regulars and militia, and having collected a sufficient number of batteaux, he pushed off in the forenoon of the 4th of October, under cover of a cannonade from Prescott, with twenty-five batteaux escorted by two gun-boats. They advanced without opposition, until mid-channel, when the enemy opened a tremendous discharge of artillery, which checked their progress. A confusion immediately ensued, and they were compelled to make a precipitate retreat, with the loss of three men killed and four wounded. The americans were commanded by brigadier general Brown, and behaved with much coolness and intrepidity. This enterprise, undertaken without the sanction of the commander of the forces, was censured by him; and the public opinion condemned it as rash.

On the ninth of October, the armed brig Detroit, recently taken at Detroit, and the brig Caledonia, with a quantity of furs belonging to the north-west company, having arrived the preceding day from Detroit, with prisoners, were boarded opposite Fort Erie, before the dawn of day, by a party of upwards of two hundred americans, in boats manned by seamen. They succeeded in cutting the cables, and the vessels drifted towards the american shore. The Caledonia grounded at Black Rock, and the Detroit upon Squaw Island, a small distance from the american side. The crew, after a severe contest being made prisoners, a party of men from Fort Erie, succeeded in boarding and dismantling her in a fog, amidst a warm fire of the enemy, and at about ten at night she was blown up. Some lives were lost upon this occasion; among the americans a major Cuyler, who was killed by a shot from Fort Erie, as he was riding along the beach on the opposite side of the river.

General Brock, who with unwearied diligence had watched the motions of the american forces upon the Niagara frontier, commanded by major general Van Ransalaer, was convinced from the movements he had observed on that shore, that an invasion was premeditated, and kept his slender force upon the alert. On the 4th of October a spy was sent over to the british side, who returned with information

Chap. XV.
1812.

that general Brock had moved on to Detroit, with all the force that could be spared. Encouraged by these news, every preparation was taken for a descent upon Queenston. On the morning of the 11th, their forces were concentrated at Lewiston, opposite that place, with a view of making an attack upon the latter; but through the neglect or cowardice of the officer entrusted with preparing and conducting the boats to the place of embarkation, the attack miscarried. Early in the morning of the 13th, their forces were again concentrated at Lewiston, and the troops embarked under cover of a battery of two eighteen and two six pounders. This movement being soon discovered, a brisk fire was opened upon them from the british shore, by the troops, and from three batteries. The americans commenced a cannonade to sweep the shore, but with little effect. The first division under colonel Van Ransalaer, effected their landing unobserved under the heights a little above Queenston, and mounting the ascent, attacked and carried an eighteen pounder battery, and dislodged the light company of the 49th regiment. The enemy were in the meantime pushing over in boats, and notwithstanding the current and eddies, here rapid and numerous, and a tremendous discharge of artillery which shattered many of their boats, persevered with dauntless resolution, and effected a landing close upon Queenston, where they were opposed by the grenadiers of the 49th regiment and the York volunteer militia, with a determination verging upon desperation. The carnage became terrible. The british being overwhelmed with numbers, were compelled to retire some distance into a hollow. General Brock, who was at Niagara, a short distance below, having heard the cannonade, arriving at that moment, the grey of the morning, with his provincial aid-de-camp, Lt.-col. M'Donnell, from that place, and having rallied the grenadiers of his favorite 49th, was leading them on to the charge, when he received a musket ball in his breast, which almost immediately terminated his existence. In the interim, the light company, supported by a party of the Yorkers, rallied, and reascended to dislodge the enemy from the heights. They formed and advanced to the charge, exposed to a smart fire, but finding the enemy posted behind trees, so that a charge could have little effect, they desisted, and separating, posted themselves in like manner, and kept up a sharp fire for some time. Lieut. col. M'Donnell who had joined them while forming for the charge, and was encouraging the men, received a ball in his back, as his horse, which had been wounded, was in the act of wheeling. He survived his wound but twenty-four hours, in the most excruciating pain. The americans having effected their landing with an overwhelming force, the british were obliged to give way, and suspend the fight until the arrival of reinforcements, leaving the americans in possession of the heights.

General Sheaffe soon after came up with a reinforcement of three hundred men of the 41st regiment, two companies of militia, and two hundred and fifty Indians. Reinforcements having also arrived from Chippawa, the general collected his whole force, amounting to upwards of eight hundred men, and leaving two field pieces, with about thirty men under lieutenant Holcroft of the royal artillery, in front of Queenston, as a check to prevent the enemy from occupying the village, proceeded by a circuitous route to gain the rear of the heights upon which the enemy were posted. The indians, being more alert than the troops, first surmounted the hill, and commenced the attack, but were repulsed and fell back upon the main body, who formed with celerity, and upon the word, advanced to the charge under a heavy shower of musketry. The british sat up a shout, accompanied with the war-whoop of the indians, and advanced at the double quick pace, when the americans struck with terror, gave way and fled in all directions, some concealing themselves in the bushes, others precipitating themselves down the precipice and being either killed by the fall, or drowned in the attempt to swim the river. A terrible slaughter ensued, by the indians, whose vengeance it was impossible to restrain, until a white flag was observed ascending the hill with offers of an unconditional surrender, which were accepted. An armistice of three days was proposed by the american and granted by the british general, in order to take care of their wounded and bury their dead, on condition of destroying their batteaux, which was immediately complied with. One general officer, (Wadsworth) two lieutenant-colonels, five majors, a multitude of captains and subalterns, with nine hundred men, one field-piece, and a stand of colours, were the fruits of this important victory; the enemy having lost in killed, wounded, missing, and prisoners, upwards of fifteen hundred men. General Van Ransalaer, before the arrival of the reinforcements from Niagara, under general Sheaffe finding the fate of the day still undetermined, his troops almost exhausted with fatigue, and falling short of ammunition, had returned to the american shore, to urge across reinforcements, from the embodied militia; but they, notwithstanding every menace, and entreaty, on his part, unanimously refused. In this dilemma, he wrote a note to general Wadsworth, who remained with the americans, on the Queenston heights, informing him of the situation of things, and leaving the course to be pursued, much to his own judgment, assuring him that if he thought best to retreat, he would send as many boats as he could command. and cover his retreat, by every fire he could make. But before the latter had time to resolve upon any mode of security or retreat, the spirited advance of the british had decided the fate of the day.

Thus ended, in their total discomfiture, the second attempt of the americans to invade

Upper Canada. The loss of the british is said to have been about twenty killed, including Indians, and between fifty and sixty wounded. The fall of general Brock, the idol of the army, and of the people of Upper Canada, was an irreparable loss, and cast a shade over the glory of this dear-bought victory. He was a native of Guernsey, of an ancient a reputable family, distinguished in the profession of arms. He had served for some years in Canada, and in some of the principal campaigns in Europe. He commanded a detachment of his favorite 49th regiment, on the expedition to Copenhagen with lord Nelson. He was one of those men who seem born to influence mankind, and mark the age in which they live. As a soldier he was brave to a fault, and not less judicious than decisive in his measures. The energy of his character was expressed in his robust and manly person. As a civil governor, he was firm, prudent and equitable. In fine, whether, viewed as a man, a statesman, or a soldier, he equally deserves the esteem and respect of his contemporaries and of posterity. The indians, who flocked to his standard, were enthusiastically attached to him. He fell at the early age of forty-two years. The remains of this gallant officer were, during the funeral service, honored with a discharge of minute guns from the american, as well as british batteries, and with those of his aid-de-camp lieutenant colonel M'Donnell, interred in the same grave at Fort George, on the 16th October, amidst the tears of an affectionate soldiery and a grateful people, who will revere his memory, and hold up to their posterity the imperishable name of Brock.

Chap. XV.
1812.

The civil and military commands in Upper Canada now devolved upon major general Sheaffe, a friend and fellow soldier of his predecessor. He paroled general Wadsworth and some of the principal officers. The remainder were sent to Quebec. Among the american prisoners, twenty-three men were found, who having declared themselves british born subjects were sent to England for trial as traitors. This gave occasion to retaliate upon british prisoners in America, and a like number of the latter were put into close confinement as hostages for the safety of the traitors, by order of the american government. This circumstance led to discussions that will be noticed in their proper place.

On the eighteenth of October, general Smyth assumed the command at Niagara, and applied to the british general for an armistice which was agreed upon, and to continue until thirty hours after notice of its termination.

On the 23d of October, a party of near four hundred americans from Plattsburg under major Young, surprised the picquet at the indian village of St. Regis. Twenty-three men were made prisoners, by the enemy, and lieutenant Rototte, sergeant M'Gillivray and six men slain. The piquet consisted of a detachment of canadian voyageurs. The americans in plundering the village found an ensign or Union Jack, in the house of the interpreter, usually hoisted upon a flag staff, at the door of the chief, on Sundays or holy-days. This piece of murder and thievery was magnified into a feat—"*these being,*"—said the american major, in an order issued upon the occasion—"*the first colours taken during the war.*"* This occurrence was, however, counterpoised by an attack upon a party of americans at Salmon river, near St. Regis, on the 23d November, by detachments of the royal artillery. 49th regiment, and Glengary light infantry, amounting to seventy men, with detachments from the Cornwall and Glengary militia, of near the same number, the whole under the command of lieut. col. M'Millan. In this affair, the enemy took to a block house, but finding themselves surrounded, surrendered prisoners of war. One captain, two subalterns, and forty-one men became prisoners on this occasion, and four batteaux, and fifty seven stand of arms were taken.

Notwithstanding the vicissitudes of war, and the internal difficulties with which the american government had to struggle, the most active preparations were in progress for invading the Canadas. Major-general Dearborn was at the head of ten thousand men, on the confines of Lower Canada: our fleet, though superior to theirs in the spring and summer on lake

---

* The taking, indeed, of a fortress and its flag, by storm or otherwise, as well as the colours of an enemy in action, in open and honorable warfare, is quite another thing, and truly would be creditable to the captors.

Ontario, dare not now even contest with the americans for the command of the lake.— General Smyth had an army of six thousand men on the Niagara frontier, and general Harrison on the river Raisin, over-awed Detroit with his Ohio and Kentucky men. From these hostile appearances it was evident that the enemy still meditated a combined movement, but the uncertainty of the point against which their main strength would be aimed, kept our army constantly on the alert. On the ninth of November, the american fleet consisting of seven sail, with a considerable number of troops, after chasing the Royal George into Kingston channel, cannonaded her for some time; being, however, warmly received by the batteries as well as the ships, they hauled off and bet up under a heavy fire to Four Mile Point, and anchored, with a view of renewing the attack, at a more favorable opportunity. Early on the ensuing morning they got under way, and beat out of the channel, under a heavy press of sail, to the open lake, where they fell in with the governor Simcoe, from Niagara, running for Kingston, and chased her into the harbour; she eluded their pursuit, by running over a reef of rocks. The weather becoming boisterous, the fleet bore away for Sacket's Harbour, after having taken in their cruise two schooners, in one of which captain Brock, pay-master of the 49th regiment, was made prisoner. He was paroled by commodore Chauncey, who generously restored the plate and effects taken with him, belonging to his late relative, genl. Brock. The american forces, under general Dearborn, had, in the mean time, gradually approached the frontier of Lower Canada, and early on the seventeenth of November, 1812, major De Salaberry, of the canadian Voltigeurs, commanding the cordon and advanced posts on the lines, received information at St. Phillip's, that the enemy, to the number of ten thousand, were advancing upon Odelltown. He accordingly strengthened his position, at the river La Cole, by two companies of canadian Voltigeurs, three hundred indians, and a small body of militia volunteers, from the neighbouring parishes. The enemy occupied Champlain Town, two or three miles from the lines, and an earnest invasion was momently expected. Nothing occurred, of any consequence, until the 20th, in the morning, when the captain of the day, visiting the picket, between three and four o'clock, perceived the enemy fording the river La Cole, and, at the same instant, heard them cock their firelocks in the surrounding woods. He had scarcely time to apprise the picquet of their danger, when the enemy, who had surrounded the guard-hut on all sides, discharged a volley of musketry so close that the wads sat fire to the roof and consumed the hut. The militia and indians discharged their pieces, and pushing through the ranks of the enemy, escaped unhurt, while the americans, who had forded the river in two places, mistaking each other in the darkness and confusion of the night, for the enemy, kept up a brisk fire for near half an hour, at each other, in which they killed and wounded several of their own people. After discovering their error, they retired to Champlain, leaving five men wounded, and three or four killed, who were found by the indians on the same day. This party is said to have consisted of fourteen hundred men and a troop of dragoons, and was commanded by colonels Pyke and Clarke.

This movement of the enemy, gave room to expect another more vigorous attempt to invade Lower Canada, and on the 22d, the Governor, by a general order, directed the whole militia of the province, to consider themselves commanded for active service, and to be prepared to move forward to meet the enemy, as soon as required. Lieut. colonel Deschambault was ordered to cross the St. Lawrence at Lachine to Caghnawaga, with the Pointe Claire, Rivière du Chêne, Vaudreuil and Longe Pointe battalions, and to march upon l'Acadie. The volunteers of the 1st battalion of Montreal militia, the flank companies of the second and third battalions, and a troop of militia dragoons crossed the river to Longueuil and Laprairie, and the whole population in the district of Montreal made a simultaneous movement towards the point of invasion, with an enthusiasm unsurpassed in any age or country. General Dearborn, who, no doubt was well informed of the state of the public mind in Lower Canada, at this crisis, foresaw, from the multitude assembled to oppose his progress, and the the hostile spirit of the canadians, the fruitlessness of an attempt to invade Lower Canada, began to withdraw his sickly and already enfeebled host, into winter quarters at Plattsburg and Burlington. Whether he earnestly contemplated an invasion, or only intended this movement as a feint to create a diversion in favor of the army under general Smyth, on the Niagara frontier, remains a question. All apprehensions of an invasion of Lower Canada, for the present season, having disappeared, the troops and embodied militia were on the 27th November, ordered into winter quarters. The armistice concluded between generals Smyth and Sheaffe, after the battle of Queenston, terminated on the 20th November, pursuant to notification to that effect from the former. This, and the former armistice, without affording any present advantage, proved in the event, of material prejudice to the british on lake Erie. The americans availed themselves of so favorable an occasion to forward their naval stores, unmolested, from Black Rock to Presque Isle, by water, which they could not otherwise have effected, but with immense trouble and expense, by land, and equipped at leisure the fleet which afterwards wrested from us the command of that lake.

General Smyth also had, during the armistice, exerted himself in preparing boats for another attempt to invade the upper province, near Fort Erie, at the foot of that lake.*

_{Chap. XV. 1812.}

---

* The proclamation, rather an original thing of the kind, issued by this gentleman, in contemplation of his intended invasion, is as follows:—

"TO THE SOLDIERS OF THE ARMY OF THE CENTRE.

"*Companions in arms!*—The time is at hand when you will cross the streams of Niagara to conquer Canada, and to secure the peace of the american frontier.

"You will enter a country that is to be one of the United States. You will arrive among a people who are to become your fellow citizens. It is not against *them* that we come to make war. It is against that government which holds them as vassals.

"You will make this war as little as possible distressful to the canadian people. If they are peaceable, they are to be secure in their persons; and in their property, as far as our imperious necessities will allow.

"Private plundering is absolutely forbidden. Any soldier who quits his rank to plunder on the field of battle, will be punished in the most exemplary manner.

"But your just rights as soldiers will be maintained; whatever is *booty* by the usages of war, you shall have. All horses belonging to the artillery and cavalry; all waggons and teams in public service, will be sold for the benefit of the captors. Public stores will be secured for the service of the U. States. The government will, with justice, pay you the value.

"The horses drawing the light artillery, of the enemy, are wanted for the service of the United States. I will order TWO HUNDRED DOLLARS for each to be paid the party who may take them. I will also order FORTY DOLLARS to be paid for the arms and spoils of each savage warrior, who shall be killed.

"*Soldiers!* you are amply provided for war. You are superior in number to the enemy. Your personal strength and activity are greater. Your weapons are longer. The regular soldiers of the enemy are generally old men, whose best years have been spent in the sickly climate of the West Indies. They will not be able to stand before you,—you, who charge with the bayonet. You have seen indians, such as those hired by the british to murder women and children, and kill and scalp the wounded. You have seen their dances and grimaces, and heard their yells. Can you fear them? No, you hold them in the utmost contempt.

"*Volunteers!*—Disloyal and traitorous men have endeavoured to dissuade you from your duty. Sometimes they say, if you enter Canada, you will be held to service for five years. At others, they say, you will not be furnished with supplies. At other times, they say, that if you are wounded, the government will not provide for you by pensions. The just and generous course pursued by government towards the volunteers who fought at Tippecanoe, furnishes an answer to the last objection. The others are too absurd to deserve any.

Chap. XV. 1812.

Early on the morning of the 28th Nov. the enemy effected a landing on the british side, with a division of fourteen boats rowed by sailors, with about thirty men each, at the upper end of Grand Isle between Fort Erie and Chippawa. They were resolutely opposed by lieutenant King of the royal artillery, and lieutenant Lamont and Bartley with detachments of thirty and thirty five men each, of the 49th regt. Lieutenants King and Lamont were wounded, and their men being overwhelmed by numbers gave way, after spiking the guns; these two officers with about thirty men, were made prisoners and sent over to the american side. Lieut. Bartley in the meantime, after a determined resistance, by which his force was reduced to seventeen effective men, was compelled to retire, being threatened by a movement of the enemy on his flank. In the interim, the boats with the prisoners and as many americans as could crowd into them,

---

" *Volunteers!* I esteem your generous and patriotic motives. You have made sacrifices on the altar of your country. You will not suffer the enemies of your fame to mislead you from the path of duty and honor, and deprive you of the esteem of a grateful country. You will shun the *eternal infamy* that awaits the man, who having come within sight of the enemy, *basely* shrinks in the moment of trial.

" *Soldiers of every corps!* It is in your power to retrieve the honor of your country and to cover yourselves with glory. Every man who performs a gallant action shall have his name made known to the nation. Rewards and honours await the brave. Infamy and contempt are reserved for cowards. Companions in arms! You came to vanquish a valiant foe, I know the choice you will make. Come on, my heroes! And when you attack the enemy's batteries let your rallying word be, " *The Cannon lost at Detroit or Death!*"

ALEXANDER SMYTH,
Brigadier general commanding.

Camp near Buffalo, 17th Nov., 1812.

returning, left captain King, aid-de-camp to the american general, with a few officers and about forty men, who moved down the shore of the river, but being pursued by major Ormsby, from Fort Erie, were made prisoners, after a feeble resistance. At about seven o'clock in the morning, another division of eighteen boats were seen advancing to effect a landing two miles lower down than the former. Colonel Bishopp having, upon the first alarm, moved from Chippawa, had now formed a junction with major Ormsby, from Fort Erie, and commanding a force of nearly eleven hundred men, consisting of detachments of the 41st, 49th and royal Newfoundland regiments, a body of militia under lieut. col. Clark and major Hall, and some indians, waited for the enemy on the shore. Their approach was welcomed with three cheers, and a steady and effectual fire opened upon them from musketry and a six pounder (under the command of captain Kirby of the royal artillery) which destroyed two of their boats, threw the remainder into confusion, and compelled them to take flight. The enemy, for a part of the day, made a display of their force on their own side of the river, but perceiving the british had unspiked and remounted the guns which had fallen into their hands in the morning, they, with a view of retiring unmolested from our fire, by gaining a little time, sent over a flag to colonel Bishopp to summons the surrender of Fort Erie, to save the effusion of human blood, who laconically answered "*come and take it.*" Preparations were made for another descent on the Canada side, on the morning of the 1st of December, but through mismanagement in embarking their troops, and a deficiency of provisions, the project miscarried, and the troops were ordered to re-land and hut themselves for the winter. Murmer and discontent crept into the american camp, and general Smyth was obliged to take flight, to save himself from the indignation of his army, which, from death, sickness and defection, soon ceased to be an object of apprehension to the british in their neighbourhood. This was the termination of the third attempt to invade Upper Canada, and the result of the formidable preparations of the american government to conquer the Canadas.

The legislature of Lower Canada, assembled on the 29th of December. The governor, at the opening of the session, expressed his confidence in the people, the fruits of whose loyalty were the honorable termination of the campaign without effusion of blood, loss of territory, or a recourse to martial law :—

"The complete discomfiture of the plans of the enemy, for the conquest of Upper Canada, by the capture of Michillimackinac and Detroit, and by the surrender of the whole of the invading army, with its general—the brilliant achievement at Queenston, though clouded by the death, in the hour of victory, of the gallant and much lamented major-general Brock - together with the other recent advantages gained over the enemy, both in Lower and Upper Canada, are subjects of sincere congratulation, and demand our fervent acknowledgments to the great ruler of the universe, for these his undeserved mercies.

"But it is not only for the success with which the Almighty has blessed his Majesty's arms in the Canadas, that I have to congratulate you:—a more remote scene, where british valour has appeared in its native vigour, calls forth additional exultation, and encourages the expectation, that the miseries which have so long desolated Portugal and Spain, are at length arrested in their course, by the splendid victories lately achieved in the latter country by general the marquis of Wellington."

He thanked the house, in the name of the Prince Regent, for the assurance of attachment and support they had promised in their answer to his speech at the opening of parliament, in the preceding month of February, and acquainted them that—" his royal highness placed that confidence in the courage and loyalty of his Majesty's canadian subjects which made him equally fearless of the result of any direct attack upon them, and of any insidious attempts to alienate their affection from his government."—He informed them of the beneficial effects resulting from the army bill act, and recommended it to their further consideration.—" He had"—he observed—" according to the powers vested in him by the legislature, called forth the militia to assist in the defence of the province, and with the most cheering satisfaction had been a witness of that public spirit, that steady order, and that love of their country, their religion and their laws, which they had manifested on this occasion, and which, by animating and uniting all classes of his Majesty's subjects, could not fail, under Divine Providence, to make them safe at home and

Chap. XV.
1813.

respected abroad."—He recommended a revision of the militia laws, and concluded by urging the necessity of dispatch, in conducting the public business.

The assembly, in answer, observed:—

"It is with no common degree of satisfaction, that we receive from your excellency, such unequivocal testimony of the voluntary exertions of all ranks of people, to second your excellency in the execution of those precautionary measures which you had in your wisdom adopted, for the defence of the province, and its preservation from menaced invasion.

"We feel it incumbent on us to state to your excellency, that not only that part of his Majesty's subjects who have been placed in your immediate view, but the entire population of the country, are devoted to the cause, and will cheerfully make every sacrifice which the safety of their country and its future happiness may require, at this truly important and critical conjuncture, thereby assuring to themselves a superior claim to the confidence and affection of their beloved sovereign.

"Considering the limited resources placed in the hands of your excellency, at the commencement of the almost unexpected, and entirely unprovoked war, declared by the government of the United States of America, against his Majesty, and the contemptuous language, and inconsiderate threats, which accompanied and followed that declaration, although we were conscious that such could not fail to arouse the hereditary spirit of the country, we have great reason to rejoice that the campaign has terminated without the effusion of blood, without loss of territory, and without interruption to the most important habits of peace by a recourse to martial law. To the energetic yet mild and conciliating measures of your excellency, to the devotion of his Majesty's canadian subjects, and to the rightful cause of a beloved sovereign, we ascribe that happy and honorable termination.

"The public spirit and determined resolution, inspired by the love of their country, their religion and their laws, which were manifested by the militia, when called forth by your excellency in the defence of the province, and to which your excellency bears such strong and honorable testimony, continues to animate and unite all classes of his Majesty's subjects, and will, we trust, under the blessings of Divine Providence, ensure our safety at home, and make us respected abroad."

"The sentiments"—said his excellency, in reply—"contained in your address, are worthy of the representatives of a loyal, brave and enlightened people, and demand my warmest acknowledgments."

Among the first proceedings of the house of assembly, in this session, was an enquiry into the causes and injurious consequences that might have resulted from the delay incurred in the publication of the laws of the provincial parliament, passed in the session thereof begun and holden on the 21st February preceding. This measure, moved by Mr. James Stuart, was, for some time, persevered in with unremitted assiduity, and with the apparent intention to palliate the guilt of the rioters at Lachine, but in reality to embarrass, it was thought, the government, against which, on account of his recent dismissal, by Sir J. H. Craig, from the solicitor generalship, he now set himself in array. Among those summoned on this occasion, to attend the bar of the house of assembly, were the clerk and other officers of the legislative council, which, not having been previously consulted by the lower house, refused to allow their servants to be examined at the bar of the latter. The legislative council, however, after deliberation, permitted them to be examined by the house of assembly, under a species of protest, from a desire to remove every possible obstacle to the immediate discussion of measures requisite for the defence of the province, reserving, for a more convenient occasion, the question of their privileges in this respect. Nothing of importance resulted from the enquiry. The subject of appointing an agent in England was resumed by the house in the present session, but postponed. To support the expense of the war, an income tax upon salaries from government was proposed in the lower house, in the proportion of fifteen per cent upon every salary of £1,500 and upwards, per annum, twelve per cent upon £1,000 and upwards, ten per cent upon £500 and upwards, and five per cent upon every £250, and upwards. A bill to that effect was passed in the lower house, but rejected by the legislative council.

The assembly took into consideration, at the instance of Mr. Stuart, the power and authority exercised by his Majesty's courts in this province, under the denomination of Rules of Practice. The result, or rather progress of this enquiry, during the subsequent session, we shall notice in its turn. —The house, in taking into consideration, on motion of Mr. Stuart, that part of the governor's speech, in which reference was had to martial law, came to resolutions strongly adverse to a recourse to it.* The army bill act was renewed and extended: five hundred thousand pounds were authorised to be put into circulation, and, in order to secure their credit, commissioners were appointed to establish, at regular periods, the current rate of exchange, of bills upon London, which the holders, upon application, were entitled to obtain from government. Fifteen thousand pounds were granted by the parliament to equip the embodied militia, one thousand pounds to provide for hospitals for the militia, and twenty-five thousand pounds towards the support of the war. The further sum of four hundred pounds was granted to improve and facilitate the communication between Lower and Upper Canada; but no amendment was made to the militia laws, owing to a disagreement on the subject, between the lower and upper houses. A duty of two and a half per cent, upon all merchandise, provisions excepted, imported into the province, and two and a half

Chap. XV.
1813.

---

* " Resolved—That it is the opinion of this committee, that all occasion or pretence for recurring in this province, to martial law, in the sense, in which it is understood, in the constitutional or public law of England, hath been taken away by the act of the parliament of the united kingdom of *Great Britain* and *Ireland*, intituled, "an act for punishing mutiny and desertion, and for the better payment of the army, in their quarters;" by the " rules and articles for the better government of his Majesty's forces ;" and by the militia laws of this province; whereby the executive government hath become, and is vested with all the powers necessary to enable it to provide for the safety of this province, in the present conjuncture.

" Resolved—That it is the opinion of this committee, that the limits and operation of martial law, as above stated, could not, nor can, be legally enlarged in this province, without the authority of the provincial parliament."

These were carried by a vote of 18 to 15.

per cent more, upon merchandise imported into the province, by persons not actually therein resident six months previous to such importation, was granted for the support of the war. The legislature was prorogued on the fifteenth of February, the governor thanking the assembly for the liberality with which they had granted to his Majesty the supplies necessary for the public service:—

"The present crisis"—said his excellency,—" will, in all probability, call for sacrifices which your loyalty and patriotism will, I trust, lead you without hesitation to make—And I look forward from your good example, to a cheerful acquiescence on the part of all his Majesty's subjects in the province, in whatever may be required of them for the defence of the country, and for the preservation of the blessings they enjoy under his Majesty's mild and paternal government."

Among the miscellaneous matters of the session, the following are entitled to notice:— Mr. Lee moved that the house should go into committee of the whole to enquire into the necessity of preventing, either by bill or representation to his Majesty and the two other branches of the imperial parliament, the judges of the court of king's bench from having deliberative votes in the legislative council of this province. The consideration of the motion was postponed, but the progress of the idea will be perceived as we proceed, until it finally was realised.

The assembly made another attack, this session, upon the press. An article in "*The Quebec Mercury*," addressed "To a party leader," (understood to mean Mr. Jas. Stuart, then one of the most active, if not at the head, of the opposition,) and signed "*Juniolus canadensis*,"* being, on motion of Mr. Lee, voted

* This document is given not from any intrinsic importance, it possesses, but, that the reader may understand what constituted in those sensitive times, "a false and a scandalous libel and manifest breach of the privileges" of the house of assembly.

"LETTER TO A PARTY LEADER.

"You are now, sir, playing the most conspicuous part in a very extraordinary scene. Those who are disposed to view your actions favourably, say, that you are practising a refinement of candour and delicacy of justice, which has seldom been surpassed. You were stript of an official situation by the late governor; your friends, and perhaps some others, thought that the act was an unwarrantable stretch of authority, and executed without such sufficient grounds, as he was well known usually to act upon. He is gone; and you are determined to vindicate his memory—yes—you will sacrifice yourself to your sense of justice, and shew the public that you were really unworthy of the place you then held. You will shew them, that however insufficient in themselves, the grounds upon which the late governor proceeded, he was guided by an anticipating discernment into your character, and a provident caution against its natural effects. With a generous and excessive zeal of reparation, with a determination to do away, at any hazard, the impression of which you happened to be the cause, you have embraced the first expedient that presented itself; you have held yourself up to the general disesteem, and appeared the self devoted victim of an honorable sensibility.

"But there are others who hold such a feeling and such a result of it, to be incompatible and contradictory;—who think that a line of conduct which they deem seriously injurious to the province, could hardly have originated in a motive so refinedly generous. These men say, that either you are venting the spleen of disappointment, and reckless of the evils that you cause, are indulging your unsatisfied revenge against the government, or that you are, in truth, friendly to the interest of the United States, and wish to contribute your mite towards the advancement of their cause.—But is it not rather ambition that has fired your efforts? Is it not the thirst of fame that has urged you on to distinction? Is it not the noble yearning after an immortal name that has excited this effervescence within your breast; that has taught you to be a mischief maker in your public situation; that has bid you head a few factious underlings of the law, and, with their zealous assistance, to fill the ignorant and inexperienced with error and perplexity, and to lead them into a belief of oppression on the part of government, in an instance where its humanity was strikingly conspicuous? It is this that arms you with courage to bully and brow beat the few—alas how few! that rise up to resist you; and while you stand forth, self-invested, the champion of the people, to ply among them your engines of discordance, and lay a

F 2

Chap. XV.
1813.

"a false and scandalous libel upon this house, and a manifest breach of its privileges," it was ordered that the editor, Mr. Cary, be taken

> train which, if you were to succeed in lighting it, would blow up the foundations of their well-being. Are you determined to be somebody, and can you find no better field of exertion; or none that will involve the complication of evils that you are so prodigally scattering? You remind us of that dauntless hero of old, who, resolved that his name should go down to posterity, and yet incapable of any action that might couple it with praise, fired the far celebrated temple of Diana at Ephesus, and burnt it to the ground. His action has been perpetuated, as he expected—but his name has perished.*
>
> "At a time when the enemy is at the door, and when nothing but the cheerful alacrity, and the honorable ardour, almost unexampled, which this province has hitherto exhibited (with one or two trifling exceptions) from one end to the other, can save it from falling;—at a time when every generous spirit is roused in the consciousness of a just cause, and eager to chastise the wicked presumption of a foe at once insidious and savage; at such a time as this, what is your employment?—You are damping that alacrity; checking that generous ardour; you are busy in sowing the seeds of embarrassment and delay; you are spreading the subtle venom of mistrust and disaffection;—you are picking out flaws, with the microscope of a lawyer, in the proceedings of government; you are cavilling, you are colouring, you are inflaming, you are fomenting groundless discontent; and what is this but to create unnecessary misery? You are painting evils and passing them for real, as you hold them up to those whom, if real, they would affect. This is your chosen office; this your patriotism; and you revel in the plenitude of temporary success. Will no man then stand up in your defiance; and shall the fulminations of your violence and abuse be dreaded as the thunder of eloquence irresistible? Shall you be suffered to go on, trampling upon all rule and decorum,—committing, at every step, some action unjustifiable and irregular; turning your colleagues into a mob; simply because you have already gained and established a proud footing by such conduct?—Go on then—and treasure up for yourself the recollection of prostituted energies and perverted talents;—go and bask in the consciousness of successful exertions, directed against the vital interests of that country which gave you birth;—proceed in the great work which you have so happily begun; and if heaven avert not the consequences of your endeavours, you may yet perhaps smile at the ruin that is around you, and exclaim with genuine satisfaction and unrepressed rapture—"*I have contributed to this.*"
>
> "January 14.   JUNIOLUS CANADENSIS.
>
> "Mr. L. J. Papineau moved, seconded by Mr. Bellet, that the said article now read in english, be translated into the french language."

---

* "*This is a small mistake; his name was Erostratus*"—ED. Q. M.

into custody of the sergeant at arms, whom, however, he evaded, keeping out of his way during the remainder of the session, treating them the day after the prorogation, on finding himself again free, with the *morceau* below.*

Three hundred and ninety-nine vessels, containing in all 86,436 tons, and employing 4054 seamen, cleared during the year 1812, from Quebec. Of those vessels twenty-one were built that year in this city, containing 5898 tons. The revenue of the year amounted to £61,193, currency. The expenses of the civil government to £98,777, sterling, including upwards of £55,000 for the militia forces, and £3,424 due to Upper Canada, as its proportion of the revenue. The expenses of the legislature were £3,644, currency, besides the above.

---

* " The Editor's respects to a majority of the house of assembly, being just arrived from a tour of business, he learns that the house had evinced much anxiety to see him, during his absence. Unfortunately, his return has taken place a day too late for him to have the honor of waiting on the house. He is, however, rather at a loss to conceive how his presence could be, in any manner, useful in assisting them in their vocation of framing laws.."—*Quebec Mercury,16th Feb.*, 1813.

CHAPTER XVI.

Chap. XVI.
1813.

The americans under general Winchester, at Frenchtown, on the river Raisin, near Detroit, defeated by colonel Proctor, and made prisoners—vote of thanks by the assembly, to colonel Proctor, his officers and men—the colonel promoted to the rank of brigadier general—the session being closed the governor visits Upper Canada—successful attack over the ice upon Ogdensburgh—preparations during the winter for the next campaign—american forces and fleet on lake Ontario attack and capture York—sail thence to Niagara—thence to Sacket's Harbour, for reinforcements—return to Niagara, attack and carry Fort George—General Vincent falls back to Burlington Heights—Sir James Lucas Yeo, arrives at Quebec, from England, with a reinforcement of seamen for the lakes—expedition under the immediate command of the naval and military commanders against Sacket's Harbour—their failure and retreat to Kingston—successful attack by general Proctor on the american forces under general Harrison, on the Miami—brilliant affair at Stoney Creek, by lieut. col. Harvey—his defeat of the enemy and capture of two brigadier generals—affair at Beaver Dams, and capture of upwards of five hundred of the enemy, under lieut. colonel Boerstler—attack upon fort Schlosser and Black Rock—demonstration before Fort George—attack by general Proctor upon the american fort at Lower Sandusky, under lieut. colonel Croghan, defeated with severe loss—capture of american sloops Growler and Eagle, at *Isle aux Noix*, river Chambly—an expedition from *Isle aux Noix* visits Plattsburgh and other places, on lake Champlain—commissariat in Upper Canada ably attended to and well supplied, but at great expense—affair at Goose Creek—naval occurrences on lake Ontario.

THE american army under the command of general Harrison still hovered on the border of

Michigan territory and over-awed Detroit, where colonel Proctor with an inferior force was, as previously stated, left in command after the reduction of that post, by general Brock. On the 19th of January, information was received at Detroit, by the british commander, that a division or brigade of the american army under brigadier general Winchester, was encamped at Frenchtown on the river Raisin, twenty-six miles from Detroit, having driven in a body of militia and indians, posted there under major Reynolds, of the militia, who, after some resistance with a field piece, fell back upon Brownstown. Colonel Proctor promptly determined to attack this division, before it could be reinforced by the main body, under general Harrison, three or four days march, in the rear; and assembled his disposable force at Brownstown on the 21st, consisting of five hundred regulars, seamen and militia, and about six hundred indians. He advanced the same day twelve miles, to Stoney Creek, and at day break the next morning made a resolute attack on the enemy's camp. General Winchester himself, fell soon after the commencement of the action into the hands of the Wyandot chief *Roundhead*, who surrendered him to colonel Proctor. The americans had retreated to the houses and enclosures, from which they were making a desperate resistance through fear of falling into the hands of the indians; but upon its being represented to general Winchester, that unless a speedy surrender were made, the buildings would be set on fire, and that no responsibility would be taken for the conduct of the indians, he caused a flag of truce to be sent to his men, and agreed, on their part, to a surrender, upon condition of their being protected from the fury of the savages, and allowed to preserve their private property. In this affair the enemy lost in killed between three and four hundred men, and one brigadier general, three field-officers, nine captains, twenty subalterns and upwards of five hundred men in prisoners. The loss on the british side was also severe: twenty-four killed and one hundred and fifty-eight wounded. This spirited and vigorous measure completely disconcerted the arrangements made by gen. Harrison, for the recovery of the Michigan territory, and secured Detroit from any immediate danger. The house of assembly of Lower Canada, then in session, passed a vote of thanks to colonel Proctor, for the skill and intrepidity with which he planned and carried into execution this enterprise. A vote of thanks was also passed to the officers, non-commissioned officers and privates belonging to the line, marine and militia forces who assisted in its accomplishment, and colonel Proctor was immediately promoted to the rank of brigadier general, by the commander of the forces, until the pleasure of the Prince Regent should be known, who was pleased to approve and confirm the appointment.

The governor having closed, as before stated,

the session of the legislature, left Quebec on the 17th February, on a visit for Upper Canada. In his route thither, lieutenant colonel Pearson in command at Prescott, proposed to him as he passed, an attack upon the american post of Ogdensburgh, in retaliation for an excursion by the enemy from thence upon Brockville some days previously. The governor did not deem it expedient to order an attack upon that post, but as two men had deserted on the evening of his arrival, and had gone over to the enemy, who might, upon ascertaining the arrival of the governor, way lay him on his route, it was determined that lieutenant colonel M'Donnell, second in command at Prescott, should make a demonstration on the ice, in front of Ogdensburgh, as well with a view of engaging the attention of the enemy, as by drawing out their forces, to ascertain the strength of the garrison. On the ensuing morning, (22d February,) as the governor departed, lieut. col. M'Donnell moved with his party across the river on the ice, towards Ogdensburgh; the enemy perceiving the movement, were prepared to receive him. Impelled by that spirit characteristic of british soldiers, he turned the demonstration into a real attack.

The enemy were driven from the village after a short contest, leaving about twenty killed and a considerable number wounded. Four brass field-pieces, seven pieces of iron ordnance complete, with several hundred stand of arms, and a considerable quantity of stores fell into the hands of the victors, who lost seven killed, and seven officers (including lieutenant col. M'Donnell) and forty-one men wounded. After having destroyed two small schooners and two gun boats, left there to winter, they returned to their quarters at Prescott.

During the winter the greatest exertions were made to be in a state of preparation for the ensuing campaign. In March, a draught of militia took place, to fill up the militia battalions. A battalion (the 6th) was embodied at Quebec, from the city militia for garrison duty. The canadian regiment of Fencibles, the Glengaries and the Voltigeurs recruited with diligence and success; and the 104th (or New Brunswick regiment) marched through from Fredericton, for Upper Canada, some hundreds of miles, with extraordinary celerity in the month of March: though their route from the former place, to the river St. Lawrence, lay through an uninhabited wilderness, (now covered by snow, two or three feet in depth) never before travelled by british troops.

The american forces in the meantime augmented daily at Sacket's Harbour, and their fleet being superior to that of the british, a descent upon Kingston or its neighbourhood was confidently expected: the american government, however, deemed it too hazardous a game to stake the fate of their lake armament upon an enterprise against the principal *depôt* of the british in the upper province, where they must expect a desperate resistance, and resolved to direct their efforts against the more distant and vulnerable parts on the lake. Commodore Chauncey having accordingly equipped his fleet for an expedition, and received on board upwards of seventeen hundred troops under the command of generals Dearborn and Pike, sailed from Sacket's Harbour on the 25th of April, and on the following evening appeared off York with fourteen sail of armed vessels. On the ensuing morning, (27th) the enemy commenced a debarkation about three miles to the west of the town, but the wind blowing fresh from the eastward they fell considerably to leeward of the position fixed upon for landing, (the site of the old french fort Toronto) while they suffered much from a galling fire of the british troops, posted in a wood. They, however, accomplished their landing and compelled the british, whose whole force, regulars and militia, did not exceed six hundred men, to retire with loss. The grenadiers of the 8th regiment, who lost their captain M'Neal, were, after a desperate contest almost annihilated by the overwhelming numbers of the enemy. The latter having made their landing, formed upon the beach under the immediate orders of general Pike, while the schooners worked up to the forts, under a heavy cannonade, and assuming a position at the distance of six hundred yards from the batteries in order to make a simultaneous impression upon the works by water and by land, opened a heavy fire upon them which did great execution. The land forces under general Pike advanced through a little wood to the main works, when, at the distance of sixty rods from them, a tremendous explosion took place, from a magazine previously prepared, which discharging an immense quantity of rubbish, spread havock among their troops, and killed a number of their officers and men. General Pike, an officer much esteemed in the american army, and who seems to have been a gentleman of an amiable character in private life, received a contusion from a large stone, while leading on his men, which in a few hours put a period to his existence. General Sheaffe finding his small force unable to resist that of the enemy, retreated at two o'clock, in the afternoon, leaving lieutenant colonel Chewitt, of the militia, to treat with the enemy: and a capitulation immediately ensued, by which York was surrendered to the american forces, and the militia to the amount of more than two hundred men, with their officers, surrendered prisoners of war, on condition that all private property should be respected. The public stores of every description fell into the hands of the enemy, with the armed schooner Duke of Gloucester, undergoing repairs. A new ship which had been laid down, at this open and defenceless post, the preceding winter, and now almost completely planked, was with the naval stores set on fire by the british previous to their retreat. The loss of the british was severe, amounting to about one hundred and thirty men in killed and wounded, among the former Mr. M'Lean, the clerk of the house of assembly of Upper Canada, who had volunteered his services with a musket. The loss of the enemy though not correctly ascertained must have been heavier than that of the british. The enemy having secured their booty, re-embarked and sailed on the 2d of May for Niagara. General Sheaffe suffered much, in the public estimation, on account of his failure, in defending York, and of his retreat before the enemy on this occasion, and was shortly afterwards superseded, in the chief command, in Upper Canada, by major general de Rottenburg. On his return to the lower province, he was put in command of the troops in the district of Montreal.

The american fleet having landed the troops at Niagara, returned to Sacket's Harbour for reinforcements, and on the 25th May, their whole fleet having proceeded by detachments, were again assembled at Niagara, and general Vincent commanding at Fort George, foresaw that an attack was shortly to be made upon his post. Commodore Chauncey despatched two of his vessels to cruise vigilantly off Kingston, and concerted his arrangements with general Dearborn for a combined attack upon Fort George. Early in the morning of the 27th May, the enemy accordingly commenced a combined attack upon that fort, having previously on the 24th and 25th, materially injured the works, by a warm cannonade from their ships and batteries. A body of about eight hundred riflemen, under colonel Scott, landed near the Two Mile Creek, while the fleet ranged up in the form of a crescent, extending from the north of the light house to the Two Mile Creek, so as to enfilade the british batteries by a cross fire. The riflemen after forming and ascending the bank were met by the british, and compelled to give way, in disorder, and return to the beach, from whence they kept up a smart fire under cover of the bank. In the meantime another body, of upwards of two thousand men, under the direction of general Lewis, made a landing, and formed on the beach, under cover of a tremendous cannonade of round shot, and showers of grape and canister from the fleet, that swept the adjacent plain and compelled the british to retire. General Vincent finding the works torn to pieces, by the enemy's artillery, and no longer tenable against so overwhelming a force, caused the fort to be dismantled, and the magazines to be blown up, and retreated to Queenstown, leaving the americans to take possession of the ruins, of the fort.* The british loss consisted

---

* In the general order issued on this occasion, by the commander of the forces, we find the following:—

" Regardless of the immense superiority of the enemy, his advance was gallantly and obstinately disputed,—a judicious position was occupied by lieut. col. Myers, and when that zealous and meritorious officer was obliged to quit the field, having received three wounds, he was ably replaced by lieut. col. Harvey, and the unequal contest continued with unshaken gallantry and determination.

" Brigadier general Vincent, considering further perseverance against an overwhelming force, a fruitless sacrifice of invaluable

of fifty-two killed, and upwards of three hundred wounded and missing. The american accounts state their loss at thirty-nine killed, and one hundred and eleven wounded.

General Vincent on the ensuing day having collected the whole of the forces, from Chippawa and Fort Erie, and destroyed or rendered useless the posts and stores along that frontier, commenced his retreat toward Burlington heights, at the head of Ontario.

The arrival of Sir James L. Yeo, from England, at Quebec, on the 5th May, with several officers of the royal navy and 450 seamen for the lakes, cheered the drooping spirits of the public. Captains Barclay, Pring and Finnis, with five lieutenants of the royal navy having previously arrived over land from Halifax, with some seamen, were already at Kingston, and were putting the fleet in a state of preparation to meet the enemy. Sir George Prevost proceeded from Montreal to Kingston, with Sir James L. Yeo, who arrived at the latter place in the short time of six weeks, from his embarking at Portsmouth.

The two commanders being now at Kingston, the public was on the tip-toe of expectation for some decisive dash upon the enemy's flotilla. An attack upon Sacket's Harbour, in the absence of their fleet, at Niagara, was resolved upon. A body of eight hundred or a

---

lives, having gained by their intrepid resistance the means of dismantling the fort, and destroying the stores, he directed the troops to fall back on Queenston, which was done with perfect order."

thousand men were embarked on the 27th May, on board the british flotilla at Kingston, consisting of the Wolfe 24 guns, Royal George 24, Earl of Moira 18, and four schooners bearing from ten to twelve guns each, with a sufficient number of batteaux, and at noon on the next day they were off Sacket's Harbour. The weather was propitious, and the troops were transferred to the batteaux, to make their landing, under an escort of two-gun boats, commanded by captain Mulcaster, the whole under the immediate direction of the land and naval commanders in chief. They had proceeded but a short distance when a convoy of american boats, loaded with troops were descried doubling Stoney Point, on their way from Oswego, to Sacket's Harbour. The indians, who had previously landed, on an island, fired upon them as they passed, and threw them into confusion, while the boats and batteaux bore down and captured twelve of them, with about 150 men: the remainder escaped into Sacket's Harbour. The landing was then deferred until the next morning, while the americans raised the alarm, and withdrew a detachment of their troops, posted upon Horse Island, at the mouth of the harbour, and assumed a position on the main, opposite a ford leading from the island to the main land, where they were reinforced by a body of militia, under general Brown, and prepared for a vigorous defence. The night was dark and rainy, and at day break next morning the boats were so scattered that they were unable to effect a landing as intended, before the enemy should have time to line the woods. They first attempted to land on the main, in a cove formed by Horse Island, but on approaching it they found the enemy prepared for them, by a heavy fire of musketry, from the surrounding woods, supported by a field piece. They then pulled round and landed on the outside of the island, with little or no loss, and pushed forward to the ford, in the face of a hot fire of musketry and the field piece, which they carried in a few moments after landing, with a tumbrel and a few rounds of ammunition. The enemy retreated, and posting themselves securely behind large trees, kept up a smart fire upon the british. The fleet, in the meantime, as well as a small vessel with two six pounders, intended to have been landed in time to support the advance, of the troops, were, through light and adverse wind, a long way in the rear. Under these circumstances it was impossible to wait for the arrival of the artillery, and colonel Baynes, the adjutant general of the forces, in british N. America, who was charged with this service, ordered the detachment to divide, in order to scour the woods, by pursuing two paths which led in opposite directions round a rising ground. The enemy dislodged from the woods at the point of the bayonet, fled to their fort and blockhouses, whither they were pursued by the british, who set fire to their barracks. At this luckless juncture it was thought by the commanding officer, that the enemy's blockhouses and stockaded battery could not be carried by assault, even with the assistance of field pieces had they been landed. The fleet were still out of reach to render any assistance in battering them, while his men were exposed to the fire of the enemy secure within their works. The signal of retreat was therefore given to the indignant assailants, and the enterprise was abandoned at a moment, when the enemy had so far calculated upon a decisive victory on the part of the british, as to have set fire to their naval store houses, hospital and marine barracks, by which all the booty previously taken at York, and the stores for their new ship were consumed. They had also set fire to a frigate on the stocks, and were it is said actually retreating from the town, as untenable and lost: but, on discovering the retreat of the british, they returned and succeeded in suppressing the fire and saved her. The troops were immediately re-embarked and returned to Kingston. The loss though heavy on both sides was never correctly ascertained, or reported; among the british, capt. Gray, acting deputy quarter master general, was much regretted. He fell while reconnoitring the enemy's works, in the hopes of discovering some opening to favor an assault.

Thus terminated an expedition to the disappointment of the public, who, from the presence and co-operation of the two commanders in chief, had flattered themselves with a very different result. This miscarriage, with other untoward events, at the commencement of the present campaign, extinguished in the mind of the enemy, the ideas of invincibility with which the prowess of our arms the preceding summer had inspired him, and the military character of Sir George Prevost sustained a shock, from which, it never recovered.

From these humiliating occurrences, we turn with pride to more cheering scenes of action, which effectually retrieved the honor of the british arms, in Upper Canada. General Harrison, notwithstanding the defeat of a division of his army, under general Winchester, at Frenchtown, in February, still persevered in his preparations to recover the Michigan territory, and in pursuance of his views, had towards the spring, taken post near the foot of the rapids of the Miami, where he only waited for reinforcements, to commence active operations against the british. General Proctor, aware of his views, determined to dislodge him before the arrival of his reinforcements, and proceeded for the Miami. He reached the neighbourhood of the enemy's position on the 26th of April. The americans had, however, secured themselves, by block houses and batteries, so as to render every effort of the small artillery, of the besiegers, unavailing. In the morning of the 5th of May, a reinforcement consisting of two regiments, amounting to about twelve hundred men, under brigadier general

Chap. XVI.
1813.

Clay, having rapidly descended the river from Fort Defiance, some distance above Fort Meigs, (the american position) made a sudden attack and surprised the british batteries, on the west side of the river, seconded by a resolute and simultaneous sally from the garrison. Having carried the british batteries, they unwarily pursued the indians, who fell back skirmishing with the enemy, while the main british force coming up, by a hasty and judicious movement cut off their retreat to the river. After a desperate contest, the enemy surrendered, and upwards of 500 men were made prisoners. They who had sallied from the fort alone effected their escape, betaking themselves to their fortification. The indians, although disposed to sacrifice the prisoners according to their mode of warfare, after some excesses, were with difficulty, restrained from slaughter by the british, two or three of whom fell victims to the fury of the savages, in their endeavours to protect the defenceless prisoners. By this partial success, the enemy became so crippled as to be unable to prosecute the campaign with any prospect of recovering Detroit, and general Proctor drew off his forces and returned to Sandwich, under the apprehension of being abandoned by the indians, who, after a battle, according to their custom, retire to the enjoyment of their booty. In this affair, the british loss amounted to one officer (of the militia) and fourteen men killed, and one officer and forty-five men wounded.

Immediately after the capture of Fort George, by the enemy, general Dearborn pushed forward a body of three thousand infantry, with nine field-pieces and two hundred and fifty cavalry, as far as the Forty Mile Creek, for the purpose of dislodging general Vincent, who had assumed a position at Burlington Heights, at the head of lake Ontario; or to prevent a junction of the forces under general Proctor with those of general Vincent, which, the americans understood had been agreed upon by the british. On the 5th of June, general Vincent was apprised of the advance of the enemy, by the retreat of his advanced picquets, from Stoney Creek. Lieut. colonel Harvey, deputy adjutant general, immediately moved forward with the light companies of the 8th and 49th regiments, and having reconnoitred the enemy's position, proposed to general Vincent a nocturnal attack upon his camp, which was approved. At eleven in the evening, the general moved up with the 49th regiment and a part of the 8th (his whole effective force only 704 firelocks) toward the american camp, distant about seven miles. Lieut. colonel Harvey led the attack, in gallant style, and completely succeeded in surprising the enemy in the midst of his camp, who, notwithstanding the darkness of the night, and the consternation and disorder into which they were thrown, evinced a state of order and discipline highly creditable, in repeatedly forming, though compelled as often to disperse, before the british bayonet. Two brigadier generals, (Chandler and Winder,) seven officers of inferior rank, and one hundred and sixteen men, with three guns, one brass howitzer and three tumbrels, fell into the hands of the british by this brilliant and intrepid action, which, as it reduced the americans from offensive to defensive operations, was probably, in its result, of more real importance to the salvation of the upper province, than any other occurrence during the present campaign. The british were ordered to retreat before day light, lest their slender force, exposed to the view of the enemy, upon the return of day, might be overpowered by their superior numbers. Finding that the british had retreated, they re-occupied their camp after sun-rise, and having destroyed all their incumbrances, commenced a precipitate retreat to Forty-mile Creek, ten miles from the scene of action, where they were reinforced on the following day by general Lewis, with a detachment of the army from Fort George. The loss of the british in this affair, was one officer and twenty-two men killed, and twelve officers and one hundred and fifteen men wounded, and fifty-five missing.*

---

* The following is from the general order issued by brigadier general Vincent, after this gallant action :—

" Brigadier general Vincent is at a loss for language to do justice to the distinguished bravery and good conduct of the troops engaged.

" To lieut. colonel Harvey, deputy adjutant general, who planned the enterprise and conducted the columns to the attack, every degree of praise is due, and his distinguished services are duly appreciated. The 8th (King's) and 49th regiments, he was rejoiced to observe, vied with each other in acts of intrepidity and gallantry, though at

On the evening of the 7th, the british fleet hove in sight, and, on the ensuing morning, approached the shore and fired a few shots upon the enemy, whom they summoned to surrender prisoners of war. This was refused by the american officer, who, however, deemed it expedient to fall back upon Fort George, while the british, as they retired, pressed upon their rear, and occupied the ground they had abandoned. Twelve of their batteaux, accompanying the army on its retreat, containing principally officers' baggage, fell into the hands of the british fleet.

On the 28th of June, a party of about six hundred of the enemy, under lieut. colonel Boerstler, who had been despatched the preceding day, by general Dearborn, by way of Queenston, with a view of dislodging a detachment or picquet, posted at a place called the Beaver Dams, (a few miles from Queenston,)

---

the unavoidable expense of many of their valuable officers and men."

This gallant officer, now lieut. general Sir John Harvey, lieutenant governor of Nova Scotia, seems to have been, during this and the following campaign, almost ubiquitary in Upper Canada, as in every military enterprise, from the Niagara frontier downward, of any moment, we find him actively and vigorously engaged, and honorably mentioned, not less in private accounts, for the skill, decision, and intrepidity invariably evinced by him, on all occasions where he was concerned, than in the general orders of the day. There is not perhaps, in the british army, an officer more favorably known in Canada, than Sir John Harvey, and certainly none more so in Quebec, where, for many years after the war, he resided, as deputy adjutant general to the forces in the Canadas, esteemed by his fellow townsmen of all denominations, for his many social and domestic qualities, uniting those of a good citizen, neighbour and friend, with the sterner ones of a gallant and good soldier, and upright public man.

were surprised on their route, by a party of indians under captain Kerr, and after some skirmishing, believing themselves hemmed in by superior numbers, surrendered to lieutenant Fitzgibbon, of the 49th regiment. This officer arriving at the conclusion of the business, with a small detachment of forty-six rank and file, completed the victory, and the americans surrendered themselves prisoners, after negociating a capitulation with him, in the name of major De Haren, by whom he induced the enemy to believe themselves surrounded with considerable force. The latter officer, though not immediately on the ground, was, however, in the neighbourhood, and advancing with the light company of the 8th regiment, and the two flank companies of the 104th, with a small body of provincial cavalry, under captain Hall. The prisoners taken, were five hundred and and twelve in number, including twenty-five officers, with two field-pieces and a stand of colours.

The enemy, by these partial successes of the british, were compelled to confine themselves to Fort George and its environs; and, before the 1st of July, the british had formed a line extending from Twelve-Mile Creek, on lake Ontario, across to Queenston, on the Niagara river. From Chippawa, a descent was made on the american Fort Schlosser, on the opposite side of the river, during the night of the 4th of July, by a small party of militia and soldiers, under lieut. col. Clark, of the militia, who surprised a small guard at that post, and brought away a brass six-pounder, upwards of fifty stand of arms, a small quantity of stores, with a gun-boat and two batteaux.

Lieut. colonel Bishopp, lately commanding at Fort Erie, having obtained the approbation of the general commanding, for the execution of an enterprise, which he had previously proposed, crossed over at day-break, in the morning of the eleventh of July, with 240 men, consisting of a small party of militia, and detachments of the 8th, 41st, and 49th regiments. They effectually surprised the enemy's post at Black Rock, where they burnt his block-houses, stores, barracks, dock-yard and a vessel; but while occupied in securing the stores, to carry them away in their batteaux, the enemy, with a reinforcement of militia and some indians in their interest, under cover of the surrounding woods, opened a smart fire and compelled the british to hasten their retreat, with the loss of thirteen men killed and a considerable number wounded; among the latter, capt. Saunders, of the 41st regiment, severely, and lieut. colonel Bishopp mortally, an officer of distinguished merit, whose loss was much regretted by the militia of Upper Canada, with whom he seems to have been a favorite inspecting field-officer. Seven pieces of ordnance, two hundred stand of arms, and a great quantity of stores were brought away.

The two armies, almost in sight of each other, remained inactive, until the arrival of the commander of the forces from Kingston, when the speedy reduction of Fort George was confidently expected. The governor to ascertain, as it was pretended, the extent of the enemy's works and the means he possessed of defending the position which he occupied, determined to make a demonstration on that fort, on the morning of the 24th of August, and the army was put in movement, as if for an assault upon it. The british drove in the picquets, several of which were taken, and advanced within a few hundred yards of the enemy, who, although supported by a fire upon the british, from their batteries on the opposite shore, declined leaving their entrenchments to venture into the field. The commander of the forces did not deem it advisable, however, to risk a trial for the recovery of that post, which, as he deemed it, was not of sufficient moment to compensate the loss, that must have been experienced from an assault. The whole force in the neighbourhood of Fort George, at that period, it is true, did not exceed 2000 men, on an extended line, while that of the enemy in Fort George, exceeded 4000, totally depending upon their own resources for the subsistence of their army, and compelled to act solely on the defensive, from the hostile front assumed by the british in their neighbourhood. The *prestige* that surrounded the military character of Sir George Prevost, improved by the popularity he was acquiring as a civil governor, had been sensibly impaired by his failure at Sacket's Harbour, and the present fruitless "demonstration," as, (to cover this, his second failure,) he termed it, dispelled what little confidence in him, as commander of the forces, the army, and those in the country the best able to judge of his abilities as such, previously entertained.

From this time forward, his reputation, as a military commander, a position, to which his inadequacy was already, in various quarters, unequivocally and publicly expressed, was in the wane; but, his personal bravery has never been impeached, and to the moment of his departure from the province, his popularity with the people, as civil governor, remained unabated.

Harrison, in the meantime, was on the Sandusky river, making preparations to prosecute the war with vigour in the Michigan territory, as soon as the fleet fitting out at Erie (Presqu'isle) under captain Perry, who had been despatched thither by commodore Chauncey, towards the end of May, should be in sufficient strength to co-operate with the land forces. General Proctor again resolved to make another effort to defeat his purpose, and immediately invested the american fort at lower Sandusky, then under the command of Major Croghan, with a force consisting of near five hundred men, including regulars and militia, and between three and four thousand indians under Mr. Dixon and the celebrated indian chief Tecumseh. After a smart cannonade, on the second of August, from five six pounders and a howitzer, for the purpose of effecting a breach in the enemy's works, the british (the indians having previously withdrawn themselves out of reach of the enemy's fire) led on by brevet lieut. col. Short, advanced unperceived by the enemy under cover of a cloud of smoke to the distance of eighteen or twenty paces of the enemy's works. A heavy fire was immediately opened, which, at first, threw the assailants into disorder: they, however, immediately rallied, and having advanced to the outer works, began to leap into the ditch, when a fire of grape slugs was opened from a six pounder (which had been previously arranged so as to rake the ditch,) supported with musketry, that dealt destruction among the assailants, and compelled them to retreat with precipitancy, leaving their gallant leader, lieut. col. Short, with three officers and fifty-two men killed and missing. The wounded amounted to forty-one including three officers. General Proctor, finding his force inadequate, the indians unaccustomed to the European mode of warfare and to the delay of a siege, growing impatient, and general Harrison, at no great distance. with a respectable force, thought proper to raise the siege and retire to Amherstburgh.

The events in the lower province also deserve our attention. The old fortifications at the Isle-aux-Noix, emphatically termed the key of Lower-Canada, had been repaired, and three gun-boats sent thither from Quebec. No material occurrence transpired in that neighbourhood until the third day of June, when, early in the morning, a sail was observed from the garrison over a point of land formed by a bend in the river about two leagues above the island. This unusual appearance created an alert in the garrison, at that moment commanded by lieut. colonel George Taylor, inspecting field officer, (a Major in the 100th regiment) who, apprehending, from previous private information, a combined attack from the naval force on Lake Champlain and the troops in the neighbourhood of his post, commanded by the brigadier generals, Smith and Clarke, determined, by a decisive *coup de main*, to anticipate the views of the enemy. He lost no time in equipping the three gun-boats lying un-employed for want of seamen, and having manned them with soldiers from his regiment, with three artillery men to each boat, proceeded to engage the enemy. On doubling the point above the garrison, another vessel was discovered a short distance from the former, hitherto concealed by the intervening land. This discovery did not, however, deter him from persevering in his resolution, and the boats having advanced, a spirited engagement soon ensued, which, after some continuation, was suspended from a deficiency of ammunition, speedily supplied, however, from the garrison, when the action was renewed with augmented vigour.

Chap. XVI.
1813.

Small detachments of troops from the garrison, were landed on each side of the river, who poured a destructive fire of musketry on the enemy as in beating up they alternately approached either shore. This judicious and well timed measure, combined with a well directed fire from the gun-boats, of round and grape, completely decided the fate of the action, which the enemy most gallantly contested from half-past four, until half-past eight in the morning, and did not surrender until further resistance became utterly unavailing, one of the vessels being run aground to prevent her sinking. They proved to be the american sloops of war, Growler and Eagle (afterwards named Shannon and Broke, and subsequently, by orders from the admiralty, Chub and Finch) fitted out in the most complete manner for service, each carrying eleven guns, (eighteens, twelves and sixes,) long eighteens on pivots upon their forecastles, with complements of fifty-five men, comprehending a company of marines, which they had received on board from Champlain the evening previous to the engagement; the whole under the command of officers of the united states navy. The loss of the enemy was considerable: the prisoners amounted to one hundred men, of whom many were wounded: the killed were thrown overboard during the action. Of the captors, not a man was killed, and only three severely wounded.* The naval force of the enemy on

---

* In this affair no more than one hundred and eight men were engaged on the part of the british. It is worthy of notice, that this

lake Champlain was, by the capture of these vessels, almost annihilated, while it afforded the british, immediate and effectual means for operations on that lake, and checked the invasion meditated on the lower province. The intention of the enemy, by thus venturing so near to Isle-aux-Noix, where the river becomes so narrow as scarcely to afford room to manœuvre with safety, has never been clearly ascertained. It was thought to have been a piece of idle bravado on the part of the navy officers. in command of those vessels, who were very young and inexperienced men.

The american government, with a view of prosecuting the war against Lower Canada, had been at considerable pains and expense in erecting barracks, hospitals and stores, at different points on Lake Champlain, particularly at Burlington, Plattsburgh. Champlain and Swanton in the neighbourhood of the frontiers; and it was deemed expedient by the commander of the forces, to fit out an expedition at Isle-aux-Noix, for the purpose of destroying them, as well as to divert the attention of the enemy from the upper-province. The two armed vessels recently captured were accordingly put in commission, under capt. Pring who was sent from the fleet on Lake

---

was the first action in which the 100th regiment had been engaged; an auspicious omen of the gallantry afterwards displayed by that meritorious corps in common with the other troops at Niagara. It is also a singular fact, that the guns belonging to his Majesty's sloop of war, Alert, some time previously captured by the United States frigate Essex, were on board these vessels.

Ontario, and promoted to them by Sir James Yeo, with the rank of commander. Captain Everard, commanding the Wasp sloop of war, having arrived at Quebec, at that juncture, was ordered from thence, with his seamen to the Isle-aux-Noix, where as senior officer, he assumed the command of the two vessels and the three gun-boats, which had soon been put in a competent state of repair after the action. On the twenty-ninth of July, this small fleet was completely equipped, and having received on board about nine hundred men, consisting of a detachment of the 13th regiment, under lieut. colonel Williams, (of that regiment) second in command, and some companies of the 100th and 103d regiments, under the respective commands of lieutenant colonels Taylor and Smelt, commanding the right and left wings of the expedition, with some artillery, under captain Gordon, and a few of the embodied militia as batteaux men, the whole under the command of colonel John Murray, inspecting field officer, moved from Isle aux Noix, for lake Champlain. The expedition proceeded up the lake with much order, and on the 31st, landed, without opposition, at Plattsburgh, from whence general Moore, with a considerable body of men, (reported at about fifteen hundred,) had previously retired, on the approach of the british. Here, colonel Murray, having previously embarked all the warlike stores, of which a considerable quantity was found in the arsenal, and having destroyed such as he could not conveniently take away, set fire to the enemy's arsenal, public buildings, commissariat stores and barracks, recently erected, and capable of accommodating from four to five thousand men. While the troops were thus employed during that day and the whole of the night, captains Everard and Pring, in the Growler and Eagle, with a gun-boat, proceeded to Burlington, where general Hampton lay encamped, with four thousand men, and threw that place into the utmost consternation. Having captured and destroyed, within sight of the enemy's forces, four vessels, captain Everard returned to Plattsburgh, where the troops were re-embarked and proceeded to Swanton. Colonel Murray, while on the way thither, sent a detachment to Champlain, for the purpose of destroying the barracks and a blockhouse at that post. The main body having visited Swanton, and effected the purposes of the expedition, returned to Isle aux Noix, where they arrived on the fourth of August.

The army acting upon the extensive line of operations along the frontiers of Lower and Upper Canada, (at the lowest computation, one thousand miles from lake Champlain to Michillimakinac) was, by the able arrangements of commissary general Sir W. H. Robinson, and the unwearied exertions of the department under his directions, copiously supplied at every point with provisions and commissariat stores of all descriptions. The small post at Lachine was converted into a *depôt*, and placed under the superintendence of deputy assistant commissary general John Finlay, from whence the whole supplies for the upper province, were, by that gentleman, forwarded to Kingston, with the most indefatigable diligence.* To intercept the convoys of batteaux with provisions from that post to Kingston, the americans had sent several cruisers and privateers from Sacket's Harbour, to the vicinity of Prescott, and among the Thousand Islands. On the 20th July, the enemy having succeeded in surprising and capturing, at day-break, a brigade of batteaux loaded with provisions, under convoy of a gun-boat, with which they retired several miles up Goose Creek, on the south of the St. Lawrence, below Gananoque, three gun-boats, under the command of lieut. Scott, of the royal navy, were despatched from Kingston, with a detachment of the 100th regiment, with a view of intercepting them on their return to Sacket's Harbour. They proceeded to the lower end of Long Island, where, having ascertained the retreat of the enemy, they immediately pushed for it; but before they came in sight of the american vessels, the evening was

---

* Any one unacquainted with that service, who, at the present day (1848) travels in those splendid conveyances, the steamers from Montreal to Kingston, and thence upwards on the lakes, can have but a very faint idea of the toil, the trouble, the risk, delay, and enormous expense, at which the troops and their necessary supplies and stores of all kinds, were, in those times, forwarded from Lachine to Upper Canada, in winter by small canadian *traineaux*, each drawn by one horse, and in summer by unwieldy *batteaux* or clumsy flat-bottomed boats, manned each by five to seven canadian voyageurs, sometimes impelling their craft by rowing, at others dragging up the rapids, by lines.

too far advanced to make an attack, with any prospect of success; it was, therefore, determined to defer the attack until the next morning. Another gun-boat arriving in the course of the evening, with a detachment of the 41st regiment, they, at three o'clock the next morning, proceeded up the creek with the gunboats, in the hope of gaining the enemy's position at the dawn of day. Advancing until the channel became so narrow that the gun-boats could neither use their oars nor turn, so as to bring their guns to bear upon the banks, it was discovered that the enemy had taken precautions to obstruct their further progress by felling large trees across the creek. In endeavouring to remove these impediments they were fired upon by the american vessels, and from a gun which they had landed on the left bank, supported with musketry from the surrounding woods. A few of the soldiers who had landed on the right bank having re-embarked in the sternmost boats, leapt into the stream, and carrying their muskets on their heads succeeded, after wading through the water and swampy soil contiguous thereto, in effecting a landing on the left bank, and drove the enemy before them in gallant style, who retreated with precipitancy to their log intrenchment. This spirited advance saved the gun-boats, the foremost of which, (the only one that bore upon the enemy) exposed to a galling fire, had been disabled. Finding the enemy strongly posted, and, from the impracticability of bringing the other gunboats into action, that a further perseverance must be attended with a greater sacrifice of lives than the nature of the enterprise seemed to justify, they re-embarked and retired from the unequal contest. In this affair, captain Milnes, aid-de-camp to the commander of the forces, was mortally wounded, and died shortly after. This gallant young officer, had accidentally met major Frend in pursuit of the enemy, and impelled by a thirst of honor, had volunteered his services to assist in accomplishing his purpose.

On lake Ontario, the two naval commanders strove with indefatigable emulation for the command of the lake. Commodore Chauncey, after the capture of Fort George, returned to Sacket's Harbour to await the equipment of his new ship, the Pike; while his adversary, Sir James Yeo, scoured the lake, and supplied the british army in the neighbourhood of Fort George, with an abundance of stores. In the early part of July, Sir James Yeo fitted out an expedition of boats for Sacket's Harbour, with a view of cutting out their new ship, then almost rigged and ready to appear on the lake. He arrived unobserved at the vicinity of that port, and would probably have effected his purpose had not the escape of two deserters from his party, which had landed for refreshment, and in order to remain concealed until night should favor the enterprise, given the alarm to the enemy. This unlucky incident induced him to relinquish the undertaking and return to Kingston. Towards the end of July the american fleet again appeared with augmented force upon the lake, and commodore Chauncey having received a company of artillery, with a considerable number of troops, under colonel Scott, proceeded for the head of the lake, with a view of seizing and destroying the stores at Burlington Heights, the principal *dépôt* of the army on the Niagara frontier, then occupied by a small detachment under major Maule. The design of the enemy against this *dépôt* being suspected, lieutenant colonel Battersby, commanding the Glengary regiment, upon being notified to that effect by lieutenant colonel Harvey, deputy adjutant general, moved forward from York, and by a march of extraordinary celerity arrived with a reinforcement in time to save the place, which the enemy, on finding the british prepared to receive them, did not deem it prudent to attack. Commodore Chauncey on learning that York, by the advance of lieutenant col. Battersby to Burlington Heights, was left destitute of troops, seized the opportunity and bore away for that port, which he entered on the 31st July. Here the americans landed without opposition, and having taken possession of the small quantity of stores found at that place, they set fire to the barracks and public store-houses, and having re-embarked their troops, bore away for Niagara. It is a coincidence worthy of notice, that on the same day in which the american commander was employed in burning the barracks and stores at York, lieutenant colonel Murray was not less actively employed on the same business at Plattsburgh. The british fleet sailed from Kingston on the last day of July, with supplies for the army, at the head of the lake, and on the eighth of August looked into Niagara, where the enemy's fleet lay moored. The latter hove up, and bore down upon the british fleet, with which they manœuvred until the tenth, on which day two small vessels, of forty men each, (the Julia and Growler,) were cut off and captured by the british. Commodore Chauncey somewhat disheartened with the loss of these, and two other small vessels, the Scourge of eight, and Hamilton of nine guns, upset by a press of sail to escape the british, with the loss of all hands, except sixteen men picked up by the british, bore up for Niagara, from whence he sailed almost immediately for Sacket's Harbour, where he arrived on the thirteenth of August. Here he provisioned his fleet, and instantly made sail for Niagara, where he remained at anchor until the british fleet appeared off that harbour, early in the morning of the seventh of September, when the american fleet again weighed and bore down upon the british, with which they manœuvred until the twelfth, when the latter retired to Amherst Bay, near Kingston. During these five days, but few shots were exchanged between the larger ships, and without any injury to either side. The americans, however, had much the advantage in weight of metal and long guns. The fleets again met on the 28th September off York, when an engagement ensued for nearly two hours, in which the Wolfe, commanded by Sir James Yeo, lost her main and mizen top masts, and would probably have been captured, had not the Royal George, commanded by captain Mulcaster, run in between the Wolfe and the Pike, taking the latter in a raking position, so as to afford the Wolfe an opportunity of hauling off and clearing away the wreck. This affair terminated in the retreat of the british fleet under Burlington Heights, whither the enemy did not think proper to pursue it: a resolution, which, if adopted by the american commander, probably would have been fatal to the british fleet, on Lake Ontario. On the first of October, the american fleet set sail from Fort George, with a convoy of troops, for Sacket's Harbour, where an expedition was preparing, whose destination was as yet unknown. The british fleet left their anchorage under Burlington Heights on the next day, and came in sight of the enemy, but no attempt was made to bring on a general engagement. The american fleet in their way to Sacket's Harbour fell in with and captured five small vessels out of seven, with upwards of 250 men of De Watteville's regiment, from York, bound for Kingston, where an attack was apprehended. This loss though apparently trifling in itself, was severely felt, by reason of the few forces in the upper-province. For the remainder of the season nothing of moment occurred on this lake, and indeed the naval commanders appear to have considered the question of too great importance, to their respective governments, to stake the fate of the war, in Upper Canada, upon a decisive naval engagement.

Among the matters of "reform and progress" in those times, worthy of being noticed as of real importance to the state and its defence, as well as to the general prosperity, was the appearance, at a time when most needed, of the second steamer, (the Swiftsure) on the waters of the St. Lawrence, which is thus noticed in " *The Quebec Mercury*," of the 4th of May of the present year, as quite a prodigy. The first has been previously noticed, and the reader, by comparing that with this, and this with those splendid conveyances of the present time, (1848,) by which the traveller from Europe for Canada, arriving at Quebec, may now proceed thence, in a very few days, to the remotest points of lake Huron and Michigan, visiting by the way the principal places in Upper Canada, and appreciate the progress which, in this respect has been made, and which there is reason to believe is, comparatively to what in time it will be, little more than at the starting point, as those who are to follow us, some fifty years hence, will see amply verified.

" On Sunday at half-past two P.M., arrived in this harbour

the steam-boat Swiftsure. She left Montreal on Saturday, at half past five, A. M. She past Three Rivers at seven P. M., on Saturday, anchored at Cape Madelaine at eight, and got under weigh at four, A. M. on Sunday. The whole time under weigh being only 22 hours and a half, notwithstanding that the wind was easterly the whole time and blowing strong. She had 28 passengers. A serjeant with six privates of the royal scots, having in charge three american prisoners of war, four deserters from the 100th regiment, and one deserter from the american army.

"From an examination and comparison it appears that the Swiftsure's mechanical movements are superior to any of those established on Hudson River or Lake Champlain. One grand improvement alone is sufficient to evince the verity of our assertion.—In those engines first constructed in the United States, serious accidents might happen, and actually did occur, from the bursting of their boilers, occasioned by the too strong ignition of their furnaces, and neglect of those who had charge of keeping up the fires, as to the precise heat required, thus inducing a superabundant quantity of steam; which could not escape but by means of a valve opened occasionally by the engineer. This method was liable to accidents, to obviate which a safety valve was constructed, connected with the boiler, to convey away the superfluous vapour, which is opened by its own power, whenever the steam is too abundant for the required velocity. Thus it is obvious the boiler cannot burst, and all uneasiness upon that account is effectually removed.

"The ladies' cabin occupies the after part of the vessel, containing eight berths or couches for reposing; and is separated from the gentlemen's cabin by the staircase, the captain's, and a private staircase; the whole is painted white and decorated with curtains, mirrors, &c.

"The gentlemen's cabin is thirty feet by twenty-three, and contains ten berths or couches on each side and two forming an angle with the starboard side, calculated to lodge forty-four persons, with convenience, decorated with pilastres, medallions, cornices, curtains, &c. The steerage is fitted for the reception of troops or persons who may not be able to pay a high price for passages. One hundred and fifty persons may be there accommodated comfortably

"The Swiftsure is 130 feet keel, the breadth of beam twenty-four feet; length upon deck 140 feet.

"Great praise is due to Mr. Molson for his exertions in preparing a cheap, safe, expeditious and commodious conveyance between the metropolis of Lower Canada and Montreal, and we heartily wish him all the success his public spirited undertaking merits."

The american fleet on lake Ontario, consisted, on the first of August, of two ships, one brig, and eleven schooners, but the number of guns and weight of metal, are not stated. The british fleet consisted of the

Wolfe	23 guns,	Sir J. L. Yeo, commodore,
Royal George,	22	Wm. Howe Mulcaster, capt.
Melville	14	Edwd. Spilsbury, commander.
Earl Moira	14	H. Dodds, —— ——
Sir Sydney Smith,	12	H. C. Owen, lieut & com.
Beresford	12	H. Radcliffe, —— ——

CHAPTER XVII.

Great efforts by the americans towards the close of the campaign—general Hampton moves his forces across lake Champlain, from Burlington, to Plattsburgh—genl. Wilkinson making great preparations, at Sacket's Harbour, for a descent upon Kingston or Montreal—general Harrison equally active on the Miami, to recover the Michigan territory—naval engagement on lake Erie, and british fleet captured—evacuation of fort Sandwich and Detroit by british forces under general Proctor—pursued by american forces under general Harrison—overtaken—battle and defeat of general Proctor at the Moravian town, on the river Thames—investment of fort George, on the Niagara river, and british forces concentrated at Burlington Heights—general Hampton invades Lower Canada, entering Odelltown—retreats and moves to Four Corners, with a view of re-entering by the river Chateauguay—proclamation, by the commander of the forces, and corresponding zeal of the canadian militia—reconnaissance upon the enemy's position, by lieutenant colonel De Salaberry—defeat of the enemy on the Chateauguay—his retreat—the enemy's forces at Sacket's Harbour move—descend the St. Lawrence—defeated at Chrystler's farm—retreat across the St. Lawrence to Salmon river, where they put into winter quarters—sedentary militia dismissed with thanks—american forces evacuate fort George—cruelly destroy the village of Newark—british surprise and take fort Niagara—the american frontier laid waste, in retribution of the conflagration and cruelties at Newark.

THE campaign, towards the autumn, assumed a more systematic and menacing character. In the beginning of September, the forces at Burlington (Vermont) under general

Hampton, moved across lake Champlain to Plattsburgh, with a view of penetrating into the district of Montreal, while general Wilkinson with 10,000 men at Sacket's Harbour, was preparing, under the immediate direction of general Armstrong, the secretary at war, a numerous flotilla of batteaux and durham boats, for an expedition, supposed to be destined either against Kingston or Montreal. General Harrison, with an army of eight thousand men, on the Miami river, only waited for the equipment of the american fleet, fitting out under commodore Perry, at Presqu'Isle, to move his forces against Detroit, and to carry on offensive operations against the british, in the neighbourhood of Lake Erie. Captain Barclay, who had early in the summer, assumed the command of the british squadron on Lake Erie, blockaded the american fleet, so as to prevent their crossing the bar at Presqu'Isle (which the enemy could not effect without unshipping their guns,) until toward the conclusion of August, when having occasion to bear away for Long Point, the enemy seized the moment of his absence and crossed the bar. Finding on his return the enemy ready for the lake, and too powerful for his small squadron, he bore away, for Amherstburgh, to await the equipment of the Detroit recently launched.

Commodore Perry sailed shortly after him for the head of the lake, and appeared at the commencement of September, for several days successively off Amherstburgh, in defiance of the british squadron, retiring every evening to his anchorage at *Put-in-Bay*. The british forces in the Michigan Territory, and its neighbourhood, falling short of supplies, for which they depended solely upon the fleet, captain Barclay had no other alternative than to risk a general engagement. With this resolution, he made sail from Amherstburgh on the 9th September, manned with only fifty or sixty seamen, (including a small reinforcement of thirty-six men from Lake Ontario) and detachments from the 41st, and royal Newfoundland regiments, as marines. On the tenth, in the morning, the enemy's fleet were descried at anchor in *Put-in-Bay*, which immediately weighed and bore down upon the british squadron, while the wind blowing a gentle breeze from the south west, veering round to the south east, gave the enemy the weather gage. At a quarter before twelve, the british commenced firing, which was, in ten minutes afterwards, returned by the enemy, who bore up for close action. The engagement continued with unabated fury until half past two, when the enemy's principal ship, the Lawrence, being rendered unmanageable, commodore Perry left her in charge of his first lieutenant Yarnal, and hoisted his pendant on board the Niagara. Soon after this officer had left the Lawrence, her colours were struck, but the british, from the weakness of their crews and the destruction of their boats, were unable to take possession of her. It was at this anxious and interesting juncture, that the fate of the day seemed to poise in favor of the british; and commodore Perry even despaired of the victory, when a sudden breeze revived his hopes, and turned the scale in his favor. This fortunate commander, finding the Niagara had suffered lightly in the engagement, made a desperate effort to retrieve the fortune of the day, and taking advantage of the breeze, shot ahead of the Lady Prevost, Queen Charlotte and Hunter, raking them with her starboard guns, and engaged the Detroit, which being raked in all directions soon became unmanageable. The Niagara then bore round ahead of the Queen Charlotte, and hauling up on the starboard tack, engaged that ship, giving at the same time a raking fire with her larboard guns to the Chippawa and Little Belt, while the smaller vessels closing to grape and canister distance, maintained a tremendous and most destructive fire. This masterly, and but too successful, manœuvre, decided the contest. Captain Barclay, being severely and dangerously wounded, captain Finnis of the Queen Charlotte, killed, and every commander and officer second in command, either killed or disabled, the Detroit and Queen Charlotte, perfect wrecks, after a desperate engagement, of upwards of three hours, was compelled to surrender. By this decisive action, the whole of the british squadron on lake Erie was captured by the enemy, who now became uncontrollable masters of that lake. The enemy lost in this action, twenty-seven men in killed and ninety-six men wounded.

The prisoners were landed at Sandusky, and treated with the greatest humanity by the american commodore, who paroled captain Barclay, and treated that gallant officer with all the kindness and attention which his unsuccessful bravery deserved.

The army in possession of the Michigan territory and in the neighbourhood of Detroit, was, by this defeat, now deprived of every prospect of obtaining future supplies from Kingston, and a speedy evacuation of Detroit, and a retreat towards the head of lake Ontario, became inevitable. Commodore Perry, as soon after the engagement, as circumstances would admit, transported the american forces under the command of general Harrison, from Portage River and Fort Meigs, to Put-in-Bay, from whence they were conveyed to the neighbourhood of Amherstburgh, which they occupied on the evening of the 23d of September, general Proctor having previously fallen back upon Sandwich, after setting fire to the navy-yard, barracks and public stores, at the former place. General Proctor seeing the enemy determined to follow up his first success, by an immediate march upon Detroit, found his troops void both of resources, and too reduced in numbers to make a stand and dispute the occupancy of that post against the overwhelming force of the enemy. He, therefore, determined to retreat along the river Thames towards the head of lake Ontario. On September 26th, he evacuated Detroit and fort Sandwich, and commenced his retreat toward the Thames, having entirely destroyed the public stores at those posts. In this reverse of fortune, the indians, under colonel Elliot, of the indian department, with Tecumseh, still adhered to his standard, with unshaken fidelity, and covered his retreat. General Harrison occupied Sandwich, on the following day, (the 27th Sept.) and on the second of October, marched in quest of the shattered remains of the british forces under general Proctor, escorted by a number of batteaux, under the immediate direction of commodore Perry. On the 4th of October, he came up with the rear-guard of the british, and succeeded in capturing the whole of their ammunition and stores. General Proctor, under this second reverse of fortune, by which he was left destitute of the means of subsistence and defence, found himself compelled to stake the fate of his small army on a general engagement. He, accordingly, assumed a position on the right bank of the Thames, at the Moravian Town, (an indian village,) the left of his line resting on the river and supported by a fieldpiece, his right on a swamp, at the distance of near three hundred yards from the river, and flanked by the whole indian force attached to the division. The intermediate ground covered with lofty trees, was dry and somewhat elevated. In this position he awaited the approach of the enemy, who having, on the morning of the 5th of October, passed the river at a rapid, twelve miles below the Moravian village, by means of two or three boats and indian canoes found on the spot, and by crossing a number of infantry behind the horsemen, came up with the british in the afternoon. General Harrison drew up his men in two lines, and secured his left flank by a division thrown back *en potence*, and without any previous engagement by infantry, ordered his mounted Kentuckians (accustomed to ride with extraordinary dexterity, through the most embarrassed woods) to charge at full speed upon the british, which they effected before the latter had time to discharge their third fire. By this cavalry charge of the enemy, the soldiers worn down with fatigue and hunger, and dispirited by the unpromising appearance of the campaign, became totally routed, and for the most part, surrendered prisoners, while the general, and his personal staff, sought their safety in flight. The indians in the mean time carried on the contest with the left of the american line, with determination; but these faithful allies, finding all hopes of retrieving the day in vain, yielded to the overwhelming numbers of the enemy, and reluctantly left the field. They, however, remained in the neighbourhood, and harrassed the enemy on his retreat to Detroit and Sandwich, whither he returned immediately after the action. The british are said to have lost twelve killed and twenty-two wounded. The americans stated their own loss at seven killed

Chap. XVII. 1813.

and twenty-two wounded. Thirty-three indians were found dead on the field; among them the famous chief and warrior Tecumseh, not less celebrated for his humanity, a virtue little known among indians in a state of war, than by his bravery, his eloquence, and his influence among our indian allies. Upwards of six hundred of the british, including twenty-five officers, were made prisoners of war. Those who escaped, made the best of their way to Ancaster, at the head of the Lake Ontario, exposed, at an inclement season, to all the horrors of a dreary wilderness, of hunger, and of famine. On the seventeenth of October, they *rendezvoused* at that place, to the number of two hundred and forty-six, including the general and seventeen officers.*

---

* The british loss can be ascertained from the following extracts from the general order of the commander of the forces, of the 24th of November, 1813, relative to general Proctor's defeat, on the 5th of October :—

" His excellency the commander of the forces, has received an official report from major-genl. Proctor, of the affair which took place on the 5th of October, near the Moravian village, and he has in vain sought in it, for grounds to palliate the report made to his excellency by staff-adjutant Reiffenstein, upon which the general order of the 18th October was founded—on the contrary, that statement remains confirmed, in all the principal events which marked that disgraceful day; the precipitancy with which the staff-adjutant retreated from the field of action, prevented his ascertaining the loss sustained by the division on that occasion; it also led him most grossly to exaggerate the enemy's force, and to misrepresent the conduct of the indian warriors, who, instead of retreating towards Machedash, as he had stated, gallantly maintained the conflict, under their brave chief Tecumseh, and in their turn, harrassed the american army on its retreat to Detroit.

" The subjoined return states the loss the right division has sustained in the action of the fleet on lake Ontario, on the 10th Sept., and in the affair of the 5th October, near the Moravian village. In the latter but very few appear to have been rescued by an honorable death, from the ignominy of passing under the american yoke, nor are there many, whose wounds plead in mitigation of this reproach.

This disaster to the british arms in that quarter, seems not to have been palliated by those precautions, and that presence of mind, which,

Chap. XVII.
1813.

The right division appears to have been encumbered with an unmanageable load of unnecessary, and forbidden private baggage—while the requisite arrangements for the expedition, and certain conveyance of the ammunition, and provisions, the sole objects worthy of consideration, appear to have been totally neglected, as well as all those ordinary measures, resorted to by officers of intelligence, to retard, and impede, a pursuing enemy.—The result affords but too fatal a proof of this unjustifiable neglect. The right division had quitted Sandwich on its retreat, on the 26th September, having had ample time for every previous arrangement, to facilitate and secure that movement; on the 2d of October following, the enemy pursued by the same route, and on the 4th, succeeded in capturing all the stores of the division, and on the following day attacked and defeated it, almost without a struggle.

"With heartfelt pride and satisfaction the commander of the forces had lavished on the right division of this army, that tribute of praise which was so justly due to its former gallantry, and steady discipline. It is with poignant grief and mortification that he now beholds its well-earned laurels tarnished, and its conduct calling loudly for reproach and censure.

"The commander of the forces appeals to the genuine feelings of the british soldier, from whom he neither conceals the extent of the loss the army has suffered, nor the far more lamented injury it has sustained, in its wounded honor, confident that but one sentiment will animate every breast, and that zealous to wash out the stain, which, by a most extraordinary and unaccountable infatuation, has fallen on a formerly deserving portion of the army;—all will vie to emulate the glorious achievements recently performed, by a small but highly spirited, and well disciplined division, led on by officers possessed of enterprise, intelligence, and gallantry, nobly evincing what british soldiers can perform, when susceptible of no fear, but that of failing in the discharge of their duty.

"His excellency considers it an act of justice, to exonerate most honorably from this censure, the brave soldiers of the right division, who were serving as marines on board the squadron on lake Erie."

"RETURN OF THE RIGHT DIVISION OF THE ARMY OF UPPER CANADA.
Detachment serving as marines on board the squadron, in action, on the 10th September, 1813.

Killed, 1 lieut., 1 serjt., 21 rank and file;—Wounded, 3 serjts., 46 rank and file;—Prisoners, 2 lieuts., 1 asst.-surgeon, 4 serjts., 4 drummers, 167 rank and file.

Killed, wounded, and missing in the retreat and in the action of the 5th October, 1813.

28 officers, 31 serjeants, 13 drummers, 559 rank and file, 46 horses.

even in defeat, reflect lustre upon a commander. The bridges and roads in the rear of the retreating army were left entire, while its

Assembled at Ancaster, on the 17th October, 1813.
18 officers, including the major general, 15 serjeants, 9 drummers. 204 rank and file, 53 horses.
Total strength of the Right Division, on the 10th September, 1813. 1 maj. gen., 49 officers, 57 serjts., 26 drummers, 994 rank and file. 99 horses."

General Proctor had, to this time, served with honor and distinction in Upper Canada, and was universally considered a brave and able officer; but his retreat, and the events of this untoward day, blasted his fame and at once ruined him in the public estimation.—Some, however, were of opinion that the severity of the general order, by Sir George Prevost, on the occasion, was premature, and a prejudication of the case of his unfortunate brother in arms, who, it was thought, before so complete a condemnation from his superior officer, ought to have had the benefit of a trial. This he ultimately did get, but not until, as the reader will perceive, by observing dates, upwards of a year after the occurrence alluded to, before the expiration of which, Sir George Prevost himself, had fallen still lower than he, in the public estimation, by his own inglorious retreat from Plattsburgh, more humiliating to the national pride than even Proctor's affair. His retreat and discomfiture were of but a small and isolated division of the army, hitherto distinguished for its gallantry, but which, by the loss of the fleet, becoming destitute of resources, had no other alternative than a speedy retreat, or an immediate surrender. He took his chance of the former. The retreat, it seems, was ill-conducted; but was, in fact, that of sir George Prevost, taking all in all, any thing better? He had advanced to Plattsburgh, at the head of an effective force of at least twelve thousand troops, the *élite* of the army under his command, recently from France and Spain—men accustomed to victory, and again marching to it, as they believed—well provided with an abundant commissariat, and stores of all kinds, and led on by experienced and able officers.—These, however, on the naval defeat, (the loss of the fleets being, in both cases, the immediate cause of retreat) he countermarched, to their inexpressible humiliation and disgust, without their being allowed once to see, much less come in contact with the enemy. A further advance, after the loss of the fleet, was, indeed, out of the question; but nothing could justify the precipitancy of retreat, sacrifice of public stores, and demoralisation in the army that took place in consequence of it. The district of Montreal, was immediately in his rear, and at the short distance of three, or at most four marches from Plattsburgh, upon which he might, it was said, have fallen back at his leisure. It is, however, but justice to remark, that time has materially worn down the asperities with which sir George Prevost was also in his turn prejudged, with respect to this, to say the least of it, most unlucky expedition.

progress was retarded by a useless and cumbrous load of baggage. Whether the neglect sprung from an erroneous contempt of the

Major general Proctor being tried at Montreal, in December, 1814. on five charges preferred against him for misconduct on this occasion. was found guilty of part of them, and sentenced " to be publicly reprimanded, and to be suspended from rank and pay for six months." It was found " that he did not take the proper measures for conducting the retreat,"—that he had, " in many instances during the retreat, and in the disposition of the force under his command, been erroneous in judgment, and in some, deficient in those energetic and active exertions, which the extraordinary difficulties of his situation so particularly required."—" But as to any defect or reproach with regard to the personal conduct of major general Proctor, during the action of the 5th October, the court most fully acquitted him."

His royal highness the Prince Regent confirmed the finding of the court, but animadverted upon it rather severely, by the general order issued on the occasion, dated " Horse Guards, 9th Sept., 1815," for its " mistaken lenity" towards the accused, as the following extracts will explain :—

" Upon the whole, the court is of opinion, that the prisoner, major general Proctor, has, in many instances during the retreat, and in the disposition of the force under his command, been erroneous in judgment, and in some, deficient in those energetic and active exertions. which the extraordinary difficulties of his situation so particularly required.

" The court doth, therefore, adjudge him, the said major general Proctor, to be publicly reprimanded, and to be suspended from rank and pay, for the period of six calendar months.

" But as to any defect or reproach, with regard to the personal conduct of major general Proctor, during the action on the 5th October, the court most fully and honorably acquits the said major general Proctor.

" His royal highness the Prince Regent has been pleased, in the name and on the behalf of his Majesty, to confirm the finding of the court, on the 1st, 3d, 4th, and 5th charges.

" With respect to the second charge, it appeared to his royal highness to be a matter of surprise that the court should find the prisoner guilty of the offence alleged against him, while they, at the same time, acquit him of all the facts upon which that charge is founded; and yet, that in the summing up of their finding, upon the whole of the charges, they should ascribe the offences of which the prisoner has been found guilty, to error of judgment, and pass a sentence totally inapplicable to their own finding of guilt, which can alone be ascribed to the court having been induced, by a reference to the general good character and conduct of major general Proctor, to forget, through a humane but mistaken lenity, what was due from them to the service.

" Under all the circumstances of the case, however, and particularly those which render it impossible to have recourse to the otherwise expedient measure of re-assembling the court for the revisal of their

enemy, or from disobedience of the orders of the commanding officer, it is not well understood; but the defeat led to the harshest recrimination, and involved the division of the brave troops that had hitherto served with honor in the Michigan territory, in undeserved disgrace.

Notwithstanding these events, the british still retained possession of Michillimackinac, which secured our influence over the indian tribes of the west, and though general Harrison, contemplated an expedition aganst that post, he found the season too far advanced to undertake it, with any prospect of success. For this reason, and from a belief, that the garrison of that post, cut off from all resources must necessarily fall of itself, he abandoned the project, not aware that it might, though with some pains, be copiously supplied by way of York, or the Ottawa river. His disposable forces were therefore conveyed from the head

---

proceedings, the Prince Regent has been pleased to acquiesce in and confirm so much of the sentence as adjudges the prisoner to be publicly reprimanded; and in carrying the same into execution, his royal highness has directed the general officer commanding in Canada, to convey to major general Proctor, his royal highness's high disapprobation of his conduct; together with the expression of his royal highness's regret, that any officer of the length of service and of the exalted rank he has attained, should be so extremely wanting in professional knowledge, and so deficient in those active and energetic qualities, which must be required of every officer, but especially of one in the responsible situation in which the major general was placed.

" His royal highness the commander in chief directs that the foregoing charges preferred against major general Proctor, together with the finding and sentence of the court, and the Prince Regent's pleasure thereon, shall be entered in the general order book, and read at the head of every regiment in his Majesty's service.

" By command of his royal highness the commander in chief.

" H. CALVERT, adjutant general."

of Lake Erie to Buffalo, from whence they were forwarded to Niagara and Fort George, to supply the detachments which had moved from thence to Sacket's Harbour.

The commander of the forces, whose headquarters were at Kingston, having cause to suspect an attack at that point, by the armament preparing at Sacket's Harbour, re-called major general De Rottenburgh with a part of his force from the Niagara frontier, leaving major general Vincent to continue the investment of Fort George. No sooner had these orders been carried into effect, for the security of Kingston, than general Vincent ascertained by several expresses from general Proctor, his retreat from Amhertsburgh, and his total discomfiture at the Moravian village. So circumstanced, he judged it expedient, for the succour of the broken remains of the right division retreating towards the head of the Ontario. as well as for the safety of his army, to raise the investment of Fort George and to fall back and concentrate his forces at Burlington Heights, lest general Harrison, by a bold and rapid march, or by a sudden descent in the fleet from Amherstburgh, should pre-occupy that important position, which, if effected by the enemy, would place him between the two hostile armies.

To retire with order and safety, at a moment when the enemy, emboldened by recent triumphs, and the advantage of superior numbers, might, by a decisive stroke, have dispersed our forces on the Niagara frontier, was a movement of the utmost consequence to the security of Upper Canada. The british line extending in front of Fort George from the Four-Mile Creek on Lake Ontario, to the cross roads and St. David's, was so extremely weakened by sickness, as to be scarcely able from three or four thousand men, to exhibit one third of that number of effective firelocks, in case of emergency: but the superior advantages of decision and method, in effecting the retreat, amply provided for the safety of the movement. Early in the morning, of the 9th of October, the main body with the baggage fell back in silence and with good order, while the picquets remained at their posts, in front of Fort George, in order to engage the attention of the enemy, who were not aware of the retreat until the evening, when the picquets retired. Seven companies of the 100th and the light company of the 8th regiment, and a few indians, the whole under the command of colonel Murray, constituted the rear guard, and covered the retreat of the main body. This small but effective force, and which during the investment had participated in all the fatigues and privations, incident to that service, proceeded in the rear of the army, by slow and deliberate marches, and though closely pressed for several days, by a brigade of 1500 men, under brigadiers general M'Clure and Porter from Fort George, so effectually checked their pursuit as to afford time to general Vincent to

119

Chap. XVII.
1813.

ains of the right division, under
r, and to prepare himself against
urlington Heights.
w days march and constant
ith M'Clure's division, the rear
ssumed a position at the already
oney Creek, from which the
think it prudent to attempt to

inder of the forces having left
De Rottenburgh in charge of the
iry commands in Upper-Canada,
ontreal, toward the end of Sep-
et the invasion with which the
ned the lower province. Gen-
after having transported his
ake Champlain, lay encamped
s, at Cumberland Head, near
On the 20th of September, he
r Canada, (his advanced guard
ed a small picquet early in the
)dclltown, with upwards of five
The road leading from thence
l the open country, in the neigh-
Montreal, passed through a
l of upwards of five leagues
n cut up and rendered impracti-
tis the preceding campaign, by
under lieutenant colonel De
l was now guarded by a few of
ight Infantry, and some indians
tion of captain Mailloux. These
itely reinforced, by the flank

companies of the 4th battalion of embodied militia under major Perrault, and the canadian Voltigeurs under lieutenant col. De Salaberry, who commanded in the advance. Had Hampton, immediately, sent forward a body of rifleman through the woods, he might, without much difficulty, have obtained a footing in the open country near St. Johns, which, if he could have succeeded in occupying, must have led to the surrender of the Isle-aux-Noix. He, however, seems not to have been aware of our weakness, or to have placed little reliance in the discipline and perseverance of his troops. On the 22d September, he evacuated Odelltown, and moved with his whole force westward, toward the head of Chateauguay river, under pretext of the impracticability of advancing through the Odelltown road, for want of water for his cavalry and cattle, owing to the extraordinary drought of the season.

At this momentous crisis, the commander of the forces issued a proclamation, calling for the exertions of the people in repelling the threatened invasion; and the militia in the district of Montreal, turned out with the same ardour and alacrity as in the preceding campaign.

Lieut. colonel De Salaberry, with the canadian Voltigeurs, on ascertaining the route the enemy had pursued, moved in like manner to Chateauguay, where he was ordered by the commander of the forces, to proceed to the enemy's camp at Four Corners, at the head of the

Chateauguay, in order to create an alarm, and if possible dislodge him by a surprise. To effect this service (the accomplishment of which appeared quite impracticable to lieutenant col. De Salaberry, with the very limited force under his command) he proceeded through the woods along the Chateauguay, with one hundred and fifty of his Voltigeurs, the light company of the canadian Fencibles, and about one hundred indians, under the direction of captain Gaucher; and on the afternoon of the first of October, arrived, unobserved, at the vicinity of the enemy's camp. By the indiscretion of one of his indians, who had discharged his piece, an alarm was created, when lieut. colonel DeSalaberry finding himself discovered, immediately collected fifty of his Voltigeurs, with whom, and his indians, he pushed into the enemy's advanced camp, consisting of two light battalions, of about four hundred men each, and drove them for a considerable distance, until perceiving the enemy making movements to cut off his retreat he fell back, and took up his former position at the skirt of the woods. From this point he made another charge, but the alarm being now universal in the camp, and the indians having fallen to the rear, he retired. Of the enemy, one officer and one man were killed, and only one wounded, by their own statement; though other more probable accounts, state their loss at twenty-five killed and wounded. This affair, afforded an occasion to lieut. col. DeSalaberry, of leading his Voltigeurs for the first time into action, and probably gave him a just confidence in the valour of his countrymen, which a few days afterwards they so well exemplified, under their gallant leader at Chateauguay. After this incursion he returned to Chateauguay, taking the precaution of breaking up the road in his rear, and acquainting himself with the ground over which Hampton was expected to make his way into the province, and finally assumed a judicious position in a thick wood, on the left bank of the Chateauguay river, at the distance of two leagues above the fork or confluence of that and the English river, where he threw up temporary breast works of logs, covering his front and right flank by extended abattis, his left being secured by the river.

Here he resolved to await the enemy and maintain his ground with a handful of canadians, against the whole strength of the invading army. In his rear there was a small rapid, where the river was fordable; this he covered with a strong breast work and a guard; keeping at the same time a strong picquet of the Beauharnois militia, in advance on the right bank of the river, lest the enemy, approaching under cover of the forest, might cross the ford, and dislodge him from his ground. The occupancy of this position, Hampton justly considered of the first importance to the ulterior object of the campaign, as the country from thence to the mouth of the Chateauguay, being principally open and cultivated, afforded no strong points to check his progress to the St. Lawrence, and prevent his junction with general Wilkinson's division, which, in fact, was not yet in readiness to move.

General Hampton, in the meantime, to distract and divide the attention of the british, directed colonel Clark to carry on a petty warfare on the eastern side of lake Champlain, and that ruthless depredator accordingly infested the settlements in Missiskoui Bay, where he plundered the inhabitants in the most wanton manner.

On the 21st of October, general Hampton again entered Lower Canada, having early in the morning of that day despatched his light troops and a regiment of the line, under brigadier general Izard, to dislodge a small picquet of sedentary militia, and a few indian warriors, at the junction of the Outarde and Chateauguay rivers, where the main body arrived on the 22d. On the 24th, having opened and completed a large and practicable road from his position at Four Corners, (a distance of 24 miles.) through woods and morasses, which lieut. colonel De Salaberry, on returning from Four Corners, had broken and embarrassed with abattis, the whole of his artillery (10 field pieces) and stores were brought forward to his new position, about seven miles from lieut. colonel De Salaberry's post.

From this point he despatched colonel Purdy, with a light brigade, and a strong body of infantry of the line, at an early hour in the night of the 25th, with orders to gain the ford, and fall on the rear of lieut. colonel De Salaberry's position; while the main body were to commence the attack in front. Purdy's brigade proceeded, but getting bewildered in the woods, either through the ignorance or treachery of the guides, did not gain the point of attack as directed. General Hampton, however, advanced next morning, (26th Oct.) under the expectation of hearing of the intended attack at the ford, and at ten o'clock made his appearance, with about three thousand five hundred men, under general Izard, on the high road, leading to the abattis, and drove in a small picquet of twenty-five men, who, falling back upon a second picquet, made a resolute stand, and maintained a smart fire upon the enemy. Lieut. colonel De Salaberry, upon hearing the musketry, advanced with the light company of the canadian Fencibles, commanded by captain Ferguson, and two companies of his Voltigeurs, commanded by captains Chevalier and Juchereau Duchesnay. The first of these companies he posted on the right, in front of the abattis, in extended order, its right skirting on the adjoining woods and abattis, among which were distributed a few Abenaqui indians. Captain Chevalier Duchesnay's company of Voltigeurs in extended order, occupied the ground from the left of this company to the river Chateauguay, and the third company, under captain L. Juchereau Duchesnay, with about thirty-five sedentary militia, under capt. Longtain, were thrown back *en potence* along the margin of the river, for the purpose of flanking, or preventing a flank fire from the enemy in the event of his appearance on the opposite side of the river. The enemy, in the mean time, advanced with steadiness in open column of sections to within musket shot, when lieutenant colonel De Salaberry discharged his rifle as a signal to commence firing, at which a mounted officer was seen to fall. The bugles sounded and a quick fire was immediately opened upon the enemy, who wheeled up into line, and commenced a fire in battalion vollies, which, from the position of their line, was almost totally thrown to the right of the canadians, and of no effect whatever. They, however, soon changed their front parallel to their adversaries, by facing to the right, and fyling up with speed, when the engagement became general. The retreat of a few skirmishers, advanced in the centre of the line, being mistaken by the enemy for a flight, an universal shout ensued, which was re-echoed by the canadians, and the reinforcements in reserve under lieutenant colonel M'Donnell, while lieutenant colonel De Salaberry, as a *ruse de guerre*, ordered the bugles placed at intervals, in the abattis, to sound an advance: this had the desired effect and checked the ardour of the enemy, who suspected that the canadians were advancing in great numbers. The noise of the engagement brought on colonel Purdy's division, on the opposite side of the river, which, having driven in the picquet of the sedentary militia, under captain Brugueire, were pressing on for the ford, at which lieut. colonel De Salaberry ordered the light company of the 3d battalion embodied militia, under captain Daly, to cross and take up the ground abandoned by the picquet. Captain Daly, with his company, crossed at the ford, and having advanced fell in with, and drove back the advanced guard of the americans upon the main body, which still pressed forward and compelled him, in his turn, to fall back. Having repulsed captain Daly's company, they were moving on in overwhelming numbers, with eagerness and speed, close on the bank of the river, until opposite to captain L. Juchereau Duchesnay's company, which hitherto lay concealed, and now at the word of command from lieutenant colonel De Salaberry opened so unexpected and effectual a fire upon the enemy, as to throw him into the utmost disorder, and immediately to occasion a tumultuous and precipitate retreat.

General Hampton finding his arrangements disconcerted, by the total route of the division on the right bank, withdrew his forces in good order, at half past two in the afternoon, without having made a single effort to carry the abattis and entrenchments, at the point of the bayonet, leaving lieut. colonel De Salaberry, with scarcely three hundred canadians, masters of the field of action. Towards the close of the engagement Sir George Prevost, with major general De Watteville, arrived on the ground, and witnessed in person, the judicious arrangements lieutenant colonel De Salaberry had made, whose prowess and that of his gallant comrades and countrymen on the occasion, called forth the warmest encomiums of the commander of the forces. Upwards of forty of the americans were found dead on the field. The loss of the canadians amounted to five killed and twenty in wounded and missing.*

General Hampton having re-occupied his late position, called a council of war, where it was determined to fall back and occupy the former position at Four-Corners, to secure their communication with the United States; from thence, either to retire into winter quarters or to be ready to re-enter Lower-Canada. Pursuant to this determination, the army retired to Four-Corners, while the canadians hung upon their rear, and harrassed their retreat.

From the fatigues and privations experienced by this division, exposed for several weeks to the inclemency of the season, it had become incapable of co-operating with Wilkinson's

---

* The commander of the forces was pleased to acknowledge the distinguished support which lieut. col. De Salaberry experienced from the zeal and exertions of captain Ferguson of the Canadian Fencibles, and from the captains Chevalier and L. Juchereau Duchesnay, from adjutants O'Sullivan and Hebden, and captain Lamotte, of the indian warriors. Sir George Prevost, in his official despatch on this occasion, solicited from the Prince Regent, as a mark of his gracious approbation of the embodied battalions of the Canadian Militia five pairs of colours, for the 1st, 2d, 3d, 4th and 5th battalions which were accordingly granted.

division, in the combined movement against Montreal. It, therefore, shortly after, fell back upon Plattsburgh, and retired to winter quarters.

The plan of the campaign adopted by the american government, as subsequently developed by the publications of sundry documents submitted to Congress, was, by hastily withdrawing their forces from Fort George to Sacket's Harbour, to make a sudden descent upon Kingston, before the british forces could be called in from the Niagara frontier; while Hampton was to make a simultaneous movement on Lake Champlain, indicating an intention of attacking Montreal and its dependencies, and really to attack them, if to reinforce the upper province, these posts should be materially weakened. The lingering progress of the armament at Sacket's Harbour, afforded time to call in reinforcements to Kingston, and after some discussion between general Wilkinson and the secretary of war, it was determined, at the instance of the latter, to leave that post in the rear, and proceed down the St. Lawrence for Montreal. The american forces, to about ten thousand men, accordingly rendezvoused towards the end of October, on Grenadier Island, in the neighbourhood of Kingston, where general De Rottenburgh, confidently expecting an attack, was prepared for the event. From this point, after experiencing much foul weather, Wilkinson commenced his movement, under cover of the american fleet, and on the 3d November proceeded down the St. Lawrence, with a flotilla of upwards of three hundred boats of various sizes, escorted by a division of gunboats. He continued to within three miles of Prescott, and landed his troops on the american shore, who proceeded downwards by land to a bay or cove, two miles below that post, in order to avoid the british batteries, while the flotilla passed them in the night of the sixth, without sustaining any material injury in their passage by the cannonade.

The movement of the flotilla down the St. Lawrence, being ascertained at Kingston, gen. De Rottenburgh detached a small force from that post, consisting of the 49th regiment, commanded by lieutenant colonel Plenderleath, the 89th regiment and some Voltigeurs, which, when reinforced by lieutenant colonel Pearson, with a party of the canadian Fencibles from Prescott, amounted to about eight hundred rank and file, the whole commanded by lieut. colonel Morrison, of the 89th regiment, and accompanied by the deputy adjutant-general, lieutenant colonel Harvey. This corps of observation proceeded under the escort of a small division of gun-boats, commanded by captain Mulcaster, R. N., in pursuit of the enemy, and on the eighth came up with them at Point Iroquois. General Wilkinson had, on the preceding day, directed colonel Macomb to land on the british shore with 1200 men, in order to clear the coast down to the head of the Long Sault, of the militia collecting along the shores from various parts of the country. On the 18th, this division was reinforced by brigadier general Brown's brigade, with a body of dragoons from the american shore. On arriving at the head of the Long Sault, the whole of the effective men, except such as were required for navigating the boats down the rapid, were landed under the orders of brigadier general Boyd, who was to proceed down by land in the rear of general Brown's division to the foot of the Long Sault. On the tenth, lieutenant colonel Morrison with the gun-boats visited the american post at Hamilton, where he landed and took possession of a considerable quantity of provisions and stores belonging to the american army, with two pieces of ordnance. Lieutenant col. Harvey, in the meantime, followed up the enemy, who, in the evening, were observed advancing from the woods in considerable numbers with a body of cavalry, but upon receiving a few rounds from three field pieces, and probably finding their pursuers better prepared than they expected, fell back for the night.* On the ensuing day, lieut. colonel Morrison pressed so closely upon the rear of general Boyd's division, as to compel him to concentrate his forces and give battle, a description of which cannot be more accurately conveyed than by quoting lieutenant colonel Morrison's

---

* Some smart cannonading, in the mean time, took place between the gun-boats.

official despatch on the occasion:—" The enemy's force, consisting of two brigades of infantry, and a regiment of cavalry, amounting to between three and four thousand men, moved forward about two o'clock in the afternoon, from Chrystler's Point, and attacked our advance, which gradually fell back to the position selected for the detachment to occupy, the right resting on the river, and the left on a pine-wood, exhibiting about seven hundred yards. The ground being open, the troops were thus disposed:—

" The flank companies of the 49th regiment, the detachment of the canadian regiment, with one field piece, under lieutenant col. Pearson, on the right; a little advanced on the road—three companies of the 89th regiment, under captain Barnes, with a gun formed in echellon with the advance on its left, supporting it. The 49th and the 89th thrown more to the rear, with a gun, formed the main body and reserve, extending to the woods on the left; which were occupied by the Voltigeurs, under major Herriot, and the indians under lieutenant Anderson.—At about half-past two the action became general, when the enemy endeavored, by moving forward a brigade from his right, to turn our left, but was repulsed by the 89th regiment forming *en potence* with the 49th regiment, and by moving forward, occasionally firing by platoons; his efforts were next directed against our right, and to repulse this movement, the 49th regiment took ground in that direction, in echellon, followed by the 89th. When within half musket shot, the line was formed under a heavy but irregular fire from the enemy—the 49th was directed to charge their guns, posted opposite to ours, but it became necessary, when within a short distance of them, to check this forward movement, in consequence of a charge from their cavalry on the right, lest they should wheel about, and fall upon the rear, but they were received in so gallant a manner by the companies of the 89th under captain Barnes, and the well directed fire of the artillery, that they quickly retreated, and by a charge from those companies, one gun was gained.—The enemy immediately concentrated their force to check our advance, but such was the steady countenance and well directed fire of the troops and artillery, that about half-past four, they gave way at all points from an exceeding strong position, endeavouring by their light infantry to cover their retreat, who were soon driven away by a judicious movement made by lieutenant colonel Pearson. The detachment, for the night, occupied the ground from which the enemy had been driven."

This, (called the battle of Chrystler's farm, from the ground on which it occurred,) is, in the estimation of military men, considered the most scientific military affair during the late war, from the professional skill displayed in the course of the action, by the adverse commanders; and when we consider the prodigious preparatives of the american government for that expedition, with the failure of which their hopes of conquest vanished, the battle of Chrystler's farm may, probably, be classed as the most important, and the best fought, that took place during the war.

The american division, after leaving the field, re-embarked in haste, while the dragoons with five field pieces of light artillery proceeded down towards Cornwall, in the rear of general Brown's division, who, unaware of the battle, had continued his march for that place. The enemy lost an able officer, in the person of brigadier general Covington, who, while animating his men to the charge, received a mortal wound, which he survived only two days. The loss of the enemy, by their own official statements, amounted to three officers and ninety-nine men killed, and sixteen officers and one hundred and twenty-one men wounded. The loss of the british amounted to three officers (captain Nairne of the 49th regiment and lieutenants Lorimier and Armstrong,) and twenty-one men killed, and eight officers and one hundred and thirty-seven wounded, and twelve missing.

General Wilkinson, who, during the action, lay confined to his barge, from a protracted illness, in his official despatch to his government, bears faithful testimony of the loyalty of the inhabitants on the Canada side of the Saint Lawrence, and of the bravery and discipline of the troops he had to contend with at Chrysler's farm.*

The day after the engagement, the american flotilla proceeded down the Long Sault and joined near Cornwall, the division which had moved on under general Brown, towards that place, where general Wilkinson confidently expected to hear of the arrival of general Hampton, on the opposite shore, to whom he had written on the 6th, to that effect, not being then acquainted with his late defeat. Here, to his unspeakable mortification and surprise, he received a letter from general Hampton, informing him that the division under his command was falling back upon lake Champlain. This information, with the countless difficulties momently crowding upon the american army, effectually blasted every prospect of further success. So circumstanced, the american commander imme-

---

* Lieut. colonel Morrison concludes his despatch by the following testimony, of the zeal and bravery manifested by the officers and men under his command :—

"It is now my grateful duty to point out to your honor, the benefit the service has received from the ability, judgment, and active exertions of lieut. col. Harvey, the deputy adjutant general, for sparing whom to accompany the detachment, I must again publicly express my acknowledgments. To the cordial co-operation and exertions of lieut. col. Pearson, commanding the detachment from Prescott, lieut. col. Plenderleath, 49th regiment, major Clifford, 89th regiment, major Herriot, of the Voltigeurs, and captain Jackson, of the royal artillery, combined with the gallantry of the troops, our great success may be attributed; every man did his duty, and I believe, I cannot more strongly speak their merits than in mentioning that our small force did not exceed eight hundred rank and file.

"To captains Davis and Skinner, of the quarter-matser general's department, I am under the greatest obligations for the assistance I have received from them; their zeal and activity, have been unremitting. Lieut. Haggerman, of the militia, and lieut. Anderson, of the indian department, have also, for their services, deserved my public acknowledgments.

diately held a council of war, in which it was unanimously resolved—" That the attack on Montreal should be abandoned for the present season, and that the army near Cornwall should immediately be crossed to the american shore, for taking up winter quarters," which, on the ensuing day, was accordingly carried into effect, by their proceeding for Salmon River, where their boats and batteaux were scuttled, and extensive barracks for the whole army erected with extraordinary celerity, and surrounded on all sides by *abattis*, so as to render a surprise impracticable.

Wilkinson's intention was to have landed on the Isle Perrôt, which is separated from the Island of Montreal, by a small channel, over which he intended to throw a bridge of boats, and thence to fight his way to the city.

Every appearance of danger having subsided, the commander of the forces dismissed the Sedentary Militia, by a general order of the 17th November,* with acknowledgments of the

---

* " HEAD QUARTERS, Lachine, November 17, 1813.

" GENERAL ORDER.—The divisions of sedentary militia called out by the general order of the 8th instant, are to be disbanded and to return to their respective homes, in the following order.

" His excellency the governor in chief and commander of the forces, in dispensing, for the present, with the further services of the militia, feels the greatest satisfaction in acknowledging the cheerful alacrity with which they have repaired to their respective posts, and the loyalty and zeal they have manifested at the prospect of encountering the enemy—although he has been checked in his career by the bravery and discipline of his Majesty's troops in the Upper Province, and thus frustrated in his avowed intention of landing on this island, his excellency feels confident that had he been enabled to reach it, whatever might have been his force, he would have met with that steady and determined resistance from the militia of the province.

cheerful alacrity, with which they had repaired to their posts, and the loyalty and zeal they had manifested, at the prospect of encountering the enemy.

With these operations terminated the campaign of 1813, in the lower province, but new triumphs still awaited the british arms, in the province of Upper-Canada.

which would have terminated his third attempt for its invasion, like those which preceded it, in defeat and disgrace.

" The Montreal Volunteers, to march from Lachine, at 10 o'clock to-morrow morning, to Montreal.

" The 1st batt. of Montreal militia, at 8 o'clock on Friday morning.

" The 2d batt. at 10 o'clock, and the 3d batt., at 12 o'clock, on the same day.

" The above corps are to remain embodied until the 24th instant, on which day a corps of the line will relieve them.

" On the 20th inst., col. McGill will allow the whole of the men belonging to the second class of sedentary militia to return to their respective homes.—Upon proper certificates being produced to the commissariat at Montreal, each captain or commanding officer of a company of sedentary militia is to receive for every private man, returning home, at the rate of 1s. 3d. currency, and non-commissioned officers in that proportion, for every five leagues that they have to travel—this allowance is, for that period, in lieu of pay and rations.

" Colonel La Croix's division, now at Lower Lachine, is to march from thence on the 20th inst., so as to arrive on the Champ de Mars, at Montreal, by 10 o'clock in the morning of that day, for the purpose of piling their arms, and returning into store their accoutrements, ammunition, blankets, haversacks, and canteens.

" Lieut. col. M'Kenzie's battalion will march from its present quarters so as to arrive on the Champ de Mars, at 12 o'clock on the same day,—and lieut. col. Leprohon's at 2 o'clock.

" Lieut. col. Cuthbert's division is to arrive on the Champ de Mars, at 10 o'clock on the 21st inst.—The batt. placed under the command of lieut. col. Boucherville will leave the ground it at present occupies on the 22d, and proceed to Montreal on its route to Three Rivers.—The one confided to the command of lieut. col. Deschambault will commence falling back to Montreal on the 23d inst.—The remaining battalions of the sedentary militia are to commence their march for their respective parishes on the 23d.

" The quarter-master general of the forces will make the necessary arrangements for relieving capt. Platt's troop of Volunteer Cavalry from its present duty, on or before the 24th inst. when it is to return to Montreal for the purpose of being dismissed until further orders.

" By his excellency's command,

" Edward Baynes, adjt.-general."

Major general De Rottenburgh was relieved in the command of Upper Canada, early in December, by lieutenant general Drummond, who proceeded from Kingston to York, and from thence to the head of the lake, where the army again resumed an offensive posture, with a view to regain possession of Fort George. General M'Clure, who, on the breaking up of the investment of Fort George, had issued a proclamation, in which he affected to consider Upper Canada as abandoned by the british army, and offered the friendship and protection of his government to the people of that province, on the approach of the british under colonel Murray, precipitately evacuated that post on the 12th December, and retreated across the Niagara, having, pursuant to the directions of the american secretary of war, most inhumanly, on the 10th of December, set fire to the flourishing village of Newark, containing about one hundred and fifty houses; which were reduced to ashes, leaving the wretched and forlorn inhabitants with upwards of four hundred women and children houseless, and exposed to the accumulated horrors of famine and the inclemency of a canadian winter. The british under the command of colonel Murray, scarcely amounting to five hundred men, including indians and militia, immediately occupied Fort George. The barbarous policy of the american government, in destroying Newark, exasperated the army as well as the inhabitants on the frontier, of whose impatience for retaliation, general Drummond promptly availed himself, after the occupation of Fort George, and accordingly adopted the resolution of carrying the american fort Niagara by surprise.

Having only two batteaux at his disposal, in the Niagara river, he deferred the attack until a sufficient number of batteaux could be conveyed over land, several miles, from Burlington at the head of the lake, which was effected by the exertions of captain Elliot, of the quarter master general's department. Having made every necessary arrangement, the batteaux were launched, and the troops were embarked on the night of the 18th December, consisting of a small detachment of royal artillery, the grenadier company of the royal scots, the flank companies of the 41st and 100th regiment, amounting in the whole to five hundred and fifty men, under the immediate command of colonel Murray. This small force having crossed the river, assisted by the Provincial Corps, as boatmen, landed with the utmost silence and good order, at the Five Mile Meadows, distant four and a half miles from the Fort. From this point, colonel Murray moved towards the Fort, having previously detached the advance of his division, under captain Fawcett, and lieutenant Dawson of the 100th regiment, who gallantly executed the orders entrusted to them, by cutting off two of the enemy's picquets, and surprising the sentinels on the glacis and at the gate, from whom the watch-word was obtained, and the entrance into the Fort, thereby greatly facilitated, which was rapidly effected through the main gate, before the enemy had time to sound the alarm. The assailants having obtained possession of the works, the enemy made for some time a feeble resistance, but finally surrendered at discretion. The valour of the troops engaged on this service, particularly of the 100th regiment, under lieutenant colonel Hamilton, was conspicuous. The loss of the british amounted to only one officer (lieut. Nolan.) and five men killed, and two officers and three men wounded. The loss of the enemy in slain amounted to sixty-five men and two officers, and twelve rank and file in wounded. The prisoners amounted to upwards of three hundred effective men of the regular army of the United States. An immense quantity of commissariat stores with upwards of three thousand stand of arms, a great number of rifles and several pieces of ordnance, of which, twenty-seven of different calibres were mounted on the works, fell into the hands of the victors. Major general Riall, who had crossed over immediately after col. Murray, with the whole body of western indians, and the 1st battalion of Royal Scots, and 41st regiment, in order to support the attack, upon ascertaining its success, immediately marched along the river upon Lewiston, where the enemy had established a force and had erected batteries with the avowed purpose of destroying the town of Queenstown, situated directly opposite. The enemy, upon the approach of this division, abandoned their position, leaving two guns, a twelve and a six pounder, which fell into the hands of the british, with a considerable quantity of small arms and stores. In retaliation for the conflagration of Newark, the indignant troops and the auxiliary indians were let loose upon the enemy's frontier, and Lewiston, Manchester and the circumjacent country were laid in ruins. General Drummond determined to follow up these successes, which he could not deem complete until he had chased the enemy from the whole frontier, and taken ample vengeance for his cruelties toward the inhabitants of Newark. He, therefore, moved his forces up to Chippawa where he fixed his head quarters, on the 28th December, and on the following day, approached to within two miles of Fort Erie, where having reconnoitred the enemy's position at Black Rock, he determined to attack him in the course of the night. He, accordingly, directed general Riall to cross the river with four companies of the King's regiment and the light company of the 89th, under lieutenant colonel Ogilvy; two hundred and fifty men of the 41st, and the grenadiers of the 100th regiment, under major Frend, together with about fifty militia volunteers and a body of indian warriors. This division completed its landing about midnight, two miles below Black Rock, its advanced guard having surprised and captured the greater part of a picquet of the enemy, and secured the bridge over the Conguichity Creek, from which the enemy made several attempts to dislodge them. The boats and batteaux after having crossed this division were tracked up as high as the foot of the rapids below Fort Erie, in order to convey across the royals, under lieutenant col. Gordon, who were destined to land above Black Rock, for the purpose of turning the enemy's position, while he should be attacked in front by the troops, who had landed below. The delay occasioned by the grounding of the boats, which detained them until morning, and exposed them to the open fire of the enemy, caused the royals some loss, and prevented them from effecting a landing, in sufficient time to fully accomplish the object intended. At day break major general Riall moved forward; the King's regiment, and the light company of the 89th leading, and the 41st and Grenadiers of the 100th forming the reserve. On gaining the town a very spirited attack was made upon the enemy, who were in great force and strongly posted, and on the arrival of the reserve, the action became general. The enemy maintained his position with obstinacy for some time, but, upon the advance of the british he was compelled to give way, and and was driven through his batteries in which were a twenty-four pounder, three twelves and a nine pounder. From Black Rock, the fugitives were pursued to the town of Buffalo, about two miles distant, where they rallied and showed a large body of infantry and cavalry, and attempted to oppose the advance of the british by the fire of a field piece, posted on a height commanding the road : finding this ineffectual, they retreated in all directions, leaving a six-pounder brass field piece, one iron eighteen, and one six-pounder, and betook themselves to the woods.

General Riall, having dispersed this force, immediately detached captain Robinson of the King's regiment, with two companies, to destroy three vessels of the enemy's lake squadron, a short distance below the town, with their stores, which he effectually accomplished.

The americans in this affair, were not less in number than 2,500, and are supposed to have lost in killed and wounded from three to four hundred men. Only one hundred and thirty men were made prisoners, and among them colonel Chapin. The british lost 31 men killed, and four officers and sixty-eight men wounded, and nine men missing. The small towns of Buffalo and Black Rock having been deserted by the inhabitants, were, with all the public stores, containing considerable quantities of clothing, spirits and flour, which could not be conveniently brought away, set on fire and entirely consumed.

These measures of retribution extinguished the resources of the enemy on the Niagara frontier, and although victims of the retributive vengeance brought on their heads, by the barbarity of their own commanders, the suffering inhabitants are said to have admitted the justice of it, loudly reprobating the conduct of their own army in destroying Newark. —Such were the rapid successes that attended the british arms in the Canadas, and cheered the hopes of the people at the close of the campaign, which a few weeks previously, threatened the total subjugation of these provinces.

Ample vengeance having been taken by lieutenant general Drummond, upon the Niagara frontier, for the wanton conflagration and the cruel outrages committed upon the defenceless inhabitants of Newark, the commander of the forces, on the 12th of January, 1814, issued a proclamation,* in which he strongly deprecated

---
* " By his excellency lieut. general Sir George Prevost, Baronet, commander of his Majesty's forces in North America, &c., &c.,&c.

" To the inhabitants of his Majesty's provinces in North America.

" A PROCLAMATION.

" The complete success which has attended his Majesty's arms on the Niagara frontier, having placed in our possession the whole of the enemy's posts on that line, it became a matter of imperious duty to retaliate on America, the miseries which the unfortunate inhabitants of Newark had been made to suffer from the evacuation of Fort George. The villages of Lewiston, Black Rock, and Buffalo have accordingly been burned.

" At the same time the commander of the forces sincerely deprecates this mode of warfare, he trusts that it will be sufficient to call the attention of every candid and impartial person amongst ourselves and the enemy, to the circumstances from which it has arisen, to satisfy them that this departure from the established usages of war, has originated with America herself, and that to her alone, are justly chargeable, all the awful and unhappy consequences which have hitherto flowed, and are likely to result from it.

" It is not necessary to advert to the conduct of the troops employed on the american coast, in conjunction with his Majesty's squadron, under admiral Sir John B. Warren, since, as they were neither within the command, nor subject to the controul of his excellency, their acts cannot be ascribed to him, even if they wanted that justifi-

Chap. XVII.
1813.

the savage mode of warfare to which the enemy by a departure from the established usages of war, had compelled him to resort. He traced

cation which the circumstances that occasioned them so amply afford.

"It will be sufficient for the present purpose, and in order to mark the character of the war, as carried on upon the frontiers of these provinces, to trace the line of conduct observed by his excellency, and the troops under his command, since the commencement of hostilities, and to contrast it with that of the enemy.

"The first invasion of Upper Canada took place in July, 1812, when the american forces under brigadier general Hull, crossed over and took possession of Sandwich, where they began to manifest a disposition so different from that of a magnanimous enemy, and which they have since invariably displayed, in marking out, as objects of their peculiar resentment, the loyal subjects of his Majesty, and in dooming their property to plunder and conflagration.

"Various instances of this kind occurred, both at Sandwich and in its neighbourhood, at the very period when his Majesty's standard was waving upon the fort of Michillimackinac, and affording protection to the persons and property of those who had submitted to it:— Within a few weeks afterwards, the british flag was also hoisted on the fortress of Detroit, which, together with the whole of the Michigan territory, had surrendered to his Majesty's arms.

"Had not his excellency been actuated by sentiments far different from those which had influenced the american government, and the persons employed by it, in the wanton acts of destruction of private property, committed during their short occupation of a part of Upper Canada, his excellency could not have availed himself of the opportunity which the undisturbed possession of the whole of the Michigan territory, afforded him of amply retaliating for the devastating system which had been pursued at Sandwich and on the Thames.

"But strictly in conformity to the views and disposition of his own government, and to that liberal and magnanimous policy which it had dictated, he chose rather to forbear an imitation of the enemy's example, in the hope, that such forbearance would be duly appreciated by the government of United States, and would produce a return to more civilized usages of war.

"The persons and property, therefore, of the inhabitants of the Michigan territory, were respected, and remained unmolested.

"In the winter of the following year, when the success which attended the gallant enterprise against Ogdensburgh had placed that populous and flourishing village in our possession, the generosity of the british character was again conspicuous, in the scrupulous preservation of every article which could be considered as private property, such public buildings only being destroyed as were used for the accommodation of troops and for public stores.

"The destruction of the defences of Ogdensburgh, and the dispersion of the enemy's force in that neighbourhood, laid open the whole of their frontier on the St. Lawrence, to the incursions of his Majes-

with precision, the conduct that had marked the progress of the war, on the part of the enemy, and concluded by lamenting the neces-

ty's troops, and Hamilton, as well as the numerous settlements on the banks of the river, might, at any hour, had such been the disposition of his Majesty's government, or of those acting under it, been plundered and laid waste.

"During the course of the following summer, by the fortunate result of the enterprise against Plattsburgh, that town was for several hours in the complete possession of our troops, there not being any force in the neighbourhood which could attempt a resistance.— Yet even there, under circumstances of strong temptation, and when the recent example of the enemy in the wanton destruction at York, of private property, and buildings not used for military purposes, must have been fresh in the recollection of the forces employed on that occasion, and would have justified a retaliation on their part, their forbearance was strongly manifested, and the directions his excellency had given to the commander of that expedition, so scrupulously obeyed, that scarcely can another instance be shewn in which, during a state of war, and under similar circumstances, an enemy, so completely under the power and at the mercy of their adversaries, had so little cause of complaint.

"During the course of the same summer, forts Schlosser and Black Rock, were surprised and taken by a part of the forces under the command of major-general De Rottenburg, on the Niagara frontier, at both of which places personal property was respected, and the public buildings were alone destroyed.

"It was certainly matter of just and reasonable expectation, that the humane and liberal course of conduct pursued by his excellency on these different occasions, would have had its due weight with the american government, and would have led it to have abstained, in the further prosecution of the war, from any acts of wantonness or violence, which could only tend unnecessarily to add to its ordinary calamities, and to bring down upon their own unoffending citizens a retaliation, which, though distant, they must have known would await and certainly follow such conduct.

"Undeterred, however, by his excellency's example of moderation, or by any of the consequences to be apprehended from the adoption of such barbarous measures, the american forces at fort George, acting, there is every reason to believe, under the orders, or with the approbation of their government, for some time previous to their evacuation of that fortress, under various pretences, burned and destroyed the farm houses and buildings of many of the respectable and peaceable inhabitants of that neighbourhood. But the full measure of this species of barbarity remained to be completed at a season when all its horrors might be more fully and keenly felt, by those who were to become the wretched victims of it.

"It will hardly be credited by those who shall hereafter read it in in the page of history, that in the enlightened æra of the nineteenth

VOL. II.   N

sity imposed upon him of retaliating upon the citizens of America, the miseries inflicted upon the inhabitants of Newark, but, at the same century, and in the inclemency of a canadian winter, the troops of a nation calling itself civilized and christian, had wantonly, and without the shadow of a pretext, forced 400 helpless women and children to quit their dwellings, and to be the mournful spectators of the conflagation and total destruction of all that belonged to them.

" Yet such was the fate of Newark on the 10th of December, a day which the inhabitants of Upper Canada can never forget, and the recollection of which cannot but nerve their arms when again opposed to their vindictive foe. On the night of that day, the american troops under brigadier general M·Clure, being about to evacuate fort George, which they could no longer retain, by an act of inhumanity disgraceful to themselves and to the nation to which they belong, set fire to upwards of 150 houses, composing the beautiful village of Newark, and burned them to the ground, leaving without covering or shelter, those " innocent, unfortunate, distressed inhabitants," whom that officer, by his proclamation, had previously engaged to protect.

" His excellency would have ill consulted the honour of his country, and the justice due to his Majesty's injured and insulted subjects, had he permitted an act of such needless cruelty to pass unpunished, or had he failed to visit, whenever the opportunity arrived, upon the inhabitants of the neighbouring american frontier, the calamities thus inflicted upon those of our own.

" The opportunity has occurred, and a full measure of retaliation has taken place, such as it is hoped will teach the enemy to respect, in future, the laws of war, and recal him to a sense of what is due to himself as well as to us.

" In the further prosecution of the contest to which so extraordinary a character has been given, his excellency must be guided by the course of conduct which the enemy shall hereafter pursue. Lamenting as his excellency does, the necessity imposed upon him of retaliating upon the subjects of America the miseries inflicted on the inhabitants of Newark, it is not his intention to pursue further a system of warfare so revolting to his own feelings, and so little congenial to the british character, unless the future measures of the enemy should compel him again to resort to it.

" To those possessions of the enemy along the whole line of frontier which have hitherto remained undisturbed, and which are now within his excellency's reach, and at the mercy of the troops under his command, his excellency has determined to extend the same forbearance and the same freedom from rapine and plunder, which they have hitherto experienced ; and from this determination the future conduct of the american government shall alone induce his excellency to depart.

" The inhabitants of these provinces will, in the mean time, be prepared to resist, with firmness and with courage, whatever attempts the resentment of the enemy, arising from their disgrace and their

time, declared it not to be his intention further to pursue a system of warfare so revolting to his own feelings, and so little congenial to the british character, unless he should be so compelled by the future measures of the enemy.

merited sufferings, may lead them to make, well assured that they will be powerfully assisted at all points by the troops under his excellency's command, and that prompt and signal vengeance will be taken for every fresh departure by the enemy, from that system of warfare, which ought alone to subsist between enlightened and civilized nations.

" Given under my hand and seal at arms at Quebec, this 12th day
" of January, 1814.

"GEORGE PREVOST

" By his excellency's command,
E. B. BRENTON."

CHAPTER XVIII.

Meeting of parliament—topics of the speech—address in answer—proceedings in the legislature—chief justice impeached at the instance of Mr. Stuart—articles of impeachment—they are presented to the governor, who refuses to suspend the chief justice—resolutions of the assembly thereupon—Mr. Stuart named agent for prosecution of the impeachments—failure of the appointment from the want of an appropriation—address to the Prince Regent on the state of the province—Mr. Bedard agent—failure of the appointment—prorogation and speech—finances, &c.—hostages and proceedings respecting them, between the two governments—preparations during winter for the ensuing campaign—troops and seamen come through from New Brunswick to Canada in February—an embassy of indian warriors from the west visits Quebec—attack by american forces under general Wilkinson on La Cole mill—repulsed.

Chap. XVIII.
1814.

On the thirteenth of January, the Legislature met for the despatch of public business.—The Governor, in his speech on opening the session, after congratulating parliament on the defeat of the enemy at Chateauguay, by a handful of brave canadians; and on the brilliant victory obtained by the small corps of observation, on the banks of the St. Lawrence, over the formidable armament commanded by major general Wilkinson; events that had nobly upheld the honor of his Majesty's arms, and effectually disconcerted all the plans of the enemy, for the invasion of this province, continued:—

"It is also a matter of further and sincere congratulation, that, notwithstanding the various events of the last summer by which a footing was gained by the enemy in the upper province, they have since been compelled to abandon the greater part of it; and that the theatre of war has been transferred into their own territory, where Niagara, their strongest fortress, and the important posts of Black Rock and Buffalo, have lately been wrested from them by british valor and enterprize.

"In reviewing these events, I cannot but contemplate with pride and satisfaction, the zealous discharge of duty which I have witnessed as well in the militia, as in all classes of his Majesty's subjects in this province, and which I consider the surest indication of their loyalty to their Sovereign, and of their determination to defend, to the last extremity, this valuable portion of his dominions.

"Notwithstanding the present favourable aspect of our affairs, and the security in which the province is now placed, from this discomfiture of the enemy's late attempts to invade it, we must still be prepared to meet with firmness, and to repel with vigour, whatever measures his presumption may again dictate for the accomplishment of his avowed object.—I trust, therefore, to your wisdom and vigilance to suggest whatever may be necessary for this purpose, and to your loyalty and patriotism to submit to whatever further sacrifices the war may require,—assuring you that his Majesty's government, not unmindful of the exertions the province has hitherto made in its defence, is using every possible effort, consistent with the important demands upon it for other services, to strengthen and increase the military establishments under my command.

"Deeply sensible, that the situation in which I am placed is as arduous and difficult as it is important—I am, notwithstanding, cheered and animated in the discharge of its duties, by the conviction that I shall always meet with your support, in maintaining the honor and promoting the service of my Sovereign. To forward the prosperity, and to preserve the integrity of this province, are objects of which

I shall never lose sight; and confidently relying on your cordial assistance for the attainment, it will be my great ambition to be able faithfully to represent to his royal Highness the Prince Regent, the loyalty, zeal, and unanimity of his Majesty's canadian subjects, and to carry with me, whenever I shall return into the royal presence, the good opinion and the affection of the people of this province."

In answering his excellency's speech, the assembly said,—

" Our sincere acknowledgments are due to your Excellency for the testimony you have been pleased, in reviewing these events, to express of the zealous discharge of duty you have witnessed, as well in the militia as in all classes of his Majesty's subjects in this province. It has been their good fortune to have been rescued under your Excellency's administration, from the most unfounded imputations which had been industriously attempted, under the preceding administration, to fix on their character, and our gratitude is therefore heightened by the assurance thus given by your Excellency, that they have justified the good opinion you had formed of them. The conduct they have exhibited in strict conformity with the sentiments by which they have always been actuated, and, we are persuaded, may be considered as a sure indication of their loyalty to their Sovereign, and of their determination to defend to the last extremity, this valuable portion of his dominions.

" We are highly flattered by the confidence your Excellency expresses in the support you expect from us in maintaining the honor and promoting the service of our gracious Sovereign, and we shall always cheerfully co-operate with your Excellency, in any measures for effecting these important purposes.

" We have gratefully acknowledged in your Excellency, an anxious desire to forward the prosperity, and to preserve the integrity of this province. For the attainment of these objects, your Excellency has been guided by a just and liberal policy, towards his Majesty's canadian subjects, by which their loyalty, zeal and unanimity, have been cherished and promoted, and we are assured that a corresponding sense of obligation for such an important benefit has been impressed on their minds, and that whenever the public service may withdraw your Excellency from the administration of the government of this country, which we hope will be a remote occurrence, your Excellency will carry with you the good opinion and affection of the people of this province."

The Governor, in a secret and confidential message to the house of assembly informed that body, that in order to carry on the public service he had found it indispensably necessary to direct an issue of army bills, to a greater amount than five hundred thousand pounds, the sum authorized by the army bill act, and recommended to the immediate and serious consideration of the house, the expedience of extending the provisions of the act. The house accordingly took the subject into consideration, and passed a bill extending the issue of army bills, to fifteen hundred thousand pounds. The militia laws underwent some discussion, but were not altered, the legislative council not concurring with some clauses, which, it had been found expedient to introduce into the bill, sent up for their concurrence. A bill to disqualify the Chief Justices and the Judges of the courts of King's bench, in the province, from being summoned to the legislative council or sitting or voting therein, was introduced, and having passed the lower house, was sent up to the legislative council for their consideration. Here it was unanimously resolved that the matters contained in the bill were unparliamentary and unprecedented, and intrenched upon the prerogative of the crown, and the rights and privileges of that house; and it was, therefore, also unanimously resolved to proceed no further in the consideration of the bill. The house of assembly upon finding it to be laid aside, appointed a committee, to search the journals of the legislative council, to ascertain, officially, what proceedings had taken place, with respect to it. The committee having taken information on the subject, reported the fate of the bill, as collected from the journals of the legislative council, and the house among other counter resolutions, indignantly resolved, "that the legislative council, by their refusal to proceed on that bill, had excluded from their consideration a measure highly meriting the attention of the legislature of the province, and had, therefore, afforded additional evidence of its expedience." A bill was again introduced as in the preceding session, "to grant to his Majesty a duty on the income arising from civil offices, and on pensions, to be applied for the defence of the province in the present war with the United States of America." This bill, also, was rejected by the legislative council. The bill for the appointment of an agent in Great Britain, was also sent up to the legislative council, where it likewise was laid aside.

The house of assembly unanimously passed a vote of thanks to lieutenant col. De Salaberry, and the officers under his command for their distinguished exertions, on the 26th October,

1813, in the action on the Chateauguay river, and directed the speaker to signify the same to lieutenant colonel De Salaberry and the officers present on that occasion; and that the house highly felt and acknowledged the distinguished valour and discipline conspicuously displayed by the non-commissioned officers and private soldiers, and militia-men of the little band under his immediate command, in the signal defeat of the american army under gen. Hampton, at Chateauguay. To lieut. colonel Morrison, of the 89th regiment, and to the officers and men under his command, a similar vote of thanks was also passed for their exertions on the 11th November, 1813, at Chrystler's Farm, in the defeat of the american army under general Wilkinson.

Chap. XVIII.
1814.

The house of assembly at an early period of the session, on motion of Mr. J. Stuart, resolved that it would take into consideration the power and authority exercised by the courts of justice in this province, under the denomination of rules of practice, and the clerk of the court of appeals, as well as the prothonotaries of the courts of King's bench, for the districts of Quebec and Montreal, were respectively ordered to lay before the house, certified copies of the rules of practice of those courts. On the 4th of February, the subject having been previously discussed in committee, the house adopted several resolutions, concerning those rules of practice, which it considered rather in the sense of legislative enactments, and, therefore, an encroachment upon the privileges of the legislature, than as simple rules or regulations for the guidance of judicial proceedings. The rules in question had first been framed and introduced into the provincial court of appeals, (where the chief justice of the province, and the chief justice of Montreal, alternately presided) in January, 1809, and in the same year, the courts of King's bench, at Quebec and Montreal, followed the example of the court of appeals, under the sanction of an act of the provincial legislature, giving to the different " courts of judicature, in the province, power and authority to make and establish orders and rules of practice in the said courts, in all civil matters, touching all services of process, executions and returns of all writs, proceedings for bringing causes to issue, as well in term time as out of term, and other matters of regulation within the said courts." It, was, however, now maintained in the house of assembly, that these rules affected the civil rights of his Majesty's subjects, and were contrary to and subversive of the laws of the province: that they rendered the enjoyment of liberty and property altogether insecure and precarious, and gave to the judges an arbitrary authority over the persons and property of his Majesty's subjects in the province. For these, and other specific political high crimes and misdemeanors, alleged to have been committed, in the course of the late administration of the colonial government, by sir J. H. Craig, tending to mislead and deceive that officer in the exercise of his authority, to oppress the people and alienate their minds from his Majesty's government in order (as it was contended) to favor the progress of american influence in the province, the two chief justices were formally impeached by the commons of Lower Canada, these being the first impeachments brought forward against any public functionaries.

Chap. XVIII.
1814.

These heads of accusation or articles of impeachment, by the house of assembly, deserve. perhaps, some further attention than is bestowed upon them above. The first and second articles are as follows :—

First—that the said Jonathan Sewell, chief justice of the province of Lower Canada, hath traitorously and wickedly endeavoured to subvert the constitution and established government of the said province. and instead thereof, to introduce an arbitrary tyrannical government against law, which he hath declared by traitorous and wicked opinions, counsel, conduct. judgments, practices and actions.

Secondly—that. in pursuance of those traitorous and wicked purposes, the said Jonathan Sewell, hath disregarded the authority of the legislature of this province, and in the courts of justice wherein he hath presided and sat. hath usurped powers and authority which belong to the legislature alone, and made regulations subversive of the constitution and laws of this province.

Chap. XVIII.
1814.

The *third* charges him with having in furtherance of those views, made and published, as president of the provincial court of appeals, various regulations under the name of "*rules and orders of practice,*" repugnant, and contrary, to the laws of the province, with a view, "wickedly and traitorously," in as far as in him lay to subvert, or cause the court to do so, the laws of the said province, which he was sworn to administer, thereby assuming legislative authority, and imposing illegal burthens and restraints upon his Majesty's subjects, in the exercise of their legal rights—altogether inconsistent with the duties of the said court, and subversive of the liberty and rights of his Majesty's subjects, in the province.

The *fourth* charges him in like manner as chief justice, presiding in the court of king's bench at Quebec.

The *fifth* alleges—that as president of the court of appeals, he had set aside the laws and substituted his will and pleasure therefor, to the injury and oppression of his Majesty's subjects, and in subversion of their most important political and civil rights.

The *sixth*, that being chief justice, and also speaker of the legislative council, and chairman of the executive council—he had by false and malicious slanders against his Majesty's canadian subjects and the assembly of the province, poisoned and incensed the mind of sir James H. Craig, the Governor-in-chief, misled and deceived him, and that he did on the 15th May, 1809. induce him to dissolve the provincial parliament, without any cause whatever to palliate or excuse the measure; and advised him to make on the occasion a speech, in gross violation of the constitutional rights of the assembly, insulting its members, and misrepresenting their conduct.

The *seventh*—that he had " in pursuance of his wicked and traitorous purposes aforesaid," and to oppress his Majesty's subjects and prevent all opposition to his tyrannical views, counselled and advised sir J. H. Craig to remove and dismiss divers loyal and deserving subjects, from offices of profit and honor, without the semblance of reason to justify it: but, merely, because they were inimical or supposed to be, " to the measures and policy of the said Jonathan Sewell, and in order, in one instance, to the advancement of his brother." This alluded to Mr. Stuart's dismissal from the office of solicitor general, who was succeeded in the appointment by Mr. Stephen Sewell, the chief's brother.

The *eighth*—that " in order in the strongest manner to mark his contempt for the liberties and rights of his Majesty's subjects and his disrespect for their representatives, and for the constitution of the province;" he had, in 1808, procured among other dismissals, from office, that of Jean Antoine Panet, esquire, then and during fifteen years preceding, speaker of the assembly, from his rank of lieutenant colonel in the militia, without any reason to palliate or excuse such an act of injustice."

The *ninth*—that he had induced P. E. Desbarats, printer of the laws of the province, to establish a newspaper, under the name of the " *Vrai Canadien*," to promote his factious views, and for the purpose of calumniating and vilifying part of his Majesty's subjects, and certain members of the assembly obnoxious to him"—and had compromised the honor and dignity of his Majesty's government by pledging its support to that paper.

The *tenth*—that intending to extinguish all reasonable freedom of the press, destroy the rights, liberty and security, of his Majesty's subjects in the province, and suppress all complaint of tyranny and oppression, he had, in March, 1810, advised and approved the sending of an armed military force to break open the dwelling house and printing office of one Charles Le François, " and there arrest and imprison him, and seize and bring away forcibly a printing press, with various private papers, which measure, of lawless violence, was accordingly executed; and that the said press and papers have since remained deposited in the court house, in the city of Quebec, with the knowledge and approbation and under the eye of the said Jonathan Sewell."

The *eleventh*—that with the intention of oppressing individuals supposed to be suspicious of his character and views, and inimical to his policy, and to ruin them in the public estimation, and prevent their re-election as members of the assembly, he had advised the arrest of Messrs. Bedard, Blanchet and Taschereau, upon the false and unfounded pretext of their having been guilty of treasonable practices, whereby they might be deprived of the benefit of bail, and caused them to be imprisoned on the said charge, for a long space of time, and at length to be discharged without trial.

The *twelfth*—that he had instigated and promoted, in pursuance of his traitorous and wicked purposes aforesaid—various other similar acts of tyranny and oppression of individuals, in other parts of the province, upon the false pretext of having been guilty of treasonable practices, and that one of them, François Corbeil, being old and infirm, was, by the rigour of his imprisonment, deprived of life.

The *thirteenth*—that he had advised sir J. H. Craig " to issue a proclamation, extraordinary as well in style as in matter, wherein the imprisonment of Messrs. Bedard, Blanchet and Taschereau, was referred to in a manner to induce a belief of their guilt, and subject them to odium, and to induce a belief that the province was in a state approaching open rebellion ;" whereby the character of his Majesty's subjects was most falsely calumniated, great injustice done to private individuals, and foreign states may have been drawn, and there is reason to believe, from subsequent events, were drawn into a belief of such disloyalty in his Majesty's canadian subjects, as would render the province an easy conquest."

The *fourteenth*—that he had read the said proclamation " in pursuance of his wicked and traitorous purposes aforesaid," in the term of the court of criminal jurisdiction, in March 1810, for the purpose of influencing the minds of the grand and petit juries, in the exercise of their respective duties.

The *fifteenth*—that in pursuance of such, " his traitorous and wicked purposes aforesaid," he had endeavoured to produce in his Majesty's government an ill opinion of his Majesty's canadian subjects, with a view to oppress them and favour the progress of american influence in this province, and " traitorously and wickedly abused the power and authority of his high offices, to promote the advantageous establishment of americans, being subjects of the United States of America, in this province, and to pave the way for american predominance therein, to the great injury of his Majesty's canadian subjects, and with a view to the subversion of the government."

The *sixteenth*—that " influenced by a desire to accelerate a political connexion of this province, with part of the United States of America, and to deprive her Majesty's canadian subjects of their present constitution and laws—he had in January, 1809, entered into a base and wicked confederacy with one John Henry, an adventurer of suspicious character, for the purpose of sowing dissension among the subjects of the government of the United States, producing insurrection and rebellion, and a consequent dismemberment of the union, and that by artful and false representations and advice, he had induced sir J. H. Craig to send Henry on a mission, for those purposes, to the neighbouring states—that he also became the channel of correspondence, by which conduct the said Jonathan Sewell hath exposed his Majesty's government to imputations reflecting on its honor, and hath rendered himself unworthy of any place of trust, under his Majesty's government."

The *seventeenth*—that he had laboured, and still did labour, to promote disunion and animosity between the legislative council and assembly ; and exerted his influence as speaker of the council to prevent the passing therein of salutary laws, which had been passed in the assembly—and had, during the present war with the United States, fomented dissension in this province, and endeavoured by various arts and practices to prevent a reliance on the loyalty and bravery of his Majesty's canadian subjects, and produce a want of confidence in the administration of his Majesty's government, and thereby weaken its exertions.

" All which crimes and misdemeanors were done and committed by the said Jonathan Sewell, &c., whereby he hath traitorously, &c., laboured to alienate the hearts of his Majesty's subjects, &c., and to cause a division between them, and to subvert the constitution, &c., and to introduce an arbitrary and tyrannical government, &c., and thereby hath not only broken his own oath, but the king's also,

Chap. XVIII 1814.

to the people, as far as in him lay, &c.; for all which the said commons do impeach the said Jonathan Sewell, hereby reserving to themselves the liberty of exhibiting at any time, hereafter, any other accusation or impeachment against the said Jonathan Sewell, and adopting such conclusions and prayer upon the premises, as law and justice may require."*

---

* Serious charges, certainly; but mostly, if not all together, gratuitous. Those against Mr. Monk were not of so complex and grave a nature. Chief justice Sewell was an eminent lawyer, profoundly versed in the civil law and ancient jurisprudence of the country, as well as in the criminal law of England, and withal a man of mild and agreeable manners, universally esteemed by the british community amongst whom he resided; but the other public stations which he occupied had mixed him up with the politics of the times, and subjected him as a political character to party obloquy. He, however, came from the ordeal unscathed, and lived to see Mr. Stuart, in his turn, carried away, as attorney general, in the same torrent of prejudices which the latter had appealed to against him. In those accusations, savouring less perhaps of patriotism than of resentment, the british commercial world in Canada, did Mr. Stuart the justice, or injustice, of believing him actuated by the double motive of personal hostility to the chief justice, and the expectancy of succeeding him. However this may have been, it is certain that availing himself of the antipathies of the french canadian population, whom, as a party leader, he then headed in the assembly, and set on against that gentleman, he gave him much annoyance, trouble, and no doubt, distress of mind. But " there is a tide in the affairs of men," and a season of retribution also, as Mr. Stuart afterwards, when attorney general, found to his cost, he himself becoming, in turn more unpopular than ever Mr. Sewell had been, being, as he might have expected, persecuted by his former colleagues in persecution, and, finally, dismissed (unjustly, as the writer ever has thought,) from his office, through their agitation and hatred of him. He it was, who first taught them how to impeach public functionaries, and it must be acknowledged that they liberally, and as some thought, suitably repaid him for his instruction.

Mr. Stuart, after some ups and downs in public life, is finally on the bench as chief justice of Lower Canada, to which he was raised by the Earl of Durham; and has, subsequently to his appointment to that important office, been also made a baronet of the United Kingdom, at the recommendation, it seems, of the late lord Sydenham. It does not appear, however, that he has taken any steps towards rescinding the obnoxious rules of practice, for which he impeached his worthy predecessor. Probably the elevation has given him more extend-

Mr. Stuart was named agent for the purpose of prosecuting the impeachments with effect, on behalf of the commons of Lower Canada, who, in a revenue bill they had passed, appropriated the sum of two thousand pounds, in order to enable him to proceed to England, but in consequence of the tacking of which to the bill, it was amended by the legislative council, by striking out that appropriation, and sent back to the assembly, which, not recognising the right in that body to alter money bills, the measure was lost. The wrong lay, however, it was said with the assembly, in improperly "*tacking*" to the bill a matter foreign to it, and unconstitutional. The bill contained also a grant of £20,000, for the militia, and a like sum for the support of the war. The impeachments having been digested, as observed, into the seventeen different heads specified against the chief justice of the province, and into eight heads against the chief justice of Montreal, (the latter being charged among other things, with promoting and advising certain criminal prosecutions at Montreal, and sitting in judgment upon them; and with having refused a writ of *Habeas Corpus* to persons legally entitled thereto,) the house of assembly, on the 3d of March, went up to the

---

ed and juster views of them than he previously had, when thundering from the less profitable benches of the assembly his anathemas against the chief, his predecessor. The exclusion of the judges from the political cares of the country, in which they ought never to have been allowed to meddle, may spare him the annoyances to which that gentleman was subjected.

Castle with their speaker, and presented an address to the governor, praying him to transmit the impeachments, with an address to the Prince Regent, drawn up for the occasion, to his Majesty's ministers, to be laid before his royal highness. They at the same time suggested the propriety of suspending the chief justices from their public functions, until the Prince Regent's pleasure should be known.

The governor replied that he would take an early opportunity of transmitting the address, with the articles of accusation against the chief justices, to his Majesty's ministers; but that he did not think it expedient to suspend the chief justices from their offices upon an address to that effect from one of the branches of the legislature alone, founded on articles of accusation, on which the legislative council had not been consulted, and in which they had not concurred. This answer, in which the articles of impeachment were denominated " articles of accusation," gave umbrage to the house, which, upon returning from the Castle, resolved—" that the charges exhibited by the house against Jonathan Sewell and James Monk, esquires, were rightly denominated " *heads of impeachment ;*" and " that his excellency the governor in chief, by his answer to the address of the house, had violated the constitutional rights and privileges thereof." * On the seventh of

---

* The following were the resolutions on the occasion:—

" On motion of Mr. Stuart, seconded by Mr. Papineau.

" Resolved, That the charges exhibited by this house against

March, the house, probably influenced by a sense of justice towards the governor, whose conduct it had so recently censured, in mitigation of its late resolution again resolved,—" that notwithstanding the wicked and perverse advice given to his excellency on the subject of the constitutional rights and privileges of the house, and the endeavours of evil disposed advisers to lead him into error and to embroil him with his Majesty's faithful commons of this province, the house had not, in any respect, altered the opinion it had ever entertained, of the wisdom of his excellency's administration, and that it was determined to adopt the measures it had deemed necessary for the support of the government and the defence of the province."

To repel these accusations, the chief justice

Jonathan Sewell and James Monk, esquires, were rightly denominated *Heads of Impeachment.*

" Resolved, That it is the unquestionable constitutional right of this house, to offer its humble advice to his excellency the governor in chief, upon matters affecting the welfare of his Majesty's subjects in this province, without the concurrence of the legislative council.

" Resolved, That it is peculiarly incumbent on this house to investigate abuses, calculated to deprive his Majesty's subjects of the benefit of their constitution and laws, and of the pure administration of justice, and that in bringing under the view of his excellency the governor in chief, the gross abuses and high offences referred to in the address to his excellency, this house hath performed the first and most essential of its duties, to the people of this province.

" Resolved, That it is the indubitable right of this house, to exhibit accusations, to which it is constitutionally competent, without consulting or asking the concurrence of the legislative council, and that in framing and exhibiting the heads of impeachment referred to in the address to his excellency the governor in chief, this house hath exercised a necessary and salutary power, vested in it by the constitution.

" Resolved, That his excellency the governor in chief, by his said answer to the address of this house, hath violated the constitutional rights and privileges of this house."

<small>Chap. XVIII.
1814.</small> Sewell, resolved to proceed to England, for which he accordingly sailed in June, receiving before his departure, addresses the most gratifying, from the members of the executive and legislative councils, and from the merchants and principal inhabitants of Quebec.*

---

* " To the honorable Jonathan Sewell, chief justice of the province of Lower Canada, &c. &c.

We, the undersigned members of his Majesty's executive council, residing in, and near the city of Quebec, feel, that having had the best opportunities of knowing your principles, and of observing the conduct that has been built upon them, we should be failing, not only in sensibility, but in justice, if we withheld, upon your departure from the province, the public declaration of our esteem of your character, as a most upright, loyal, and indefatigable servant of your sovereign, and as a warm, steady friend, to the true interests of your fellow subjects.

" That conspicuous ability, that comprehensive knowledge, that patient candour, that liberal respect for the opinions of others, and that equability and gentleness of temper, which you have brought to every discussion, and which in every discussion are so favorable to the attainment of truth, cannot but make your absence from this province felt, as greatly detrimental to his Majesty's service, as well as particularly painful to ourselves.

" Upon the causes, which have produced the necessity of that absence, we forbear, for obvious reasons, to make any observation: respecting its result, we have neither anxiety, nor doubt.

" Accept, sir, the assurances, that you carry with you our sincere regrets, and our cordial good wishes; and that we shall hail the moment of your return, as highly auspicious to the interests of his Majesty's government, and the general welfare of his subjects in this province.

(Signed) " J. QUEBEC,   A. L. J. DUCHESNAY,
F. BABY,   J. KERR,
P. A. DE BONNE,   ROSS CUTHBERT,
J. WILLIAMS,   JOHN MURE,
J. IRVINE,   OLIVIER PERRAULT."

" We the undersigned members of the legislative council of the province of Lower Canada, feel it highly incumbent on us, from motives of a public as well as of a private nature, to express, at the moment of your departure from this province on your voyage to England, the strong sense that we entertain of the important services, which you have been constantly occupied in rendering to this province, and of the regret that we feel at the prospect of being deprived of them, even for a short period.

" We regret, sir, to think that your laudable exertions in preserv-

The expediency of appointing an agent in England was again considered, and it was resolved—" that it is necessary for the interests of the inhabitants of this province, that a person fitly qualified, be appointed as agent

Chap. XVIII.
1814.

ing the public tranquility, and your unremitted zeal in devoting your high professional acquirements to the establishing of order by a regular system of practice in his Majesty's courts of justice in this province, should have exposed you to the extraordinary and unfounded charges which have been preferred against you. You must, however, recollect, sir, that such has not unfrequently been the reward of those who have best deserved the gratitude of their country.

" You go, sir, to a country where we have no doubt, your long and eminent services will be duly appreciated, and honourably distinguished.—Permit us to congratulate you on your visiting her at the proud moment of her triumph, when having established the social order, the peace, and the well regulated liberties of Europe, she has, we trust, for ever destroyed throughout the world, the hopes of those, who seek their own aggrandisement, in diminishing the consideration due to virtue and talent, in the production of anarchy, and in the subversion of established authorities. We take leave of you, sir, with the warmest sentiments of personal regard, and the most sincere anxiety for your early return to those elevated stations which you have filled with so much honor to yourself and advantage to the public.

(Signed) " J. QUEBEC,
P. R. DE ST. OURS,
FRS. BABY,
CHARTIER DE LOTBINIERE,
JENKIN WILLIAMS,
CHARLES DE ST. OURS.
JOHN HALE,

A. L. J. DUCHESNAY.
HERTEL DE ROUVILLE.
JOHN CALDWELL,
H. W. RYLAND.
JAMES CUTHBERT.
JOHN BLACKWOOD.
WM. M'GILLIVRAY."

" Quebec, 13th Jue, 1814."

" To the honorable Jonathan Sewell, chief justice of the province of of Lower Canada, and the honorable James Monk, chief justice of the district of Montreal.

" We the seigniors, landowners, and other proprietors of real estate, barristers, merchants or principal inhabitants of the city and neighbourhood of Quebec, whose names are hereunto subscribed, beg leave to address your honors on occasion of the accusations brought against you by the assembly of this province, during the last session of the legislature.

" Deeply impressed with the beneficent intentions of the mother country, in giving us a constitution, as nearly similar as our local circumstances would admit, to that excellent system whereby her own happiness has been so long secured, it is with the utmost regret that we feel ourselves compelled to animadvert upon the proceedings near his Majesty's government, in the United Kingdom of Great Britain and Ireland, for the purpose of soliciting the passing of laws, obviating misrepresentations, and for the transacting of such public matters as shall be, from

of any part of the constituted authorities; but when we see one branch of those authorities led by the violence of party spirit to attack another branch equally sacred, not only without adequate cause, but even without any application for such interference, and in the heat of that attack to infringe the principles which provide for personal security, as well as those which ensure the constitution itself, silence, under such circumstances, would be disgraceful.

"Of the numerous provisions whereby the laws of the british empire secure the lives and liberties of the subject, those regulations have ever been considered as pre-eminent in excellence, which allow no accusations to be received unsupported by evidence—provide before putting any man on his trial, for the examination of that evidence by the impartial judgment of an inquest of the country—and finally, before inflicting any punishment, secure to him a fair and open trial by his Peers. Of these salutary principles, we have, in the attacks made upon your honors, witnessed the total neglect—we have seen you accused, without the production of a single complaint to support the charges made in the assembly—we have seen those accusations adopted by that house, without examination, and, as we believe, without the existence of any evidence to support them—and finally, have witnessed an attempt to bring upon you, without trial, and on the mere allegations of the house itself, those inflictions which are due only to the guilty.

"Of constitutional principles, none can be more important than those which secure that equal balance amongst the respective public authorities, which has so long formed the peculiar and happy distinctions of the british government; and of these we have ever considered the independence of the judiciary power, as one of the most material; nor can we forget the sanction afforded to this principle, on the happy accession of our beloved sovereign, in the solemn confirmation then given to the salutary provision established by the same act, which secured the succession of the present royal family, that no judge should be removed, except on a joint address to the crown from both branches of the legislature: an admirable regulation, providing as well against any encroachments of the executive power, as against the excesses of party spirit in either branch of the legislature; notwithstanding the evident importance of this constitutional principle, and the high authority by which it is sanctioned, we have, in the proceedings of the late assembly, witnessed not only its total neglect but have seen measures adopted, which must evidently lead to its utter destruction.

"Independent of these general principles, on which we deprecate the proceedings into which the late assembly has allowed itself to be

time to time, committed to his care, for the good of the said province." A bill for appointing an agent in the United Kingdom was, accordingly passed, Mr. Bedard, who had not

hurried, if, having witnessed as we have done, in every instance where the proceedings of your respectable courts have come to our knowledge, the unremitting assiduity, the distinguished ability and perfect impartiality, with which your honors have administered your high and important offices, we were to fail, on this occasion, to bear testimony thereto; sensible also, as we all are, and benefited as many of us have been, by the improvements introduced into the practice of the courts, we cannot omit stating our decided opinion, that the charges made against you are unfounded in fact, false as far as we can judge in argument, and certainly so in the motives imputed; nor finally unconscious, as we ourselves are, of any cause of complaint against your honors, and ignorant even of the existence of a single individual justly deeming himself aggrieved by you, can we be deterred from expressing our belief, that the proceedings against you originate wholly in personal prejudice or party violence.

" Confident of the justice of your cause, we have learnt with the highest satisfaction, the intention of your honors to court the strictest investigation: the result, we are satisfied, will, before an impartial and enlightened tribunal, be the confusion of your accusers, and the complete vindication of your characters: and we cannot doubt, that when this shall be made apparent, a wise and liberal government will feel it incumbent, as an act of justice and public example, to testify its sense of your long and zealous services, by some distinguished mark of its approbation; we entertain also a lively hope, that such further measures will be devised by his Majesty's ministers, as shall in their wisdom appear adequate, to prevent the recurrence of similar injustice to that which you have experienced: so that, instead of being deterred from a bold and independent discharge of their duties, by the obloquy to which your honors have been so undeservedly exposed, all others, in like high stations may, by the ultimate result, be encouraged to a similar performance of their respective duties.

" We request your honors, in the mean time, to permit us to assure you of our profound respect, as well as of our ardent wishes for whatever can augment your happiness or good fame, and especially, that, animated by the testified approbation of a revered sovereign, you may long continue to exercise those high functions which you have hitherto discharged with such eminent advantage to the whole community.

" Quebec, 8th June, 1814."

This address was supported by upwards of two hundred signatures, comprising those of the principal proprietors and merchants, as well as the most influential and respectable citizens.

long since been promoted to the bench as provincial judge, at Three Rivers, being the agent named in the bill by the assembly, and the bill was, accordingly, sent up to the legislative council for its concurrence. While the bill was under consideration in the council, a message was sent by the assembly to that body " to invite their honors to join a second person to Pierre Bedard, esquire, to be agent for this province, and to acquaint their honors that the house of assembly will concur in their nomination." In answer to this, a message came down acquainting the assembly, " that as the message of the eleventh instant, received by the legislative council from the assembly, on that day, relates solely and entirely to the subject matter of the bill, intituled, " An act for appointing an agent in the United Kingdom of Great Britain and Ireland," which bill having been received by the legislative council from the assembly on the tenth instant, was, at the time of the delivery of the said message, in possession of the legislative council, cannot but observe this unusual proceeding on the part of the assembly, and do desire that the assembly, in future, will take no notice of the subject matter of any bill of which the legislative council shall be possessed, until the legislative council shall desire a conference thereon, with the assembly; a course which the legislative council will always observe, towards the proceedings of the assembly, as they conceive that the contrary is not compatible with the privileges of either house;" and here the matter rested for the present.

The House also drew up an address to the Prince Regent, on the state of the Province, and the progress of the war with the United States, in which the exertions of the people and the urgency of early assistance was briefly expressed.* It was at the same time voted " that Pierre Bedard, esquire, provincial judge at Three Rivers, be appointed by the house to present the said address to his royal highness the Prince Regent." An address, at the same time, was voted to the governor, praying him to advance to Mr. Bedard, out of the unappropriated monies, a sum of three thousand pounds currency, one half immediately, and the other in six months from that date, and that the house would make good the same, during the session. It was also ordered that a copy of the address to the Prince Regent, be communicated to the governor. The house, on the following day, rescinded its order naming Mr. Bedard, substituting an address to the governor, praying his excellency to transmit the address by such messenger, as he might be pleased to appoint for the purpose, and to advance a thousand pounds for the purpose, which the house would make good. The governor, in reply, informed the

---

* The strength of the six battalions of canadian embodied militia, amounted, in the month of December, 1813, according to a return submitted to the house of assembly, to 3,893 men, exclusive of the Voltigeurs, the Frontier Light Infantry, and other militia and Provincial Corps.

messengers that he acceded to the request of the assembly, and would name a proper person or persons to present the address to his royal highness, so soon as there were an appropriation made to that effect. But as his answer seemed not to have been accurately reported to the assembly, as expressed by him, he sent down a message in writing stating that, in order to prevent any mistake or misunderstanding with regard to the verbal answers given by him to the addresses of the assembly on the matter in question, he informed them that whenever a sum of money should be appropriated by the legislature for that service, he would take into his consideration the nomination of a person or persons as a messenger or messengers for transmitting the address.—This not being done owing to the disagreement between the two houses, the intended mission of Mr. Bedard, to wait upon the Prince Regent, with the address, did not take place, nor does it appear how the address was forwarded.

Such were the principal affairs that occupied the house of assembly, during the present session, which, on the seventeenth of March, was prorogued by the Governor, putting an end to the seventh parliament of Lower Canada, his excellency remarking, as follows :—

" It would have afforded me sincere gratification to have witnessed that unanimity and despatch amongst yourselves, and that liberal confidence in me, which the emergencies of the times, the situation of the province, and the assurances contained in your addresses, gave me a right to expect from you, and I have seen with regret, that my disappointment in this expectation has been attended with serious inconveniences to the public service.

"Gentlemen of the house of assembly,—I cannot but lament, the course of proceeding adopted by you, has occasioned the loss of a productive revenue bill, and of the liberal appropriations you had made for the defence of the province, and for ameliorating the situation of the militia; and I regret that in sacrificing these desirable objects, you should have been swayed by any considerations which seemed to you of higher importance than the immediate security of the country, or the comfort of those engaged in its protection.

"Gentlemen of the legislative council, gentlemen of the house of assembly,—The pacific rumors which have prevailed since I last addressed you, not affording any certain ground, for belief, that peace is at hand, our vigorous and united exertions will still be required to maintain the decided ascendency with which the Divine Providence has been pleased to bless our efforts in the present contest; I, therefore, earnestly entreat you to impress, by your precept and example, on all around you, a respect for the laws by which they are governed, as well as a just confidence in those who administer and execute them, and to cherish and encourage that spirit of loyalty and attachment to his Majes'y's person and government, which has hitherto proved the firmest barrier against all the attempts of the enemy.

"As the period fixed by law for the duration of the provincial parliament will shortly expire, I shall avail myself of an early opportunity to recur to the sense of the people, for the election of a new house of assembly. It is, therefore, my earnest recommendation to you, to endeavour in your several stations, to give to the inhabitants of this province, a true idea of the nature and value of the constitution which they possess;—that in the choice of their representatives, their attention may be directed to those, who, duly estimating its advantages, will endeavour faithfully to uphold it, and thereby effectually to promote the safety, welfare, and prosperity of the province."

The revenues of this, considerably exceeded those of the previous year, amounting to £99,602 currency; the expenses to £183,033 sterling, including £121,366, on account of militia services. But 198 vessels had cleared out from Quebec during the season, containing 46514 tons, and employing 2230 men—eight of those vessels were built at Quebec; tonnage 2658. The general elections took place in April and May, and for the most part were warmly contested.

It has been already mentioned that among the prisoners taken at the battle of Queenston, in the autumn of 1812, twenty-three men were recognised as deserters, and british born subjects. As traitors to their country, the commander of the forces had sent them to England for trial. This circumstance being made known to the american government, by the american commissary of prisoners at London; general Dearborn was ordered by his government, to put an equal number of british soldiers into close confinement as hostages, for the former. In consequence of this measure, the commander of the forces, by a general order of the 27th of October, 1813, made it known that he had received the commands of the prince regent to put forty-six american officers and non-commissioned officers into close confinement, as hostages, for the twenty-three soldiers confined by the american government. He at the same time apprised that government, that if any of the british soldiers should suffer death by reason of the guilt and execution of the traitors. found in arms against their country, who had been sent to England for legal trial, he was instructed to select out of the american officers and non-commissioned officers detained as hostages, double the number of the british soldiers who might be so unwarrantably put to death, and to cause them in retaliation, to suffer death immediately. In transmitting this information to the american government, the commander of the forces also notified them, that the commanders of his Majesty's armies and fleets on the coast of America, had received instructions to prosecute the war with unmitigated severity against all cities, towns and villages, belonging to the United States, and against the inhabitants thereof, if after that information should have reached the american government, they should not be deterred from putting to death any of the soldiers detained as hostages.

On the 10th of December, the commander of the forces received a communication from major general Wilkinson, by colonel Macomb, of the United States army, bearing a flag of truce, stating, " that the government of the United States adhering unalterably to the principle and purpose declared in the communication of general Dearborn, on the subject of the twenty-three american soldiers, prisoners of war, sent to England to be tried as criminals, and the confinement of a like number of British soldiers, prisoners, selected to abide the fate of the former, had, in consequence of the step taken by the british government, ordered forty-six british officers into close confinement, and that they should not be discharged therefrom until it should be known that the forty-six american officers and non-commissioned officers in question, were no longer confined."— In consequence of this, the governor ordered all the american officers, prisoners of war, without exception of rank, to be immediately placed into close confinement as hostages, until the number of forty-six were completed over and above those already in confinement. In pursuance of this order, generals Winder, Chandler, and Winchester, were conveyed from their quarters in the country at Beauport, to a private house in Quebec, where their confinement was rendered as little inconvenient as their situation could admit of.

On the fifteenth of April following, after some negociation between colonel Baynes, the adjutant general, under the direction of the commander of the forces, and brigadier general Winder, authorised on the part of the american government for the purpose, a convention was entered into at Montreal,* for the mutual release of all prisoners of war, hostages or others, with the exception of the forty-six american officers and non-commissioned officers placed in close confinement as hostages.

---

* The negociation was opened at the solicitation of the american government, in a letter from the secretary of state, to Sir George Prevost, who consented to the exchange of brigadier general Winder, for the purpose of negociating.

in retaliation for the twenty-three british soldiers, confined by the government of the United States, as hostages for the twenty-three british born subjects taken from the ranks of the enemy and sent to England for legal trial. The american government still persisted in detaining hostages for those traitors, but finding, in the correspondence that had taken place between the two negociators, Baynes and Winder, the governor firm in his determination not to yield an iota of the just grounds taken with respect to them, it finally yielded, and in July, another convention, supplementary to the former, was entered into at Champlain, between the adjutant general Baynes and Mr. Brenton, named for the purpose by the commander of the forces, and colonel Lear, on the part of the United States, by which all limitations to the previous convention were completely removed, it being here agreed, that " the twenty-three british soldiers, and the forty-six american officers, the hostages mentioned in the previous convention, were to be included, and to be released and exchanged in the same manner as other prisoners of war mentioned in the said articles, notwithstanding the exception to them therein contained ;" and the exchange was accordingly effected. Thus ended this matter, which, at one time, threatened to be the cause of some sanguinary doings, which, happily, were averted. We have never understood what became of the prisoners sent to England, but it does not appear that they were made examples of, as traitors, by capital punishment.

In the correspondence between col. Baynes and brigadier general Winder, the following articles on the subject, are so concise, clear, and satisfactory, that we cannot refrain from quoting them:—

"The british view the confinement of twenty-three soldiers as the first act of aggression; for the undoubted right that every free nation possesses of investigating and punishing the crimes committed by her own natural born subjects, in a due course of law, is too self-evident to require a comment; nor can it, by any distortion of sense or justice, be construed into a just ground, for an act of fair retaliation, exercised on twenty-three british soldiers;—the latter are characterised by their patriotism and loyalty—the former, stigmatised for their treason and rebellion.

"It would be wasting time to enter into any further discussion on this subject:—Great Britain has successfully maintained her national rights unsullied, for twenty years, against the whole world combined;—it is not to be supposed, that it is reserved for the United States, to stop the course of justice, and to dictate to England what procedure she shall observe towards her own natural born subjects, in her own courts of civil judicature, arrested in her own territories, in the actual commission of acts of treason and rebellion."

The most active exertions were made during the winter, to be prepared for the ensuing campaign. Stores of all descriptions were forwarded to Kingston, from Quebec and Montréal, on sleighs, at prodigious expense. The second battalion of the 8th regiment, commanded by lieut. colonel Robertson, marched through the woods from Frederickton to the St. Lawrence, in the month of February. A reinforcement of two hundred and twenty seamen for the lakes came by the same route. To expedite the progress of these reinforcements, the legislature of New Brunswick voted three hundred pounds, and the city of St. John's, gave a similar sum to defray the expense of conveying them on sleighs, as far as the nature of the roads would permit.

In the month of March, an embassy of chiefs and warriors from the Ottawas, Chippawas, Shawnees, Delawares, Mohawks, Saiks, Foxes, Kickapoos and Winabagoes, arrived at Quebec, to visit and hold a council with the commander of the forces. His excellency, on the fifteenth of that month, gave them an audience, and held a *Talk* or conference with them, at the Castle of St. Lewis. Their speeches were principally complimentary and expressive of their joy on beholding their father and meeting him in a council. They expressed their poverty, and requested that peace might not be concluded with the american government, until they should recover the ancient bounds of the territories of which the enemy had deprived them by fraud and violence. They represented the loss they had experienced of their young men in the war, but expressed their determination to persevere, and solicited arms for their warriors, and clothing for their women and children,—" The americans"—said one of the chiefs,—" are taking our lands from us every day, they have no hearts, father :—they have no pity for us, they want to drive us beyond the setting sun; but we hope, although we are few, and are here as it were upon a little island, our great and mighty father who lives beyond the great lake, will not forsake us in our distress, but will continue to remember his faithful red children." The governor in answer, exhorted them to persevere in the contest against the common enemy, in order to regain the territory lost in the last campaign. He expressed his sorrow for the loss of one of their warriors, (Tecumseh) and for that of many other valliant chiefs during the war. He charged them upon all occasions, to spare and shew mercy to all women, children and prisoners that should fall within their power, an injunction to which the listening chiefs unanimously murmured approbation. After some days residence at Quebec, they were loaded with presents, and despatched for the Upper Province, on their way homewards, to prepare their tribes for the approaching compaign.

On the twenty-sixth of March, his excellency issued a general order, expressing the approbation of the Prince Regent, of the affair at Chateauguay, and his " peculiar pleasure at finding that his Majesty's canadian subjects had at length had the opportunity of refuting, by their own brilliant exertions in defence of their country, the calumnious charge of disaffection and disloyalty with which the enemy had prefaced his first invasion of the province."— To lieut. col. De Salaberry in particular, and to all the officers and men under his command, the sense entertained by his Royal Highness of their meritorious and distinguished services was made known. The commander of the forces at the same time acquainted the militia of the determination of his Royal Highness to forward colours for the five battalions of embodied militia, feeling that they had evinced an ability and disposition to secure them from insult, which gave them the best title to such a mark of distinction. So flattering a testimony of the regent's approbation could not fail to raise the honest pride of the provincial militia.

A movement of the american forces in the neighbourhood of Lake Champlain, towards the conclusion of March, gave room to expect an invasion of the district of Montreal. Brigadier general Macomb, with a division of the american forces from Plattsburgh, crossed Lake Champlain upon the ice and entered St. Armands, where he remained some days without molestation, while general Wilkinson prepared for an attack upon the outposts of Odelltown, and the La Cole Mill, a stone building which had been converted into a block house. On the morning of the thirtieth of March, (General Macomb having suddenly withdrawn his division from St. Armands and rejoined the main body,) the american forces, consisting of five thousand men, commanded by general Wilkinson, in person, entered Odelltown. Major Handcock, commanding the block-house, received intelligence at eight o'clock in the morning, of the approach of the enemy, and immediately sent off a despatch to the Isle-aux-Noix for a reinforcement, from whence a picquet of the 13th regiment, under the command of captain Blake, was despatched to his aid. The enemy halted for a short time at the village, and then made a demonstration upon Burtonville with a part of their force. Their advance in that direction was checked by part of the grenadiers of the canadian fencibles, under captain Cartwright, and a few of the frontier Light Infantry, under captain Barker. At one o'clock the enemy was seen deploying in the neighbouring wood, with the intention of surrounding the block-house, a fire was immediately commenced which they did not return for some time, but appeared determined to carry the place by assault, as they advanced cheering; the heavy fire obliged them to relinquish their plan and retreat to the wood, where they were completely sheltered. A twelve pounder was brought to bear upon the building, but, so badly served, that during a cannonade of two hours and a half, only four shots struck it; the gun being within the range of musketry the artillery suffered severely, and in fact were unable to take aim with any degree of precision. The flank companies of the 13th regiment were ordered to charge the enemy in front—they advanced as far as the wood in line, but the difficulty of marching through the snow against a galling fire in front, compelled them to retire to the block house. The grenadiers of the canadian Fencibles and a company of the Voltigeurs, just now arriving from Burtonville, major Handcock ordered them to support the flank companies of the 13th regiment in a second charge, to which they advanced in column of sections.* The americans had now concentrated their whole force close to the gun, but did not attempt to fire until the british had advanced to within twenty-five yards of their centre, and were completely flanked on both sides: the first discharge of musketry, from the enemy, was so effectually destructive that these companies were entirely broken and compelled to retreat in disorder. All attempts to rally them were ineffectual, and they were recalled by the bugle to the Block house; the gun was spiked by the enemy during the first charge. The americans exhausted with cold and fatigue, finding it impossible to carry the place without heavy artillery, which, from the state of the roads, could not be brought forward, withdrew in good order from the contest, at five o'clock in the afternoon, without being pursued in the retreat. The british loss amounted to ten men killed and four men missing, and two officers and forty-four men wounded. The american loss though considerable, has not been precisely ascertained. Having failed in the attempt to carry a block-house, scarcely deserving the appellation of a military post, the enemy fell back upon Champlain town, from whence they soon retired to Plattsburgh.

---

* The force in the mill, when attacked, was 160 men. The reinforcements which arrived during the action, amounted to about two hundred men. Some accounts (which have been considered probable) state the american loss at 13 killed, and 123 wounded and 30 missing

CHAPTER XIX.

Military occurrences in Canada during the winter of 1814—campaign opens in Upper Canada—successful attack upon Oswego—british squadron blockade Sacket's Harbour—misadventure of captains Popham and Spilsbury at Sandy Creek—invasion of Upper Canada, by american forces under general Brown—surrender of fort Erie—battle of Chippewa—battle at Lundy's lane—american fleet on the lake—two american armed schooners captured by captain Dobbs—unsuccessful assault by the british upon fort Erie—Michillimackinac supplied and reinforced by lieut. col. McDouall, via the Nottawasaga—capture of *Prairie du Chien*—expedition against Michillimackinac, by the americans—operations by british forces under Sir John Sherbrooke, from Halifax—Castine and Machias captured—arrival of reinforcements from the british army in France—remarkable general order relating to the dress of officers belonging to them—forces concentrated between Laprairie and Chambly, preparatory to an invasion of the State of New York—advance upon Plattsburgh—fleet advances—engages the enemy, defeated and taken—troops fall back from Plattsburgh without assaulting it—great discontent and outcry in consequence of the loss of the navy on lake Champlain, failure of the expedition, and discreditable retreat of the army—*sortie* by the american forces at fort Erie upon the british before it on hearing the news—Sir James L. Yeo in command of lake Ontario—commodore Chauncey retires to Sacket's Harbour—predatory incursions of the enemy upon settlements on lake Erie—troops and embodied militia in Lower Canada sent into winter quarters—legislature meets—proceedings, &c.—official news of peace announced—militia disbanded—assembly vote £5,000 for a service of plate to Sir George Prevost—grant of £500 to Joseph Bouchette, esquire, as an aid to publish his map of Upper and Lower Canada—prorogation and speech—Sir George Prevost recalled, to answer charges preferred by Sir James L. Yeo—and superseded in the government by Sir Gordon Drummond—departs for England, via St. Johns, N. B.—addresses to him from Quebec and Montreal previous to his departure—general order to the troops on his taking leave—his decease in England previous to time fixed for his trial—steps by his brother and widow to clear up his character—result—remarks on his administration.

In Upper Canada the occurrences during the winter, were of small importance, being principally confined to incursions reciprocally practised by the troops, in advance, along the frontiers with various success. One of the most successful enterprises effected, in the course of the present season, was planned and executed by captain Sherwood, of the quartermaster-general's department. That officer with a subaltern, and a small detachment of twenty rank and file of the marines, and ten men of the embodied militia, under captain Kerr, proceeded over the St. Lawrence, on the night of the 6th of February, from Cornwall in Upper Canada, to Madrid, on Grass river, fourteen miles beyond the village of Hamilton, and brought away a considerable quantity of merchandize, (having pressed all the horses and sleighs he could find for that purpose) plundered from british merchants, near Cornwall, in October preceding, when on their route to Upper Canada. These effects were to have been sold on account of the United States government, notwithstanding an agreement for

Chap. XIX.
1814.

their restitution entered into on the 10th of November, by judge Ogden and Mr. Richardson on the part of the United States, and lieut. colonel Morrison and captain Mulcaster, (royal navy) on the part of the british government. The inhabitants made no opposition to the seizure and transportation of these effects, nor did they experience any molestation from the party, who, at two o'clock on the ensuing day, returned to their quarters with the most valuable of the merchandize, for which they had proceeded to Madrid.

A slight loss was experienced in an unsuccessful effort, made by a detachment consisting of the flank companies of the royal Scots, and the light company of the 89th regiment, under the command of captain Barsden of the 89th, for the purpose of dislodging a strong party of the enemy, who had taken post at Longwood, in the advance at Delaware town. The enemy had secured themselves on a commanding eminence, behind log intrenchments, and were attacked at five o'clock, in the afternoon, of the 4th of March, by this force, supported by a flank movement to the right, of a company of militia Rangers, under captain Caldwell, with a detachment of the Kent militia, and a similar movement by a party of indians to the left. After several repeated but unsuccessful efforts to dislodge the enemy, in a spirited contest of an hour and a half, the troops having suffered severely, were withdrawn. The enemy soon afterwards abandoned the position. The british lost two officers and twelve men killed. and three officers and forty-nine men wounded, including an officer and six men of the Kent militia volunteers, who distinguished themselves on the occasion.

The campaign was opened in Upper Canada, by sir Gordon Drummond and sir James L. Yeo, under the most cheering auspices. The american forces along the Lake Champlain, after leaving small garrisons at Plattsburgh, Burlington and Vergennes, moved early in the spring towards Lake Ontario and the Niagara frontier, with a view of resuming offensive operations against the Upper Province, as soon as the fleet at Sacket's Harbour (considerably augmented during the winter) should be in a state to co-operate with the land forces. The principal naval stores, for the equipment of the fleet, were forwarded to Sacket's Harbour, by the way of Oswego; and as the british naval force at Kingston, strengthened by two additional ships, the Prince Regent and Princess Charlotte, were ready to appear on the Lake, early in the season, it became an object of importance to intercept the enemy's supplies and by that means retard his preparations for invasion. An expedition against Oswego was, therefore, determined upon, and general Drummond having embarked a considerable force consisting of six companies of De Watteville's regt., the light companies of the Glengaries, the second battalion of the Royal Marines, with a detachment of royal artillery and two field pieces, a detachment of a rocket company, with a few sappers and miners, set sail from Kingston on the fourth of May, and at noon on the following day, made the port of Oswego, when a heavy gale from the north-west sprung up, and obliged the squadron to gain the offing. On the morning of the sixth, a landing was effected by about one hundred and forty of the troops, under lieut. colonel Fischer: and two hundred seamen, armed with pikes, under the command of captain Mulcaster, R. N., in front of a heavy discharge of round and grape from the battery, and of musketry from a detachment of about three hundred men, of the american army, posted on the brow of the hill, and in the skirts of the neighbouring wood. The british, on landing, pressed up the hill towards the enemy's battery, which the americans (upon finding the british determined to carry it by storm) relinquished, leaving about sixty men, principally wounded.

The land and naval commanders having taken possession of the stores found in the fort and its neighbourhood, and having dismantled the fortifications, and destroyed the barracks, re-embarked on the seventh of May, and returned to Kingston.

The loss of the british troops amounted to one captain (Holtaway of the marines) and eighteen men killed, and two officers and sixty men wounded. That of the navy amounted to three men killed, and four officers and seven men wounded. Captain Mulcaster, while entering the fort, at the head of his men, received a very severe and dangerous wound. Captain Popham was also severely wounded. Although the service derived much benefit from this expedition, the main object in contemplation was not accomplished, the principal part of the naval stores being saved by the enemy, who had taken the precaution of depositing them at the Falls, some miles from Oswego, up the river.

The flotilla at the Isle-aux-Noix, under the command of captain Pring, proceeded up the Lake Champlain, on the ninth of May, with a detachment of marines, for the purpose of capturing or destroying the new vessels recently launched at Vergennes, or of intercepting the stores and supplies intended for their armament and equipment. On the 14th capt. Pring reached his destination at Otter Creek, but, finding the enemy prepared for his reception, he judged it expedient to abandon his intended plan of attack, and returned to the Isle-aux-Noix.

The british squadron having, for the present, a decided ascendency on Lake Ontario, blockaded Sacket's Harbour, in order to intercept the supplies which might, from time to time, be forwarded from Oswego, for the equipment of the american fleet. On the morning of the 29th of May, a boat laden with two twenty-four pounders, and a large cable for one of the american ships of war, was captured on the way to Sacket's Harbour from Oswego, from whence it had sailed in company with fifteen other boats, loaded with naval and military stores. This intelligence induced the naval commander to despatch captains Popham and Spilsbury, with two gun-boats and five barges, in quest of the enemy's boats, which these officers ascertained to have taken shelter in Sandy Creek, whither they proceeded with the resolution of capturing or destroying them, if the attempt, should be found practicable. On the morning of the 31st of May, the boats from the british squadron entered the Creek, and captains Popham and Spilsbury, having reconnoitred the enemy's position, determined on an immediate attack, which, although aware of the hazard of the enterprise, they determined to risk, as the stores in possession of the enemy were of the utmost importance to the armament of their squadron. The boats advanced cautiously up the Creek to within half a mile of the enemy, when parties were landed on either bank, who advanced on the flanks of the gun-boats, to a turning which opened the enemy's boats full to their view—It was at this juncture, when, by some accident, a sixty-eight pounder carronade in the bow of the foremost gun-boat being disabled, it became necessary to pull her round to bring the twenty-four pounder in her stern to bear upon the enemy. The americans taking this movement for the commencement of a retreat advanced with their whole force, consisting of one hundred and fifty riflemen, near two hundred indians, and a strong body of militia and cavalry; who after a short though desperate contest, from which it was impossible to effect a retreat, overpowered the british party, consisting of about two hundred men, of which, it is said, eighteen were killed and fifty wounded. Captain Popham in his official despatch to sir James L. Yeo, on this affair, acknowledged with the warmest gratitude the humane exertions of the american officers of the rifle corps, commanded by major Appling, in saving the lives of many of the officers and men, whom the american soldiers and indians were devoting to slaughter.

The american forces concentrated at Buffaloe, Black Rock, and other places, on the Niagara frontier, under the command of major general Brown, in momentary expectation of the co-operation of the squadron on lake Ontario, were ready at the end of June, to invade Upper Canada. On the morning of the third July, the enemy embarked in boats and batteaux, and effected a landing on the Canada side, without opposition, with two strong brigades, under brigadiers Scott and Ripley, at two points on the shore above and below fort Erie, each about a mile distant from that post, then under command of major Buck, of the 8th regiment. This officer had been active in putting fort Erie in a state of defence, and with a small detachment of about seventy men was left in charge of it, more with a view of causing a temporary check to an invading force, than for the purpose of defending it against a regular siege, which was not intended. It would have been impossible to maintain fort Erie, for any length of time, against the overwhelming force of the enemy, but a resistance of even a few hours, might have been of material consequence, and have enabled general Riall to repell the invasion at the outset. The able dispositions which had been made by the forces under that officer, along the Niagara line, by the direction of lieut. general Drummond, who had anticipated an invasion at the point where it commenced, were such, that the least impediment to the progress of the invaders, would have enabled general Riall to have concentrated his troops, and to fall upon and disperse the enemy, before they could have time to be prepared for an effectual resistance. Under these circumstances, it was a matter of regret, that fort Erie was tamely surrendered to the enemy, without firing a shot or making even a shew of resistance. The americans after the acquisisition of this important post, advanced with confidence in the afternoon of the ensuing day, to the plains adjacent to Chippawa, and were making preparations to carry that post, when general Riall, to anticipate their design, having collected his forces, marched on the evening of the fifth, from his lines, and gave them battle. The enemy had much the advantage in numbers and fought with determined bravery. His right rested on some buildings and orchards on the brink of the Niagara, and was strongly supported by artillery. His left was skirted by a wood, with a considerable body of indians and riflemen in front. The militia and indians engaged the enemy's riflemen, who, at first, checked their advance, but being supported by the arrival of light troops, consisting of the light companies of the Royal Scots and 100th regiment, with the 2d Lincoln militia, under lieut. colonel Pearson, they were dislodged after a very sharp contest. Two light twenty-four pounders and a howitzer were brought into action against the enemy's right, which was also engaged by the King's regiment, while the Royal Scots and 100th regiment, after deploying with the utmost steadiness, opened a heavy fire upon his left and advanced to the charge, with the most intrepid gallantry, under a destructive fire. In this attempt they suffered so severely that it was found necessary to withdraw them and desist from a contest, which, from the great superiority of the enemy's numbers, must have been unavailing. General Riall accordingly fell back upon Chippawa in the evening, and to prevent the enemy from occupying Burlington Heights, by a forced march, as intended, threw such reinforcements as he could spare into forts George, Niagara, and Mississaga, and retired to Twenty-mile Creek, on the route to Burlington, where he prepared for a vigorous stand against the progress of the enemy to that post. The American squadron was not, however, ready to appear upon the lake during these occurrences; a circumstance peculiarly fortunate, as their appearance would have so emboldened their army, far superior in numbers to the british, as probably to have led to the reduction of forts George and Niagara. The militia, under lieut. colonel Dickson, who was wounded, behaved with gallantry. The british lost six officers and one hundred and forty-two men killed, and twenty-six officers (among them lieut. col. the marquis of Tweedale, severely) and two hundred and ninety-five men wounded, and one officer and forty-five men missing. The enemy stated their loss at seventy men killed, and nine officers and two hundred and forty men wounded, and nineteen missing.

The enemy, after this affair, gradually advanced along the Niagara, and occupied Queenston, from whence he made demonstrations upon forts George and Mississaga, but finding lieut. col. Tucker, who had been left in command of those posts, on the alert, and determined to make a resolute defence, he desisted from further attempts to carry them.

General Brown, finding a stouter resistance than he expected, fell back upon Queenston, from whence, on the 25th of July, he retreated with his whole force upon Chippawa, having previously set fire to the village of St. David's.*

---

* This, it would seem, however, was contrary to the orders and instructions of the general commanding, who, in general orders, expressed his displeasure at the circumstance, and desired lieut. colonel Stone, commanding at that village, to retire from the army in consequence of his conduct. This officer was afterwards dismissed the service on account of this business, without a hearing.—The village of Long Point, was also reduced to ashes by these incendiaries.

General Riall immediately put his advance in motion, and was moving on to support it, when the enemy wheeled about with a view of overpowering his forces, before they could be assisted by the reinforcements which were expected to join him. General Drummond, with lieut. col. Harvey, had that morning arrived at fort George, from York. The proceedings which immediately succeeded his arrival, cannot be more concisely and clearly explained than in his own official despatch, after the battle of Lundy's Lane, which is quoted as the best relation to be found, of that hard fought action :—

Chap. XIX
1814.

" I embarked on board his Majesty's schooner Netley, at York, on Sunday evening, the 24th instant, and reached Niagara at day-break, the following morning. Finding from lieutenant colonel Tucker that major general Riall was understood to be moving towards the falls of Niagara, to support the advance of his division, which he had pushed on to that place, on the preceding evening, I ordered lieut. colonel Morrison, with the 89th regiment, and a detachment of the Royals and King's, drawn from forts George and Mississaga, to proceed to the same point, in order that, with the united force, I might act against the enemy (posted at Street Creek, with his advance at Chippawa) on my arrival, if it should be found expedient. I ordered lieut. colonel Tucker, at the same time, to proceed on the right bank of the river, with three hundred of the 41st, and about two hundred of the Royal Scots, and a body of indian warriors, supported (on the river) by a party of armed seamen, under captain Dobbs, royal navy. The object of this movement was to disperse or capture a body of the enemy, which was encamped at Lewiston. Some unavoidable delay having occurred in the march of the troops, up the right bank, the enemy had moved off previous to lieutenant colonel Tucker's arrival. I have to express myself satisfied with the exertions of that officer.

"Having refreshed the troops at Queenston, and having brought across the 41st, Royals, and Indians, I sent back the 41st and 100th regiments to form the garrisons of the forts George, Mississaga, and Niagara, under lieutenant colonel Tucker, and moved, with the 89th, and detachments of the Royals and King's, and light company of the 41st, in all about 800 men, to join major general Riall's division at the Falls.

"When arrived within a few miles of that position, I met a report from major general Riall, that the enemy was advancing in great force. I immediately pushed on, and joined the head of lieutenant colonel Morrison's column, just as it reached the road leading towards the Beaver Dam, over the summit of the hill at Lundy's Lane. Instead of the whole of major general Riall's division, which I expected to have found occupying this position, I found it almost in the occupation of the enemy, whose columns were within 600 yards of the top of the hill, and the surrounding woods filled with his light troops. The advance of major general Riall's division, consisting of the Glengary Light Infantry, and incorporated militia, having commenced their retreat upon fort George, I countermanded these corps, and formed the 89th regiment and the Royal Scots detachments, and 41st light companies, in the rear of the hill, their left resting on the great road; my two twenty-four pounder brass field guns a little advanced in front of the centre on the summit of the hill; the Glengary Light Infantry on the right, the battalion of incorporated militia, and the detachment of the King's regiment on the left of the great road; the squadron 19th Light Dragoons in the rear of the left, on the road. I had scarcely completed this formation, when the whole front was warmly and closely engaged. The enemy's principal efforts were directed against our left and centre. After repeated attacks, the troops on the left were partially forced back, and the enemy gained a momentary possession of the road. This gave him, however, no material advantage, as the troops which had been forced back formed in the rear of the 89th regiment, fronting the road, and securing the flank. It was during this short interval that major general Riall, having received a severe wound, was intercepted as he was passing to the rear, by a party of the enemy's cavalry, and made prisoner. In the centre, the repeated and determined attacks of the enemy were met by the 89th regiment, the detachments of the Royals and King's, and the light company of the 41st regiment, with the most perfect steadiness and intrepid gallantry, and the enemy was constantly repulsed with very heavy loss. In so determined a manner were these attacks directed against our guns, that our artillerymen were bayoneted, by the enemy, in the act of loading, and the muzzles of the enemy's guns were advanced within a few yards of ours. The darkness of the night, during this extraordinary conflict, occasioned several uncommon incidents: our troops having for a moment been pushed back, some of our guns remained for a few minutes in the enemy's hands; they were, however, not only quickly recovered, but the two pieces, a six pounder and a five and a half inch howitzer, which the enemy had brought up, were captured by us, together with several tumbrils; and in limbering up our guns at one period, one of the enemy's six pounders was put, by mistake, upon a limber of ours, and one of our six pounders limbered on one of his; by which means the pieces were exchanged; and thus, though we captured two of his guns, yet, as he obtained one of ours, we have gained only one gun.

"About nine o'clock (the action having commenced at six) there was a short intermission of firing, during which it appears the enemy was employed in bringing up the whole of his remaining force, and he shortly afterwards renewed his attack, with fresh troops, but was everywhere repulsed, with equal gallantry and success. About this period the remainder of major general Riall's division, which had been ordered to retire, on the advance of the enemy, consisting of the 103d regiment, under colonel Scott; the head-quarter division of the Royal Scots, the head quarter division of the 8th (or King's;) flank companies 104th; some detachments of militia, under lieutenant colonel Hamilton, inspecting field-officer, joined the troops engaged; and I placed them in a second line, with the exception of the Royal Scots, and flank companies 104th, with which I prolonged my front line on the right where I was apprehensive of the enemy's out-flanking me. The enemy's efforts to carry the hill were continued until about midnight, when he had suffered so severely from the superior steadiness and discipline of his Majesty's troops, that he gave up the contest, and retreated with great precipitation to his camp, beyond the Chippawa, On the following day he abandoned his camp, threw the greatest part of his baggage, camp-equipage, and provisions into the rapids ; and having set fire to Street's Mills, and destroyed the bridge at Chippawa, continued his retreat in great disorder towards Fort Erie. My light troops, cavalry, and indians, are detached in pursuit, and to harrass his retreat, which, I doubt not, he will continue until he reaches his own shore.

" The loss sustained by the enemy, in this severe action, cannot be estimated at less than fifteen hundred men, including several hundreds of prisoners left in our hands: his two commanding generals, Brown and Scott, are said to be wounded; his whole force, which has never been rated at less than five thousand, having been engaged. Enclosed, I have the honour to transmit a return of our loss, which has been very considerable. The number of troops under my command did not, for the first three hours, exceed sixteen hundred men; the addition of the troops, under colonel Scott, did not increase it to more than two thousand eight hundred, of every description."

General Drummond received a severe wound in his neck, from a musket ball. He, however, concealed the circumstance from the troops, and remained on the ground, cheering on his men until the close of the action. Lieut. col. Morrison, of the 89th regiment; lieut. colonel Pearson, captain Robinson, of the King's regiment, (commanding the militia,) and several other officers were severely wounded. The bravery of the militia, in this desperate conflict, is said to have been beyond all praise, as attested by a variety of authorities, and by none more warmly (to the writer's knowledge) than by lieut. colonel (now lieut. general,) Sir John Harvey, himself no idle spectator on the occasion.—Nothing could have been more awful and impressive than this mid-night contest. The desperate charges of the enemy were succeeded by a deathlike silence, interrupted only by the groans of the dying, and the dull sounds of the falls of Niagara, while the adverse lines were now and then dimly discerned through the moonlight, by the gleam of their arms. These anxious pauses were succeeded by a blaze of musketry along the lines, and by a repetition of the most desperate charges from the enemy, which the british, regulars and militia, received with the most unshaken firmness. The american loss, by their own statement, amounted to one hundred and sixty rank and file killed, including twelve officers; and five hundred and seventeen wounded, including fifty officers, among them generals Brown and Scott. The command of the american forces, in the absence of generals Brown and Scott, who retired for the recovery of their wounds, devolved upon general Ripley. The enemy retreated, on the 27th, with his whole force to Fort Erie, and threw up intrenchments in the neighbourhood of that fort to secure himself against the british, who immediately invested their works. General Gaines, in the mean time, proceeded from Sacket's Harbour, and assumed the command at Fort Erie.

Chap. XIX.
1814.

On the 1st of August, the american fleet sailed from Sacket's Harbour, and after looking into Kingston, proceeded for the head of the lake; from whence he soon returned to port, upon finding the army far from being in a state to co-operate, cooped up at Fort Erie, and incapable of holding any direct communication with the naval force on lake Ontario.

The successful result of an enterprise by captain Dobbs, of the royal navy, in capturing, in the night of the 12th of August, with his gig and some batteaux, (conveyed over land from the Niagara river,) two of the enemy's schooners, the Ohio and Somers, lying close to Fort Erie, for the purpose of flanking the approaches to the fort, each mounting three long twelves, with complements of thirty-five men, gave spirit to the army. General Drummond, after reconnoitering the enemy's position, determined to storm the american intrenchments. He accordingly opened a battery on the morning of the thirteenth, and on the ensuing day, finding that a material effect had been produced upon their works, he made the necessary preparations for an assault. Three columns were, in the night of the fourteenth, put in movement: one under the command of lieut. colonel Fischer, of De Watteville's regiment, consisting of the 8th and De Wattville's regiments, the flank companies of the 89th and 100th regiments, with a detachment of artillery; another under lieut. col. Drummond, of the 104th regiment, consisting of the flank companies of the 41st and 104th regiments, and a body of seamen and marines under captain Dobbs, R. N., and the third under colonel Scott, of the 103d regiment, consisting of his own regiment, supported by two companies of the royals. The first of these columns was ordered to attack and turn the left of the enemy's intrenchment, on the side of Snake Hill, while the two other columns were to attack the fort and the right of their intrenchments. Col. Fischer's column had gained the point of attack two hours before daylight, and the head of the column had actually gained possession of the enemy's batteries, but the column of support, in marching too near the lake, entangled themselves between the rocks and the water, and were, by the repulse of the flank companies of the King's regiment, (which, for want of timely support, was compelled to retire upon them,) thrown into utter confusion, and suffered most severely by the fire of the enemy. The two other columns advanced as soon as the firing upon lieut. col. Fischer's column was heard, and at the same moment stormed the fort and intrenchments on the right, and after a desperate resistance succeeded in making a lodgment in the fort, through the embrasures of the demi-bastion. The enemy took to a stone building, which they maintained, with determination, for upwards of an hour and a half, against the guns of the demi-bastion, which the assailants had turned against them, until some ammunition, under the platform on which the guns were placed taking fire, (whether accidentally or by design, is not well understood,) a tremendous explosion ensued, by which almost all the troops who had entered the fort were dreadfully mangled. An immediate panic seized the troops, who could neither be rallied by the surviving officers, nor persuaded that the explosion was accidental. The enemy after having repulsed lieut. col. Fischer's column, had ordered reinforcements from the left and centre of their lines, to the assistance of the fort, who, taking advantage of the darkness and confusion of the moment, pressed forward with a heavy and destructive fire, and compelled the assailants to retire from the works they had so gallantly carried.

In this assault, the loss of the british was severely felt. Colonels Scott and Drummond, fell, while storming the works, at the head of their respective columns. Four officers and fifty-four men were returned as killed, and twenty-four officers and two hundred and eighty-five men wounded. The missing were reported at nine officers and five hundred and thirty men, afterwards ascertained to have been principally killed. The american statement of their own loss, makes it eighty-four in killed wounded and missing.

General Drummond was reinforced a day or two after this assault, by the arrival of the 6th and 82d regiments, from Lower Canada. This reinforcement was, however, no more than barely sufficient to supply the recent casualties, and the general did not, with the small force under his command, deem it expedient to hazard a second attempt to recover Fort Erie, but, by continuing its investment, he cut off all communication with the adjacent country, and in compelling the enemy to draw his resources from his own country rendered the occupation of that post, for the remainder of the campaign, of no service to the invaders.

Michillimakinac, contrary to the expectation of the enemy, had, early in the spring, been reinforced with a detachment of troops and seamen, under lieutenant colonel M'Douall. This officer proceeded by way of the Nottawasaga river, and after having, for several days, struggled against the ice and tempestuous weather, which, at this season, agitates Lake Huron, arrived at his destination on the 18th of May, with his open canoes loaded with provisions and stores for the relief of the garrison.

From Michillimakinac, lieutenant colonel M'Douall dispatched lieutenant colonel M'Kay, of the indian department, at the commencement of July, with a force of six hundred and fifty men (of which 120 were Michigan Fencibles, Canadian Volunteers and officers of the indian department, the remainder indians) to reduce the post of *Prairie du Chien*, on the Mississippi. Mr. M'Kay arrived at that place on the 17th July. Here he found the enemy in occupation of a small fort, situated on a height, with two block-houses, mounting six pieces of cannon, and in the middle of the Mississippi, immediately in front of the fort, a large gun-boat mounting fourteen pieces of small artillery. Mr. M'Kay sent a flag of truce, demanding an immediate surrender. This being refused, he opened a fire from one gun, upon the enemy's gun-boat, with such effect, after an action of three hours, as to compel her to cut her cable and run down the stream, where she took shelter under an island. In the evening of the 19th, having thrown up his breast works, at the distance of four hundred and fifty yards, he was prepared to open a cannonade upon the enemy, with a single gun which he had mounted for the purpose, when the enemy hoisted a white flag and sent an officer to acquaint the besiegers of their surrender, who immediately took possession of the garrison. The enemy's force consisted of three officers and 71 men. The reduction of this post, which was effected without the loss of a single man, was of the utmost importance to the british traders, and effectually secured the british influence over the indian tribes of of the West.

The enemy, upon ascertaining that Michillimakinac had been reinforced, fitted out an expedition which was put under the command of lieut. col. Croghan. A detachment of this force, under the command of major Holmes, an unfeeling miscreant, proceeded to Saint Marie's, where, after plundering the whole of the stores belonging to the North West Company, they reduced the buildings to ashes.*— The main body after it had been joined by this detachment consisted of about nine hundred men. This force effected a landing near the fort of Michillimakinac, on the 4th of August, in the forenoon; but the spirited opposition which it experienced from the handful of men, under lieutenant colonel M'Douall, was such as to compel them to re-embark, leaving seventeen men dead on the shore, among them major Holmes.

Though the enemy had failed in this attempt, to carry Michillimakinac, they kept their small cruisers in the neighbourhood, so as to intercept all supplies destined for the garrison. Two of these vessels the Tigress and Scorpion were carried, (the former on the evening of the 3d, and the latter in the morning of the 5th of September) by a small party of seamen, under lieutenant Worsley, R. N., and a party of soldiers, under lieutenant Bulger, of the Royal Newfoundland regiment. They carried each a long twenty-four pounder on a pivot, with complements of thirty-two men. After their capture, Michillimakinac was left unmolested.

During these events in Upper Canada, lieut. general sir John Coape Sherbooke, then lieut. governor in Nova Scotia, was successfully

---

* It is related among other traits of their cruelty, that these brigands, having made use of a horse all the day in carrying the plunder, tied him whilst harnessed in the cart, to a dwelling-house, which they set on fire, and amused themselves in admiring the unavailing efforts of the poor animal to extricate itself from the flames.

engaged in reducing a very populous and extensive portion of the enemy's territories, adjacent to the province of New Brunswick. He detached a small force from Halifax, under lieutenant colonel Pilkington which, with the Ramilies, commanded by sir Thomas Hardy, took possession, on the 11th July, of Moose Island in Passamaquoddy Bay, the garrison at fort Sullivan, consisting of six officers and eighty men, under the command of major Putnam, surrendering themselves prisoners of war. On the 26th of August, sir John C. Sherbrooke having embarked at Halifax, the whole of his disposeable forces on board of ten transports set sail, accompanied by a small squadron, under rear admiral Griffiths for Castine, on the Penobscot river, where he arrived on the 1st September, and took possession of the batteries at that place; the enemy, finding it impossible to retain the post, having previously blown up the magazine and retreated with the field pieces. The United States' frigate Adams, had some days previous to the arrival of the british at Castine, run into the Penobscot and for security had gone up as far as Hamden, where her guns had been landed and a position taken, with a view of protecting her. Captain Barrie, of the Dragon, with a suitable naval force, and six hundred picked men, under the command of colonel John, of the 60th regiment, were detached up the river, for the purpose of obtaining possession or destroying this vessel. The enemy, who at first offered a spirited resistance, after setting fire to the frigate, fled in all directions, upon finding the british resolutely advancing against their positions. Several pieces of ordnance and three stand of colours fell into the hands of the british, whose loss amounted to no more than one man killed and one officer and seven men wounded.

After the capture of Castine, lieutenant col. Pilkington was despatched with a brigade of troops for Machias, which was taken possession of on the 11th September by that officer; the detachment in Fort O'Brien, having, on the approach of the british, precipitately retreated from the fort, leaving twenty-six pieces of ordnance, with a quantity of small arms and ammunition. Lieut. colonel Pilkington was on the point of marching into the interior of the country, when he received a communication from lieutenant general Brewer, commanding the district, engaging that the militia forces within the county of Washington, should not bear arms or serve against his britannic Majesty during the war. This, with a similar offer made by the civil officers and principal inhabitants of the county, brought on a cessation of arms. By these judicious measures a populous extent of territory, stretching one hundred miles along the sea coast, including a valuable tract of country, partly separating New Brunswick from Lower Canada, submitted to the british arms without effusion of blood or waste of treasure.

Chap. XIX. 1814.

Among the casualties in advance along the lines on the Montreal frontier, in the course of the present summer, the death of captain Mailloux deserves to be remembered. This brave canadian had been remarkably vigilant and was of essential service in watching the movements of the enemy. He fell, while on a reconnoitring party, into the hands of the enemy, who had laid in ambush for him. He received several balls through the body, of which he languished some days, receiving, however, the greatest attention from the american surgeons, as well as from those of the british, who were allowed by the enemy to cross the lines to attend him. The body, after his decease, was sent to the lines, escorted by a party of the american military, with the honors of war, and every mark of respect for the memory of the deceased.

The arrival at Quebec, of a strong reinforcement of sixteen thousand men, of the Duke of Wellington's army, from the Garonne, in July and August, determined Sir George Prevost, to invade the state of New York, by the way of Lake Champlain.* The flotilla at Isle-aux

* The following general order, issued at Montreal, on the 23d of August, 1814, shortly after their arrival, gave great offence to the officers of the division of the army pointed at, and made Sir George Prevost, very unpopular in it, many of them making no scruples in expressing their conviction of his inadequacy for the position in which he was placed, and their determination to disregard the general order, as a piece of *petitesse* :—

" HEAD QUARTERS, Montreal, 23d August, 1814.

" General Order.—The commander of the forces has observed in the dress of several of the officers of corps and departments lately added to this army, from that of Field Marshal the Duke of Welling-

Noix was necessary to co-operate with the land forces, and the commissary general and quarter-master general, in order to expedite the new frigate, the Confiance, were directed to suspend every other branch of the public service which interfered with its equipment. Sir James L. Yeo was urged, by the commander of the forces, early in August, to put this division of his command into an effective state, for the contemplated service. In answer to this, he was acquainted by the commodore, that the squadron on lake Champlain was already ninety men over complete. This officer at the same time superseded captain Fisher, who, with much exertion, had almost prepared the flotilla for active service, appointing captain Downie, from the lake Ontario squadron, in his stead.

The commander of the forces, disappointed in not receiving a reinforcement of seamen from lake Ontario, applied to admiral Otway and captain lord James O'Brien, then at Quebec, who furnished a strong reinforcement from their respective ships, the Ajax and Warspite, for the service of the flotilla.

---
ton, a fanciful variety inconsistent with the rules of the service, and in some instances, without comfort or convenience, and to the prejudice of the service, by removing essential distinctions of rank and description of service

" His excellency deems it expedient to direct that general officers in charge of divisions and brigades, do uphold his Majesty's commands in that respect, and only admit of such deviations from them as may be justified by particular causes of service and climate, and even then their uniformity is to be retained.

" Commanding officers are held responsible that the established uniform of their corps is strictly observed by the officers under their command. " Ed. Baynes, adjt.-gen."

Sir George Prevost having sent to Upper Canada, a brigade of troops under major general Kempt, who was authorised to make a descent upon Sacket's Harbour, before the close of the season, if such a measure should be thought practicable, concentrated his army between Laprairie and fort Chambly, under the immediate command of major general De Rottenburgh. Although the flotilla was scarcely ready to co-operate, finding that a strong division of the enemy's forces under general Izard, had marched from Plattsburgh, to reinforce the troops at fort Erie, he, in order to check the advance of this division, put his army in movement and crossed the lines at Odelltown, on the 1st of September. On the third, he advanced and occupied Champlain Town, which the enemy abandoned upon his approach.

From this point, the whole british force marched on the fourth, in two columns, by parallel roads upon Plattsburgh, through a woody country. The column marching by the western road, (more elevated and on drier ground than the road next the lake, which was low and swampy,) commanded by majors generals Power and Robinson, was smartly opposed by the enemy's militia. It, however, drove the enemy back upon Plattsburgh on the sixth, and opened the way for the left brigade, commanded by major general Brisbane, by Dead Creek. a strong position, upon the border of lake Champlain, which the enemy had occupied in force, after destroying a bridge over the stream, which, in this place was not fordable, having so distributed their gun-boats, (ten in number, six of which carried each one long twenty-four, and an eighteen pounder carronade, the others a long twelve each,) as to take the british in flank, on their approach. The american squadron, consisting of the ship Saratoga of 26 guns; brig Eagle, 20 guns; schooner Ticonderoga, 17 guns; and the cutter Preble, of 7 guns, lay anchored in the Bay, then within reach of the protection of three batteries and redoubts, on a ridge of land on the south of the Saranac river. This position being turned, the enemy fell back upon their redoubts beyond the Saranac, keeping a vigilant outlook upon the fords of the river, with strong picquets of light troops. On the seventh, the the heavy artillery being brought forward, eligible situations were chosen to place them in battery, when it was observed that the squadron had changed their position from that of the preceding day, and were anchored out of reach of their own, as well as of the british batteries. The commander of the forces had previously acquainted captain Downie, (who was moving gradually up the lake, with his flotilla,* himself in the Confiance, rather unprepared for action, with a crew entirely strangers to her officers,) of the position of the american squadron; and that the attack, by land and water, might be simultaneous, he deferred an attack upon their

---

* Consisting of the Confiance, 36; Linnet, 18; Chub, 10; Finch, 10; 12 gun-boats. 16 guns.

works until the arrival of the squadron. This resolution, it is said, was adopted with the unanimous concurrence of the general officers present. The escape of the enemy's fleet to the narrow channels, at the head of the lake, might render it impracticable to engage them there, with any prospect of success: a final decision of the naval ascendency, on the lake, at the present juncture was, therefore, of the utmost importance to the ulterior operations of the army, and the expediency of such a measure was universally acknowledged, particularly as the strongest confidence prevailed in the superiority of the british vessels, their weight of metal, and in the capacity and experience of their officers and crews; and as the commander of the forces was informed by an officer of his staff, who had been dispatched to captain Downie, that he (capt. D.) considered himself, with his own vessel alone, (the Confiance) a match for the whole american squadron. At midnight, on the 9th September, Sir George Prevost received a communication from capt. Downie, stating that he was prepared for service, and proposed getting under way with his squadron the same night, at twelve o'clock, with the intention of doubling Cumberland Head, at the entrance of Plattsburgh Bay,) about day-break, and engaging the enemy's squadron, if anchored in a position to justify such a measure. The troops, at dawn of day, were under arms, but there being no appearance of the fleet at the expected hour, they were sent into quarters. Sir George wrote a note to captain Downie, acquainting him that the army had been held in readiness that morning for the expected arrival, and expressing his hopes that the wind only had delayed the approach of the squadron. The brave Downie, who, to the noble and manly virtues characteristic of his profession, united the nicest sense of honor, is said to have been fired with indignation at the reflection contained in the note. No communication subsequent to that of the 9th was, however, received from him at head-quarters. At dawn of day, on the 11th, the wind being observed to be favorable for the advance of the squadron, the troops were put under arms, and at seven o'clock its approach was announced by the scaling of the guns of Confiance, which rounded Cumberland Head with a leading breeze, leaving the other vessels and gun-boats far in her wake. At 8 o'clock the whole fire of the enemy's squadron, moored in line, was directed upon the Confiance, which moved gallantly into action without returning a shot, (captain Downie intending to lay his ship athwart hause of the enemy's largest ship) until within two cable lengths of the american line, when, having two anchors shot away and the wind baffling, she came to anchor, and opened a destructive fire upon the enemy. The Linnet and Chub, some time after, took their stations at a short distance, but the Chub having had her cables, bowsprit, and main boom shot away, became unmanage able and drifting within the enemy's line was obliged to surrender. Shortly after the commencement of the fire from the Confiance, her gallant commander fell, and the command of the squadron devolved upon captain Pring of the Linnet. The Confiance, after the fall of captain Downie, fought for some time most gallantly, under the command of lieutenant Robertson, but was compelled to strike her colours to the enemy's ship, the Saratoga, which at one moment had slackened her fire, several of her guns being dismounted: she, however, cut her cable, winded her larboard broadside so as to bear on the Confiance, which, being much shattered in her hull and injured in her rigging, endeavoured in vain to effect the same manœuvre. The Finch struck on a reef of rocks, to the eastward of Crab Island, early in the action, and was of no service in the engagement. The Linnet only remained; but captain Pring finding that the gun-boats had shamefully abandoned the object assigned to them, and were flying from the scene of action, while not a hope remained of retrieving the disasters of the day, his men falling fast, was compelled, reluctantly, to give the painful orders to strike his colours. The fire on both sides proved very destructive, from the light airs and the smoothness of the water: the british loss in killed and wounded was one hundred and twenty-nine, of which three officers and thirty-eight men were killed, and one officer and thirty-nine men wounded on board of the Confiance.

The batteries on shore were put into operation against the enemy's line of fortifications, as soon as the enemy's ships commenced firing. As the approach to the front of their works was rough and exposed to a fire of grape and musketry, as well as to a flank fire from a Block-house, a column of assault, under major general Robinson, was ordered to move by the rear of their bivouacs, the better to conceal their movements and cross a ford previously reconnoitred some distance up the Saranac; thence to penetrate through a wood to a clear space of ground, in the vicinity of the enemy's position, where the necessary preparations might be made to carry their works by assault, on their reverse front.

The second brigade, under major general Brisbane, was so distributed as to create a diversion in favor of the column, under major general Robinson, which, through the mistake of the guides, had been led upon a wrong path and missed the ford. Before the error could be rectified by a countermarch, shouts of huzzah, were distinctly heard by this column, in the direction of the american works. To have carried these fortifications would have been no difficult task for the brave troops composing either column, but their attainment, after the loss of the squadron, could not have been attended with any permanent advantage. Orders were, therefore, sent to general Robinson, (who upon hearing the shouts had halted and sent to Head-Quarters to ascertain the cause, and to receive such further orders from the commander of the forces as were necessary) to return with his column. The loss of the squadron gave the enemy the means of conveying their troops to such points as might be deemed expedient, and the numerous reinforcements which crowded in, gave them a disposeable force, whose superiority in numbers was such that a delay of a few hours might have placed the british in a critical situation. So circumstanced, the army indignant at being obliged to retire before an enemy their inferior in discipline and renown, fell back upon Chazy, in the evening, with little molestation from the americans. On the ensuing day they continued their retreat towards the lines, bringing away such of the ordnance and commissariat stores as had not been injured by the rain, which, from the commencement of the invasion and during the retreat of the army, had been almost incessant. The loss of stores was prodigious.*

---

* The reader may take an interest in perusing the accounts given by the respective commanders of the british and american forces, at Plattsburgh, on the events of the day alluded to, exceedingly humiliating as they were, and are, to every british subject taking an interest in the success of his country and the honor of its arms. The style of the american general Macomb, different from that of most general orders of that time, by officers of the United States' army, is free of the gasconade, and vaunting which generally characterised them, and on the whole, soldier like and patriotic, as the reader will perceive :—

" HEAD QUARTERS, Plattsburgh,
" State of New York, Sept. 11, 1814.

" My Lord—Upon the arrival of the reinforcements from the Garonne. I lost no time in assembling three brigades on the frontier

Thus terminated the luckless and humiliat- Chap.
ng expedition to Plattsburgh, with the loss of XIX.
he squadron, (the gun-boats, owing to the 1814.

f Lower Canada, extending from the river Richelieu to the St. Lawence, and in forming them into a division, under the command of 1ajor general De Rottenburg, for the purpose of carrying into effect is royal highness the Prince Regent's commands, which had been onveyed to me by your lordship, in your dispatch of the 3d June last.

"As the troops concentrated and approached the line of separation etween *this** province and the United States, the american army bandoned its entrenched camp on the river Chazy, at Champlain—a osition I immediately seized, and occupied in force on the 3d instant. 'he following day the whole of the left division advanced to the vilige of Chazy, without meeting the least opposition from the enemy.

"On the 5th it halted within eight miles of this place, having surnounted the difficulties created by the obstructions in the road from he felling of trees, and the removal of bridges. The next day the ivision moved upon Plattsburgh, in two columns, on parallel roads; he right column led by major-general Power's brigade, supported by our companies of light infantry and a demi-brigade, under majoreneral Robinson; the left by major general Brisbane's brigade.

"The enemy's militia, supported by his regulars, attempted to imiede the advance of the right column, but they were driven before it rom all their positions, and the column entered Plattsburgh.—This apid movement having reversed the strong position taken up by the nemy at Dead Creek, it was precipitately abandoned by him, and iis gun-boats alone left to defend the ford, and to prevent our restorng the bridges, which had been imperfectly destroyed, an inconvelience soon surmounted.

"Here I found the enemy in the occupation of an elevated ridge of and, on the south branch of the Saranac, crowned with three strong edoubts and other field works, and block-houses armed with heavy rdnance, with their flotilla at anchor out of gun-shot from the shore, onsisting of a ship, a brig, a schooner, a sloop, and ten gun-boats.

"I immediately communicated this circumstance to capt. Downie. vho had been recently appointed to command the vessels on lake 'hamplain, consisting of a ship, a brig, two sloops, and twelve gunoats, and requested his co-operation, and in the mean time batteries vere constructed for the guns brought from the rear.

"On the morning of the 11th our flotilla was seen over the isthmus vhich joins Cumberland-head with the main land, steering for Plattsurgh bay. I immediately ordered that part of the brigade under najor-general Robinson, which had been brought forward, consisting of four light-infantry companies, 3d batt. 27th and 76th regiments, ind major-general Power's brigade, consisting of the 3d, 5th, 1st patt. 27th, and 58th regiments, to force the ford of the Saranac, and

* The reader will observe that the despatch is dated at "Plattsburgh;" out, from the above expression, it would seem to have been written in Ca1ada. Though of little moment, this gave rise to some comment.

VOL. II.   T

Chap. XIX.
1814.

misconduct of the officer in command, excepted,*) and five hundred men of the land forces in killed, wounded, and missing.

advance, provided with scaling ladders, to escalade the enemy's works upon the heights: this force was placed under the command of major general Robinson. The batteries opened their fire the instant the ships engaged.

"It is now with deep concern I inform your lordship, that notwithstanding the intrepid valour with which capt. Downie led his flotilla into action, my most sanguine hopes of complete success were, not long afterwards, blasted, by a combination, as appeared to us, of unfortunate events, to which naval warfare is peculiarly exposed.

"Scarcely had his Majesty's troops forced a passage across the Saranac, and ascended the height on which stand the enemy's works, than I had the extreme mortification to hear the shout of victory from the enemy's works, in consequence of the british flag being lowered on board the Confiance and Linnet, and to see our gun-boats seeking their safety in flight. This unlooked for event depriving me of the co-operation of the fleet, without which the further prosecution of the service was become impracticable, I did not hesitate to arrest the course of the troops advancing to the attack, because the most complete success would have been unavailing, and the possession of the enemy's works offered no advantage to compensate for the loss we must have sustained in acquiring possession of them.

"I have ordered the batteries to be dismantled, the guns withdrawn with the wounded men who can be removed, to be sent to the rear, in order that the troops may return to Chazy, to-morrow, and on the following day to Champlain, where I propose to halt until I have ascertained the use the enemy propose making of the naval ascendancy they have acquired on lake Champlain.

"I have the honor to transmit herewith returns of the loss sustained by the left division of this army in its advance to Plattsburgh, and in forcing a passage across the river Saranac.

"I have the honor, &c. (Signed) "GEORGE PREVOST."
"To the Earl Bathurst, &c., &c."

"HEAD QUARTERS, Plattsburgh, Sept. 19, 1814.

"General Orders.—The governor general of the Canadas and commander in chief of the british forces in North America, having invaded the territories of the United States, with the avowed purpose of conquering the country as far as Crown Point and Ticonderoga, there to winter his forces with a view to further conquest, brought with him a powerful army and flotilla—an army amounting to fourteen thousand men, completely equipped and accompanied by a numerous train of artillery and all the engines of war—men who had conquered

* This gentleman, lieut. Rayot, soon after his disgraceful flight from the naval action at Plattsburgh, disappeared, while under arrest, preparatory to his trial by a naval court martial, and was struck from the navy list.

The unfortunate result of this expedition mortified the army, which felt itself disgraced in being compelled to retire before an enemy

Chap. XIX. 1814.

in France, Spain, Portugal, the Indies, and in various other parts of the globe, and led by the most distinguished generals of the british army; a flotilla also, superior to ours in vessels, men and guns—had determined at once to crush us both by land and by water.

"The governor general after boasting of what he would do, and endeavouring to dissuade the loyal inhabitants of the United States, from their allegiance by threats and promises, as set forth in his proclamations and orders, fixed his Head Quarters at the village of Champlain, to organise his army and to settle the government of his intended conquests. On the second day of the month, he marched from Champlain, and on the 5th, appeared before the village of Plattsburgh, with his whole army, and the 11th, the day fixed for the general attack, the flotilla arrived.

"The enemy's flotilla, at 8 in the morning, passed Cumberland Head, and at 9 engaged our flotilla at anchor in the bay, off the town, fully confident of crushing in an instant, the whole of our naval force, but the gallant commodore Macdonough, in the short space of two hours, obliged the large vessels to strike their colors, whilst the gallies saved themselves by flight.—This glorious achievement was in full view of the several forts, and the american forces had the satisfaction of witnessing the victory. The british army was also so posted on the surrounding heights, that it could not but behold the interesting struggle for the dominion of the lake. At the same hour the fleets engaged, the enemy opened his batteries on our forts, throwing hundreds of shells, balls and rockets, and attempted at the same time to cross the Saranac, at three different points, to assault the works. At the upper ford he was met by the militia and volunteers, and after repeated attempts was driven back with considerable loss in killed, wounded and prisoners. At the bridge near the village, he was repulsed by the picquets and the brave riflemen under capt. Grovenon, and lieuts. Hamilton and Riley, and at the bridge to the town, he was foiled by the guards, blockhouses, and the artillery of the forts served by capt. Alex. Brooks, capts. Richards and Smyth, and lieuts. Mountford, Smith and Cromwell. The enemy's fire was returned with effect from our batteries, and by sunset we had the satisfaction to silence seven batteries which had been erected, and to see his column returning to their camps, beyond the reach of our guns.

"Thus beaten by land and by water, the governor general withdrew his artillery and raised the siege, at 9 sent off his heavy baggage, and under cover of the darkness retreated with his whole army towards Canada, leaving his wounded on the field, and a vast quantity of bread, flour and beef which he had not time to destroy, besides a quantity of bombshells, shot, flints, and ammunition of all kinds which remain at the batteries and lie concealed in the ponds and rivers. As soon as his retreat was discovered, the light troops, volunteers and militia, were in pursuit, and followed as far as Chazy, capturing several dragoons and soldiers, besides covering the escape of

they had been accustomed to undervalue. The naval commander in the Canadas, Sir James L. Yeo, in his official letter to the admiralty, attributed the loss of the lake squadron, to the misconduct of the commander of the forces. Of captain Downie, it has been said that he was hurried into action, before his ship was in a state to meet the enemy, and that the commander of the forces failed to give the promised co-operation to the fleet, by not

---

hundreds of deserters, who continued still to be coming in. A violent storm and continual fall of rain prevented the brave volunteers and militia from further pursuit.

" Thus have the attempts of the invader been frustrated by a regular force of only fifteen hundred men, a brave and active body of militia of the state of New York, under gen. Mooers, and volunteers of the respectable and patriotic citizens of Vermont, led by gen. Strong and other gentlemen of distinction. The whole not exceeding two thousand five hundred men.

" The british force being now either expelled or captured, the services of the volunteers and militia may be dispensed with.

" Gen. Macomb cannot, however, permit the militia of New York, and the volunteers of Vermont, to depart without carrying with them the high sense he entertains for their merits. The zeal with which they came forward in defence of their country, when the signal of danger was given by the general, reflects the highest lustre on their patriotism and spirit. Their conduct in the field has corresponded with the laudable motives which led them into it. They have deserved the esteem of their fellow citizens and the warm approbation of their commanders. They have exemplified how speedily american citizens can be prepared to meet the enemies of their country. In testifying his sense of the merits of the troops, the general cannot but express his sorrow and regret, for the loss of some brave and virtuous citizens, and for those who have been wounded. The loss, no doubt, will be keenly felt by their friends and countrymen, but at the same time it will be borne with that fortitude and resignation which become good citizens and good christians.

" The affection of the general will accompany his brave associates in arms, wheresoever they may go, nor will anything give him more pleasure than opportunities of testifying to them individually, by actions as well as words, the high regard he cherishes for them.

" The general, in the name of the United States, thanks the volunteers and militia for their distinguished services, and wishes them a happy return to their families and friends.

" ALEX. MACOMB."

commencing an assault on the batteries, upon a signal given by the Confiance, in consequence of which the whole attention of the enemy was directed against the fleet. That if the land batteries had been assaulted in time, the american fleet would have been compelled to leave the bay, when they might have been attacked by the british squadron on the open lake, to much more advantage. On the other hand, it has been urged that captain Downie, so far from being hurried into action, entertained the fullest confidence in the superiority of his squadron, and that he felt equally certain of success, whether he should meet the enemy on the lake or attack them in Plattsburgh Bay. That there was no signal agreed upon between the commander of the land forces and captain Downie; and that the circumstance of his scaling the guns was considered by the former as no more than the usual precaution before the commencement of a naval action.* That the storming of the works on shore could not have been of any service to the british squadron, as the american

---

* Capt. Pring, in his official despatch relating to this action says,— " In consequence of the earnest solicitation of Sir George Prevost, for the co-operation of the naval force on this lake, to attack that of the enemy who were placed for the support of their works at Plattsburgh, which it was proposed should be stormed by the troops at the *same moment* that the naval action should commence in the bay. every exertion was used to accelerate the armament of the new ship, that the military movements might not be postponed at such an advanced season of the year, longer than was absolutely necessary." Capt. Pring, who was the next senior officer after the death of capt. Downie, being tried by a court martial in England, appointed to enquire into the circumstances of the loss of the squadron on lake Champlain, was, with the officers under his command, honorably acquitted.

ships during the action, were moored out of range of the land batteries. That it would have been imprudent to have carried the american batteries before the naval ascendency should have been decided, as the enemy's squadron, after such an event, by retiring to the narrows in the lake, before the british squadron should have been off Plattsburgh, to intercept their retreat, might have secured themselves against every future effort to attack them to advantage. Amidst the contradictory relations of facts and diversity of opinions, which have been given from respectable authority, spectators of the event, it is difficult to say what were the grand errors which occasioned the failure of the expedition to Plattsburgh, or whether it may not be considered as one of those misfortunes incidental to warfare, which human prudence can neither foresee nor prevent. It is confidently asserted of captain Downie, that he thought himself with his single ship, the Confiance, as previously mentioned, a match for the whole american squadron, and when we advert to the circumstance of his having gone, as it were, singly into action, while the other vessels, particularly the gun-boats, in his squadron, were far in his wake, there is room to believe that this gallant officer fell a victim to a fallacious confidence of success, which, after consecrating his life to it, we cannot but respect.

The decease of sir George Prevost, before a military court martial could investigate the charges preferred against him, renders it impossible to pronounce with any authentic certainty on the absolute propriety of his conduct, or the contrary, on that expedition: but it seems to be generally admitted by those who are supposed most capable of forming a correct opinion on the subject, that after the loss of the squadron his situation, in the enemy's country, must have been extremely precarious; and that although he might without any great exertion have carried all the enemy's works at Plattsburgh, their momentary occupation, which would have cost him some blood, would have been utterly useless. It has been asserted, however, that his great error lay in delaying all attempts to carry the enemy's works by storm until the arrival of the fleet, for which he ought not to have waited. How this may have been we cannot determine.

The enemy, at Fort Erie, on hearing the result of the expedition to Plattsburgh, and aware that the british in their neighbourhood had not been recently reinforced, made a sortie, in the afternoon of the seventeenth of September, and attacked the british lines, extending through a thick wood, with their whole force consisting of upwards of five thousand men. At the onset they gained some advantage, having from the thickness of the weather (the rain pouring in torrents) succeeded in turning the right of the british line of picquets without being perceived, and after a warm contest, obtained possession of two batteries.

As soon as the alarm was given, reinforcements were sent forward, who drove the enemy from the works, of which they had gained possession, and pursued them to the glacis of Fort Erie, whither they retired with precipitation, with the loss (by their own accounts) in killed, wounded and missing, of five hundred and nine men, including eleven officers killed and twenty-three wounded. The british loss amounted to three officers and one hundred and twelve men killed, seventeen officers and one hundred and sixty-one men wounded, and thirteen officers and three hundred and three men missing; making a total of six hundred and nine officers and men.

General Drummond, after this affair, finding his troops encamped in a low situation, now rendered very unhealthy by the late constant rains, growing sickly, raised the investment of fort Erie, and fell back upon Chippewa, on the evening of the 21st of September, without molestation by the enemy.

Sir James L. Yeo, after much exertion, completed the Saint Lawrence, a new ship of 100 guns, and on the 16th October, sailed from Kingston for the head of the lake, with a reinforcement of troops and supplies for the army, commodore Chauncey having previously retired to Sacket's Harbour, on hearing that the british squadron was prepared for the lake. General Brown, finding the american squadron incapable of co-operating with him, came to the resolution of evacuating Fort Erie, which he accordingly did, on the 5th November, after calling in his out-posts and destroying the whole works at that post, and retiring across the Niagara to his own territory, leaving the wearied inhabitants of the Upper Province, once more in repose.

The american army evinced throughout the the present campaign, a character and improved state of discipline far beyond what might have been expected from such raw materials. The barbarous conduct of a few marauders, who occasionally made incursions into the western parts of Upper Canada disgraced, however, the reputation which their regular army had acquired in the estimation of the british, ever ready to acknowledge merit in a generous enemy. The villages of Dover, and Port Talbot were destroyed by these ruthless barbarians, in the course of the summer; but the devastation which marked the course of a horde of mounted brigands from Kentucky, under brigadier general M'Arthur, in the month of November, exceeded every thing :—The country through which they passed was given up to indiscriminate plunder—the settlements were reduced to ashes, and the miserable inhabitants were left to perish with cold and hunger. This band of ruffians was arrested in its progress, on attempting to cross the Grand River, by a party of the 103d regiment and a few indian warriors, and their speedy retreat before a party of the 19th light dragoons saved them from exemplary chastisement. They made good their retreat to Detroit, whence they had set out on this excursion.

The troops and embodied militia, in the lower province, were sent into winter quarters, on the 10th of December. General Drummond and Sir James L. Yeo, after the campaign had ended in Upper Canada, came down to Montreal to concert measures with the commander of the forces, for the ensuing campaign, in the event that the negociations then in progress at Ghent should not terminate in a peace. The creation of a naval force on Lake Huron, in the ensuing season, was determined upon by these officers, as a place affording much greater security for the construction of vessels than Lake Erie, where the enemy, possessing the dominion of the Lake, could at any time destroy them.

The House of Assembly met on the 21st January.* Mr. Panet having been called up to the legislative council, L. J. Papineau, Esq.,

---

* The new assembly consisted of the following members:—
County of Quebec, Peter Brehaut and Louis Gauvreau ; County of Montreal, James Stuart and Augustin Richer ; Lower Town of Quebec, Pierre Bruneau and Andrew Stuart ; County of Hertford, Frs. Blanchet and Féréol Roi ; County of Orleans, Charles Blouin ; County of St. Maurice, Etienne Leblanc and Rémi Vallières; County of Hampshire, François Huot and George W. Allsopp ; County of Surrey, Pierre Amiot and Etienne Duchesnois ; Borough of William Henry, Robert Jones ; County of Dorchester, J. Thomas Taschereau and John Davidson ; Borough of Three Rivers, Chas. Richard Ogden and Amable Berthelot; County of Warwick, Ross Cuthbert and Jacques Déligny ; County of Effingham. Joseph Malbœuf and Samuel Sherwood ; County of Huntingdon, Austin Cuvillier and Michael O'Sullivan ; West Ward, City of Montreal—J. Louis Papineau† and James Fraser ; East Ward, Montreal—Savense de Beaujeu

† By some mistake the initials of Mr. Papineau's christian names, stand in the journals of the assembly *J L.*, whereas they, as he himself signs them, ought to be reversed and stand *L. J.*

was elected speaker of the assembly.† The militia act was revised and amended by admitting substitutes. A grant of new duties upon tea, strong spirits, and on goods sold at auction, was made to his Majesty, to supply the wants of the province. One thousand pounds were granted for the encouragement of vaccine inoculation, upwards of eight thousand pounds were appropriated for the improvement of the internal communications of the province, and a further sum of twenty-five thousand pounds for the purpose of opening a canal from Montreal to Lachine. A bill was also introduced to grant a salary to the speaker of the house of assembly of Lower Canada, to enable him to support the dignity of his office during the present parliament. The salary was a thousand pounds currency. A similar bill pursuant to a message from the governor, was also

---

and George Platt; County of Bedford, Henry Georgen; County of York, Eustache N. L. Dumont and William Forbes; County of Northumberland, Thomas Lee and Etienne C. Lagueux; County of Leinster, Denis B. Viger and Jacques Lacombe; County of Cornwallis, Joseph L. Borgia and Jos. Robitaille; County of Kent, Joseph Bresse and Noël Breux; County of Devon, Fis. Fournier and Joseph F. Couillard Després; Upper Town of Quebec, Jean Ant. Panet and Claude Dénéchau; County of Buckingham, François Bellet and James Stuart; County of Richelieu, S. Cherrier and F. Malhiot; County of Gaspé, George Brown.

† The following vote of thanks was passed by the assembly, to Mr. Panet:—

" Resolved, *nemine contradicente*, that the thanks of this house be voted to the honorable Jean Antoine Panet, esquire, late speaker of this house, for his steady, impartial, and faithful discharge of that high and important station, during twenty-two years, by supporting, on every occasion, the honor and dignity of the house, and the rights and privileges of the people.

" Ordered, that Mr. Speaker do transmit the thanks of this house to the honorable Jean Antoine Panet, esquire."

passed, granting a like salary to the speaker of the legislative council. This bill, however, for what reason it does not appear, did not pass that house. The former bill being reserved for the royal sanction was confirmed in the course of a subsequent administration.

The assembly, among other matters, came to a resolution that it was expedient to appoint an agent in Great Britain for the purpose of soliciting the enactment of laws, and for transacting such public matters as might, from time to time, be committed to his care, for the good of the province. This resolution was communicated to the legislative council, where, in opposition to the measure it was resolved, that the governor of the province was the only fit and constitutional channel, between the legislative bodies of Lower Canada and his Majesty's government in Great Britain: they, therefore, did not concur in the message of the assembly. The further consideration of this matter was then referred to a select committee, which reported on the subject as follows:—

"The necessity that the colonies should have an agent, will appear evident, if it be considered that each branch of the colonial legislature has a right to petition the branches of the imperial legislature; a right which is common to all his Majesty's subjects. Although the governor may transmit the petitions of the respective branches of the legislature, to the foot of the throne, he cannot, without much difficulty and inconvenience, transmit those to the house of lords and house of commons, and he could not support them himself before those houses, nor solicit the passing of laws, nor conduct many affairs which can only be conducted by a person resident himself in Great Britain. By whom then can this be done, unless by an agent resident therein?

"The colonial legislature would, otherwise, in certain cases, be deprived of the right of petitioning, and always restrained in its exercise; which would also be the case with respect to the imperial legislature, in the exercise of its undeniable privilege of receiving and hearing petitions from the colonies—a thing not to be supposed:—and all measures tending to deprive the colonies of that right of petitioning, and the imperial parliament of receiving the petitions, would be high infringements of the rights of the imperial parliament, and of the rights of the colonial legislatures.

"But a peculiar and pressing necessity exists that the province of Lower Canada should have an agent resident in Great Britain, to allay the uneasiness of its inhabitants; more especially at the present moment, inasmuch as they fear that endeavours are now making to prejudice against them the imperial government and the british nation, and to effect a change in the free constitution which british wisdom has conferred upon them, by means of an union of the two Canadas, of which the language, laws and usages, totally differ.—That uneasiness will cease whenever they shall have an agent resident in England. The obstacles encountered by this house, in the prosecution of the impeachments against Jonathan Sewell and James Monk, esquires, afford additional reason for the nomination of an agent for the province."

Pursuant to this report an address was voted to the Governor, praying he would be pleased to represent to his royal highness the Prince Regent, the desire of the inhabitants of this province to have an agent, resident in the United Kingdom, and, the expediency of their having an agent so resident, and to pray his royal highness to be pleased to give instructions to the governor of this province, to recommend to the provincial legislature the appointment of a provincial agent.

The assembly also adopted certain resolutions

relating to the impeachments of the chief Justices, in the previous session, and which were still pending in England, whither, as already mentioned, Mr. Sewell had proceeded to repel them.*

Whilst the attention of the colonial legislature was engaged in these concerns, news of

---

* "Resolved, as the opinion of this committee, that the heads of impeachment, by this house, in the name of the commons of the province of Lower Canada, in parliament assembled, and of all the commons of Lower Canada, against Jonathan Sewell, esquire, and James Monk, esquire, for sundry high crimes and misdemeanors, are now pending.

"Resolved, as the opinion of this committee, that it is expedient to persist in the nomination of a person as agent in behalf of the house of assembly, for the purpose of forwarding and managing in England, the impeachments exhibited by the house of assembly against Jonathan Sewell and James Monk, esquires, and for soliciting from his Majesty's government, the measures that may be necessary to enable the commons of Lower Canada, to prosecute the said impeachments with effect.

Resolved, as the opinon of this committee, that an humble address be presented to his excellency the governor in chief, informing him that his Majesty's dutiful subjects, the commons of Lower Canada, have unanimously declared, during the present session of the provincial parliament, that they persist in the prosecution of the heads of impeachment exhibited by the commons of this province during the last session of the late provincial parliament, against Jonathan Sewell and James Monk, esquires, and praying his excellency to forward to his Majesty's ministers the resolutions of this house, and the present address, by which this house persists in declaring the said Jonathan Sewell and James Monk, esquires, guilty of all the high crimes and misdemeanors set forth in the several heads of impeachment exhibited against them, reserving to themselves the right of exhibiting further and other heads of impeachment; and that this house persists in nominating James Stuart, esquire, one of the members of the house of assembly of Lower Canada, its agent for conducting and managing the prosecutions to be instituted against them, if it shall please his royal highness to permit the said impeachments to be submitted to a tribunal competent to adjudge upon them, after hearing the matter on the part of the impeachments, and on the part of the persons accused; and that this house, relying on the justice and wisdom of his royal highness the Prince Regent, rests satisfied that its humble recourse to the authority of his Majesty's government, will not prove ineffectual, but that at all times that authority will be exercised for the repression of such high public offences."

the treaty of peace was officially announced to them, on the first of March, by a message from the governor.

The embodied militia were disbanded, and as a gratuity, the legislature granted eighty days' pay to the officers.* An annuity of six

---

* "Adjutant General's Office, 1st March, 1815.

"GENERAL ORDERS.—His excellency the governor in chief and commander of the forces having received official notification that a treaty of peace and amity between Great Britain and the United States of America, was ratified and exchanged at Washington, on the 17th of February, and by which it is stipulated that all hostilities shall cease immediately—he announces the same for the information and guidance of the troops serving in British North America.

"His excellency embraces the earliest opportunity that is afforded him, of restoring to their domestic avocations the provincial corps and battalions of embodied militia, whose gallant and patriotic devotion to their country, has been so honorably evinced in their zealous services, since the commencement of hostilities, and his excellency will not fail to represent to our most gracious sovereign, the zeal, courage and loyalty that has been so conspicuously displayed by all classes of his brave subjects in both Canadas.

"The engagement of the corps of canadian Voltigeurs, terminating with the war, that corps is to march to Montreal, with all convenient expedition, for the purpose of depositing its arms, accoutrements and stores, and will there be disbanded, receiving twenty days' full pay, for every non-commissioned officer, drummer and private, in lieu of rations, which are not to be issued. The officers to continue to receive pay until further orders, but all garrison and field allowances are to cease.

"The frontier light infantry and the battalions of embodied militia will, in like manner, be disbanded and receive the same gratuity as the voltigeurs.

"The 1st battalion of embodied militia, will deposit their arms, accoutrements and stores, at Quebec—the 3d battn. at Chambly, the 2d. 4th and 5th, or Chasseurs, at Montreal.

"The corps of canadian voyageurs, is, in like manner, to be disbanded, and to cease to receive pay on the 24th inst. also, all provincial drivers, and the troop of Dorchester light dragoons, under captain Watson, and the corps of guides, under capt. Hebert, (who are held responsible for the delivery of the arms and appointments committed to their charge.)

"Major-general De Rottenburg, having received his excellency's instructions, will give the necessary orders for these arrangements being carried into effect, in the left division.

"All garrison and field allowances to the militia and militia staff, will cease on the 24th instant.

pounds was provided for such Voltigeurs and Militiamen as had been rendered, during their service, incapable of earning a livelihood. A small gratuity was also made to the widows and children of those who had been killed during the war; and the assembly in an address to the Prince Regent, recommended that a grant of lands should be made to such Voltigeurs and militia, as had served in defence of the province during the late war.

The assembly as a mark of respect for the character of the governor in chief, voted him the sum of five thousand pounds sterling, for the purchase of a service plate.* This measure

---

" The issue of rum to the troops is discontinued on the 24th inst., and is to be granted only on particular occasions, on the special sanction of general officers commanding stations and brigades.

" The establishment of regimental bat horses is cancelled: these horses are to be delivered over to the commissariat to be sold, on or before the 24th inst., in the Lower Province, and 24th April, in Upper Canada, when all allowances of forage for such horses will cease to be issued.

" No forage to be issued in kind, after the 24th of April, except to the 19th light dragoons and such light artillery as may remain horsed.

" Major general De Rottenburg will cause the sleigh establishment under the charge of lieut. Fennell, to be disbanded—the horses and sleighs delivered into the commissariat to be disposed of.

" The gun carriage establishment is no longer to be considered as a separate branch of the engineer department—the appointment of maj. Sinclair, royal artillery, to the superintendence of that duty is cancelled on the 24th inst.

" EDWARD BAYNES, adjt.-gen., N. A."

* " Resolved, that it is the opinion of this committee, that this house entertains the highest veneration and respect for the character of his excellency Sir George Prevost, governor in chief, whose administration, under circumstances of peculiar novelty and difficulty, stands highly distinguished for energy, wisdom, and ability.

" Resolved, that it is the opinion of this committee, that this house, representing the people of this province, anxiously desirous of expressing their gratitude to his excellency, for having, under providence, rescued us from the danger of subjugation to our late implacable foe, have and do hereby unanimously give and grant a service of plate,

met with the approbation of the Prince Regent, but was not carried into effect, the legislative council refusing their assent to a bill for the purpose, sent up for their concurrence in the course of the ensuing session. The assembly, just before the close of the session, resolved that the house would, at the opening of the next session, take into consideration the expediency of granting a pecuniary compensation to the hon. Jean Antoine Panet, for his long and meritorious services as speaker of the house. But the beneficence intended by the house of assembly, was not carried into effect, owing to the decease of Mr. Panet. His widow, however, received a pension in acknowledgment of his services.

---

not exceeding five thousand pounds sterling, to his excellency as a testimonial of the high sense this house entertains of his excellency's distinguished talents, wisdom, and ability.

" Resolved, that it is the opinion of this committee, that for the better carrying into execution the object this house has in view, for the purchase of the service of plate for his excellency, the speaker of this house be authorised to give directions to such persons in England, as may be best able to execute the same, and that when so completed, the said service be presented to his excellency the governor in chief, in the name and on the behalf of the commons of his Majesty's province of Lower Canada.

" Resolved, that it is the opinion of this committee, that an humble address be presented to his excellency the governor in chief, to communicate the above resolutions, humbly praying that his excellency will be graciously pleased to advance a sum not exceeding five thousand pounds sterling, to the order of the speaker of this house, for the object stated in the above resolutions, and that this house doth engage and hereby pledges itself to make good the said advance the next ensuing session of this provincial parliament."

These resolutions being presented to his excellency he answered:—
" Gentlemen of the house of assembly—I thank you for the favorable opinion you have expressed of my services, and I will transmit to his Majesty's government your address, containing sentiments so gratifying to my feelings, in order that your munificence may be governed by the commands of his royal highness the Prince Regent."

Chap. XIX.
1815.

Of the acts passed during the session, there was one granting five hundred pounds to Joseph Bouchette, esquire, the surveyor general of the province, (a gentlemen of indefatigable industry in his line, and whose labours attest his merit,) to assist him in publishing his geographical and topographical maps of Upper and Lower Canada.* The speaker of the assembly, in presenting, at the prorogation, the money bills that had been passed, for his excellency's sanction, addressed him in the following terms :—

" May it please your excellency,— His Majesty's dutiful subjects, the commons of Lower Canada, have hastened to bestow their most serious attention upon the several objects connected with the public service, which it pleased your excellency, at the opening and during the course of the present session of the provincial parliament, to recommend to their consideration. The measures which have appeared best adapted to promote the common interests of his Majesty's subjects in this province, and those of his government, which is obliged still to continue a great part of the expenses occasioned by a state of warfare, have all, in as far as it depended upon them, been adopted.

" With this view, a revenue act which was on the eve of expiring, has been continued, and a new one passed. Appropriations which will be deemed liberal, considering the means of the colony, have been granted to his Majesty.

" The people of this province having followed whithersoever the interest of his Majesty's government, the voice

---

* While mentioning this zealous and distinguished canadian topographer, who died in 1841, it is but due to his son, Joseph Bouchette, esq., to observe, that following in the track of his father and improving upon his labours, he has recently produced a map of Canada and neighbouring provinces, which, for correctness of delineation and beauty of execution, is unmatched by any thing of the kind hitherto published, and that it will probably be some time before any is produced to excel it. Towards the publication of this work also, an aid was liberally voted Mr. Bouchette, by the legislature.

of honor, the presence of the enemy, and your excellency's commands and example have called them, now contribute, by the voluntary gift of its representatives, to the expenses incurred for the support of the war—provides some indemnification to those of its citizens whom the love of their king and country had induced to accept commissions in the provincial corps, and whom the sudden return to peace will deprive of employment, until they shall be able advantageously to resume the exercise of the several professions which they had abandoned—and affords relief to the families of such of their countrymen as have fallen on the day of battle, and to those whose sufferings for life, from the honorable wounds they bear, furnish living evidence of the zeal and feelings which have animated his Majesty's canadian subjects in the defence of the rights of that empire to which it is their glory to belong, and in the defence of that constitution which has been conferred upon them, to render them the guardians of their dearest rights.

" The events of the late war, have drawn closer the bonds which connect Great Britain and the Canadas. These provinces have been preserved to her under circumstances of peculiar difficulty. At the epoch of the declaration of war, this country was destitute both of troops and of money; and your excellency was at the head of a people in whom it was pretended that half a century of repose had extinguished all military spirit.

" Superior to prejudices which had but too generally prevailed, your excellency has derived from the devotion of that brave and loyal, yet unjustly calumniated people, resources sufficient for disconcerting the plans of conquest devised by a foe at once numerous and elate with confidence. Reinforcements were subsequently received; and the blood of the sons of Canada, has flowed mingled with that of the brave soldiers sent to its defence. Multiplied proofs of the efficacious and powerful protection of the mother country, and of the inviolable loyalty of the people of this province, strengthen their claim to the preservation, and free exercise, of all the benefits which are secured to them by their existing constitution and laws.

" The pursuits of war are about to be succeeded by those of peace.—It is by the increase of population, agriculture and commerce, that the possession of this colony may become of importance to Great Britain. The improvement of internal communications, having a close connection with the progress of the prosperity of the colony, it was with lively satisfaction that the house of assembly heard your excellency recommend to their consideration that subject. To second those views, and the desire so natural in your excellency, of improving a country which you have so essentially contributed to preserve to the empire, his Majesty's dutiful subjects, the commons of Lower Canada, have voted large appropriations, in order to facilitate the opening of a canal from Montreal to Lachine, to assist in the opening of new roads, and to acquire such information as may enable them hereafter to follow up and extend that plan of improvement.

"The several acts relative to the objects which I have detailed, and to which, in the name of the commons of Lower Canada, I pray your excellency to give the royal assent, are," &c., &c.

Among the measures introduced this session, was a bill for the appointment of commissioners to examine the accounts of the receiver general, and for counting the cash in the treasury. On the other hand, that officer, Mr. Caldwell, presented a petition to the assembly, complaining of the insufficiency of his salary. This bill was introduced by Mr. Lee, but fell through. The same gentleman made also an attempt this session, to carry a measure for the improvement of the roads in the vicinity of Quebec, by establishing turnpikes, which, however, the farmers and population in the surrounding parishes being opposed to it, did not succeed,

By a return laid before the assembly, of marriages, baptisms and burials, in the districts of

Montreal, Quebec and Three Rivers, during 1814, they were ascertained to be as below.*

The revenues of the last year, (1814) amounted to £204,550, currency, and expenditure to £162,125, sterling, including £111,451 on account of military services, and £5,474 to Upper Canada, for its proportion of duties levied in the Lower Province, in 1813.—The expenses of the late general election came to £339—(a trifle to those of the present time, 1847-8) and those of the legislature not included in the above, to £3693, currency. Independently of the expenditure just mentioned, is also to be added £5,086, expenses of collection of the revenue for the year. The number of vessels cleared out from Quebec, in 1814, was 184, bearing 38,605 tons, including seven built there, in all employing 1889 hands.

The business of the session being concluded, the governor prorogued the parliament on the 25th March, with the following speech :—

"Gentlemen of the house of assembly,—The liberality with which you have provided for the advancement of purposes of high public utility, has sufficiently shewn, that you have proceeded upon those patriotic and loyal principles, which dignify when they actuate the representatives of a free people.

---

* Return of marriages, baptisms and burials in the districts of Montreal, Quebec, and Three Rivers, as laid before the house, for the year 1814 :—

	Marriages.	Baptisms.	Burials.
Montreal,	1727	7707	4601
Quebec,	653	4045	2318
Three Rivers,	260	1565	976
Total	2640	13317	7895

"Gentlemen of the legislative council, gentlemen of the house of assembly,—You will have learned with satisfaction, that the desire of his Majesty, for the renewal of amity with America, has been met by a corresponding disposition from the government of the United States, and that a peace has ensued, which it may be permitted us to hope, will, by its ultimate provisions and its permanence, compensate for the evils of war to which it has given a termination.

"I have now to inform you, that I have received the commands of his royal highness the Prince Regent, to return to England, for the purpose of repelling accusations affecting my military character, which have been preferred by the late naval commander in chief, on the lakes in Canada; and while I take my leave of you with regret, I embrace with eagerness the opportunity afforded me of justifying my reputation.

"However intent on the subject which so unexpectedly summons my attention, be assured I shall bear with me a lively recollection of the firm support I have derived from you, and I shall be gratified at an early period, in representing personally to his royal highness the Prince Regent, the zeal and loyalty evinced by every class of his Majesty's subjects in british North America, during my administration, their attachment to his august person and to his government, and most particularly, the spirit and devotion manifested by the people of the Canadas, in the late contest with the United States of America."

Sir George Prevost accordingly departed from Quebec, on the third of April, for England, by way of St. John's, (New Brunswick) passing thither over the uninhabited country between the St. Lawrence and the river St. John's. On the day of his departure, he received farewell addresses from the citizens of Quebec and Montreal, expressive of their satisfaction with his administration. He was succeeded by Sir Gordon Drummond in the government of Lower Canada, as administrator in chief, who arrived at Quebec on the same day, a few hours after the governor's departure, and assumed the command.

It was observed in the address from Montreal:—

"In your excellency's civil administration, we have seen conspicuously evinced, an anxious desire to dispense equal justice to his Majesty's subjects—to obliterate unjust and impolitic distinctions between the inhabitants of this province of different origin, and to unite them as members of one community, with the same rights and interests, for the promotion of their common welfare. Influenced by this wise and just policy, your excellency has been enabled to form a correct estimate of the character and disposition of the population of Canada, and by reposing in the loyalty and bravery of his Majesty's canadian subjects that confidence which they fully merited, your excellency has afforded practical evidence of their devoted attachment to his Majesty's government, and their capacity to yield it effectual support."

The address from Quebec was couched in still more flattering terms:—

"At the period of your excellency's arrival in this country, on the eve of a war with America, you found the majority of its inhabitants irritated by the unfortunate effects of misunderstandings of a long duration. Your excellency, consulting only the general welfare, by a strict adherence to justice and a well-timed confidence, soon allayed every discontent, and rallied the whole population for the common defence. Under the happy influence of harmony thus restored, the militia was assembled and trained, and an exhausted treasury replenished. The additional means which you thereby derived from the colony committed to your particular care, enabled your excellency to extend the handful of british troops at your disposal to the most distant parts of the Upper Province, where the long meditated attacks of the enemy were met at the outset, and his forces repeatedly overthrown with disgrace;—the happy precursor of the fate which awaited all his attempts on this province.

"If the smallness of the regular army with which your excellency was left to withstand the whole efforts of the United States for two years, and the insufficiency of the naval force of the lakes, have exposed his Majesty's troops to some reverses, it is nevertheless true, that under the auspices of your excellency the british arms have acquired new laurels amidst circumstances of extraordinary difficulty, unprecedented in european warfare; the name of the people of this country has been rendered illustrious, and a vast extent of territory protected from the ravages of war and preserved to the empire.

"Your excellency's name and services will ever be held in veneration and grateful remembrance by the inhabitants of Quebec. The whole province has assured you of its gratitude, and the imperishable evidences of your excellency's merits, though they could not appease, will easily overcome your enemies."

These addresses, it is to be observed, were principally from the inhabitants of french origin, in the cities, few of the british participating in the sentiments expressed in them. With these he was exceedingly unpopular, as well as with the army, both on account of his policy, in the administration of the civil government, stooping to adulation, as they deemed it, to propitiate the former, which gave rise to no small disgust, now increased by the recent unsatisfactory occurrences at Plattsburgh, and the retreat. After this event, the violence of the press in array against him, particularly in Montreal, knew no bounds. He was, in plain terms, reproached by it with having, on that memorable expedition, sacrificed the flotilla, and, as far as in him lay, disgraced the army under his command.

On the day of his departure from Quebec, he issued a farewell general order to the army serving in British North America.*

---

* "ADJUTANT GENERAL'S OFFICE.
"HEAD QUARTERS, Quebec, 3d. April, 1815.

"GENERAL ORDERS.—His Excellency the commander of the forces announces to the army serving in british North America, that he has received the commands of his royal highness the Prince Regent to return to England.

"In taking leave of an army he has had the honor to command from the commencement of hostilities with the United States to the termination of the war, his Excellency has great satisfaction in expressing his entire approbation and acknowledging the sense he entertains of the zeal, courage and discipline that has been so eminently displayed by this portion of his Majesty's troops.

"It has fallen to the lot of this army to struggle through an arduous and unequal contest, remote from succour, and deprived of many advantages experienced in the more cultivated countries of Europe; yet his Excellency has witnessed with pride and admiration, the firmness, intrepidity and patient endurance of fatigue and privations, which have marked the character of the army of Canada. Under all these circumstances, valour and discipline have prevailed, and although local considerations and limited means have circumscribed the war principally to a defensive system, it has, notwithstanding, been ennobled, by numerous brilliant exploits, which will adorn the page of future history. At Detroit and at the river Raisin, two entire armies with their commanding generals were captured, and greatly superior armies were repulsed. The several battles of Queenston, Stoney Creek, Chateauguay, Chrystler's, La Colle, Lundy's Lane, near the Falls of Niagara, and the subsequent operations on that frontier, will ever immortalize the heroes who were on those occasions afforded the opportunity of distinguishing themselves. The capture of Michillimackinac, Ogdensburgh, Oswego, and Niagara by assault, are trophies of the prowess of british arms. The names of the respective officers who led his Majesty's troops to these several achievments are already known to the world, and will be transmitted by the faithful historian with glory to a grateful posterity.

"Reviewing past events, it is with exultation his Excellency reflects on the complete success which has crowned the valour exertions, and perseverance of this gallant army, by terminating each successive campaign in the defeat and discomfiture of all the enemy's plans, in which the utmost energies of the government of the United States have been exhausted in vain efforts to accomplish his avowed object, the conquest of these provinces.

"Lieut. general sir John C. Sherbrooke, and the army under his immediate orders, are entitled to the highest praise for the bravery and promptness displayed in the occupation of a large district of the enemy's territory, and his Excellency requests that the lieut. general

Chap. XIX.
1815.

Great exertions were made by the advisers of the late administration, to prepossess and poison the mind of Sir George Prevost, on his arrival in Canada, against those who had been obnoxious to his predecessor. The letters in the "*Canadien,*" constituting probably the pretended " treasonable practices" imputed to them, were pointed out to him as atrocious libels upon the government, judges and other public functionaries, which ought to preclude them from his confidence and countenance. He, however, wisely disregarded all attempts to prejudice him in this way, taking by the hand, though incurring no small odium for it, those who had been recently marked as men of dubious loyalty, turning their influence with the country to account of the king's service, and conciliating through them, their compatriots galled by recent

will accept his thanks for the cordial assistance he has at all times afforded him.

" To lieut. general sir Gordon Drummond, on whom the command of the Canadas devolves, his Excellency's best thanks are due, for his unwearied exertions and support under circumstances of peculiar difficulty :—To the general officers, general staff, and officers and soldiers his Excellency feels himself highly indebted; and duly appreciates their respective merits. To major general Baynes the adjutant general, and major general sir Sidney Beckwith the quarter master general, and to the officers of his personal staff, his Excellency's thanks are also due for the judgment, alacrity and zeal evinced in the discharge of their several duties.

" His Excellency has every reason to be satisfied with the conduct and exertions of the public departments of this army, and he feels it an act of justice to express particularly his approbation of the very efficient manner in which the commissariat has been conducted, under the zealous and judicious arrangements of commissary general Robinson.

" His Excellency will have peculiar gratification in representing to his royal highness the Prince Regent the services and talents of the officers of this army, to the honourable survivors of which lieut. gen. sir George Prevost offers the heartfelt tribute of his warmest thanks."

" (Signed)   EDWARD BAYNES, adjutant general, N. A."

events. A warm and unswerving friend to the canadian population of french origin, he confided in and liberally patronised them from the commencement to the close of his administration, and they, it must be acknowledged, as generously responded to his confidence in them. No country or people ever exhibited greater unanimity and patriotism than did the people of Lower Canada, of both origins, in the war of 1812, by the United States against Great Britain—a stand the more to be remembered by her government, as these colonies, almost destitute of troops, wholly so of money, and scarcely possessing even a sufficiency of arms, and other munitions of defence, owing to the more imperious calls from other quarters, upon the home government were, at the outset of the war, in a manner left to their own action and resources, and which they nobly exemplified, single-handed as it were, throughout the first two campaigns. The principles of loyalty and duty no doubt were deeply implanted in the bosom of the people, but he it was, who exalted them into enthusiasm, and inspired the mass with a spirit and a confidence in their own exertions and a reliance upon his wisdom, fitting them for the emergency, and that bore them successfully through the contest. Whatever may be the opinion now established of his talents, by the military world, the impression which the inhabitants of french origin, in Lower Canada, universally retain of him is that of a conciliating, wise, and able civil governor, and in all the relations of private life, an amiable and estimable man.

It is due to the public and to the memory of Sir George Prevost, to give some statement of the proceedings with respect to that officer, after his return to England, to account for his military conduct at Plattsburgh, in September, 1814, at the instance of Sir J. L. Yeo, commander of the naval forces on the lakes in Canada. Some time after his arrival in England, he was induced, by the promulgation of the sentence of a naval court martial, assembled for the trial of capt. Pring and the officers under his command, for the loss of the british squadron on lake Champlain, in Plattsburgh Bay, reflecting upon the conduct of the commander of the land forces, to address a letter on the subject, to his royal highness the Duke of York. In this letter, he strongly protested against the decision of the court martial, so far as it related to him, as premature and unjust; his conduct and that of the army under his command, not being properly the subject of their enquiry; and because their opinion must have principally relied upon the bare statement and assertions of the parties whose conduct was in question, without any other than *ex parté* testimony. He complained of the peculiar injustice of this prejudication of his conduct, aggravated by the delay of his accuser to bring forward his accusations; and solicited the interposition of his royal highness with his Majesty's government, to compel him to produce his charges in due legal form, and proceed upon them, in order that an opportunity might be afforded him of vindicating his character and conduct. A copy of the charges (four in number,) given in by Sir James L. Yeo, in consequence of this remonstrance, was, by the adjutant general of the forces, transmitted from the horse-guards, on the 13th of September, to Sir George Prevost; and to afford time for the arrival of the necessary witnesses from Canada, the meeting of the general court martial was postponed till the twelfth of January, 1816. In the meantime the health of sir George Prevost naturally of a delicate cast, and impaired in the course of service, became seriously affected from anxiety of mind and the fatigue he had experienced in his journey on foot over the uninhabited country, then covered with snow, between the rivers St. Lawrence and Saint John's; and on the 5th January he died in London, leaving a disconsolate family to regret his loss, rendered doubly grievous by the reflections to which his memory was exposed, from his not having had an occasion of clearing up his conduct at Plattsburgh.

Col. William Augustus Prevost, anxious for an opportunity to retrieve the injured reputation of his brother from the obloquy which the want of an investigation of the charges preferred against Sir George Prevost, previous to his decease, must have cast upon his memory; in a letter addressed to his royal highness the commander-in-chief, after stating in the strongest light, the distressing situation in which the family and relations of the deceased were placed, requested that an investigation of his conduct might be ordered before a court of inquiry. A reference to the judge advocate was made on the subject, who was of opinion that such an inquiry could not be properly made; and indeed the objections to an investigation after the death of a party, in such an instance as the present, appear to be insurmountable, the evidence before a court of inquiry not being taken on oath, nor could any proceedings with a view to afford public satisfaction have had the desired effect, unless the prosecutors (whose characters must also have been considered to a certain degree at stake) were allowed to come forward with the whole weight of their evidence.

In consequence of this determination, lady Prevost addressed a letter to the commander-in-chief, representing to his royal highness, in the most forcible terms, the painful dilemma in which she was placed. She dwelt strongly on the injustice sustained by the memory of an injured officer, whose life had been devoted to the service of his country, and whose exertions in that service had been honored with the frequent and unqualified approbation of his sovereign and his country,—Honors, which, though the fruit of long and acknowledged services, were now in danger of being blasted by unproven and calumnious accusations. She, therefore, solicited his royal highness to extend his favor and protection to herself and family, and implored him to commisserate their multiplied afflictions, and to endeavour to obtain from his royal highness the Prince Regent, a gracious consideration of their claims for such marks of distinction as might be thought due to the memory of the deceased. His royal highness acknowledged the receipt of her ladyship's letter, and assured her that he should be glad to do any thing calculated to alleviate her distress, but declined interfering with the Prince Regent on the subject, before whom, he was of opinion, it could only be regularly submitted by his Majesty's ministers.

Lady Prevost accordingly drew up a memorial, which, with a statement of the military occurrences at Plattsburgh, she submitted to the Prince Regent through the ministers. His royal highness having taken the same into consideration, was soon afterwards graciously pleased, publicly to express the high sense he entertained of the distinguished services of Sir George Prevost, conferring at the same time, as a mark of his approbation, additional armorial bearings on the arms of his family.*

---

* The preceding twelve pages were in type and ready for the press, when in conversation with a friend, on the occurrences of the late war with the United States, the writer's attention was directed by him to the opinions expressed, at the time, by the duke of Wellington, with respect to the system to be pursued by Sir George Prevost, in defending the Canadas; and to those also in reference to his conduct after the loss of the fleet at Plattsburgh : as well as to Mr. Alison's remarks on those matters, in his history of Europe. As they are very different from the views entertained generally at that period, they are here introduced with much pleasure, for the reader's perusal, and in justice to the memory of a much injured officer, deserving, on the whole, (as the writer humbly opines) well of the country. Time, which " at last sets all things even." will do its work. Few will question the autho-

rities here quoted, both eminent in their way. The duke as a soldier and the latter as an historian, are entitled to credit, and have pronounced *avec connaissance de cause*, in favor of the late Sir George Prevost, and posterity will scarcely set aside their verdict :—

Extract from a letter to lord Bathurst, from lord Wellington, 10th February, 1813 :—

" I am glad to find that you are going to reinforce Sir George Prevost, and I only hope that the troops will go in time, and that Sir George will not be induced, by any hopes of trifling advantages, to depart from a strong defensive system. He may depend upon it that he will not be strong enough either in men or means to establish himself in any conquest he might make. The attempt would only weaken him, and his losses augment the spirits and hopes of the enemy, even if not attended by worse consequences; whereas, by the other system, he will throw the difficulties and risk upon them, and they will most probably be foiled."—*Gurwood's Despatches*, vol. x., page 109.

Extract from vol. x. of Alison's History of Europe. (last edition.)

" Thus terminated the campaign of 1813, in Canada,—and though not uncheckered by disaster, yet was it upon the whole eminently glorious, both to the arms of Britain and to the inhabitants of her noble American colonies. The superiority of the enemy, both in troops and all the munitions of war, was very great: twenty thousand regular soldiers, besides as many militia, were at their disposal; the vessels built on the lakes were at their own door, armed from their own arsenals, and manned by the picked men of their commercial marine, now thrown almost utterly idle.—On the other hand, the whole british force did not exceed *three thousand* regular soldiers, who were charged with the defence of a frontier nearly a thousand miles in length; * * * * * * * * *
* * * * * * * * —*page* 648.

" The wisdom of the measures adopted by Sir George Prevost, the vigour with which attack at all points was repelled, and the imposing celerity with which a cautious defensive was converted, at its close, into a vigorous offensive warfare, can never be sufficiently praised, and justly place this campaign on a level with any in the long annals of british glory."—*page* 649.

PLATTSBURGH EXPEDITION.

" To have carried the redoubts when the troops did get up, would have been a bloody undertaking, though probably certain of success, and would have formed a set-off at least to the naval disaster; but Sir George Prevost, deeming his instructions not to expose the troops under his command to unnecessary or useless danger, to be imperative,* being of opinion, that after the command of the lake was lost, no further advance into the american territory was practicable, and

---

* " You will take care not to expose his Majesty's troops to being cut off; and guard against whatever might commit the safety of the force placed under your command "—*Lord Bathurst's instructions to Sir George Prevost.*

consequently, that the men lost in obtaining the redoubts would prove an unavailing sacrifice, gave the signal to draw off, and soon after commenced his retreat."—*page* 685.

"Yet did his error, if error it was, originate in a sacrifice of the feelings of self to a sense of public duty.—His personal courage was undoubted; his character amiable in the highest degree; the mildness and conciliatory spirit of his government had justly endeared him to the canadians; and his general conduct in North America had been in the highest degree admirable.—Indeed, his defence of that province against the vastly superior forces of the americans, is one of the brightest pages in the military annals of Great Britain, and justly after his death called forth a public expression of satisfaction from the Prince Regent, and the conferring of additional honors on his family. The failure of the expedition against Plattsburgh was not to be ascribed to him: it arose from the unprepared state of the fleet before the expedition commenced, and the shameful desertion of the gun-boats, which deserted the heroic Downie when on the point of gaining a decisive victory. We have the authority of the greatest military master of the age for the assertion, that after the destruction of the fleet, any further advance on land could have led to no beneficial result, as the troops could not have obtained supplies, when the americans had the command on the waters."* —*pages* 686 & 687.

Chap. XIX.

1815.

In addition to the above, the writer of the present would also remark, that the affair at Sacket's harbour, which, in like manner, gave rise to much reflection upon Sir George Prevost, is, now that the passions of the moment have passed away, likely also to be better judged of, than at the time.

The american force then at that place, as it has since been ascertained, (through General Wilkinson's memoirs,) consisted of 313 light dragoons, (dismounted.) 142 artillery, 332 of the 9th, 21st and 23d regiments of infantry—in all 787—to these were added 150 volunteers and 350 militia.—The british force did not exceed 700 men. The capture of Sacket's harbour, with a view to its occupancy during the war was out of the question, and never, for a moment, intended. A surprise, during the absence of their fleet then up the lake, and destruction of the new ship of war on the stocks, public stores and barracks, was the utmost contemplated, and to effect this, by a *coup de main*, Kingston was almost drained of its forces, and, in a manner, left unprotected. The enemy's squadron might not only intercept them on their return, whether successful or not, but at the same time make sure of Kingston, through the ascendency they had, at that pe-

---

* "I approve highly; indeed, I go further; I admire all that has been done by the military in America, so far as I understand it generally.—Whether Sir George Prevost was right or wrong in his decision at lake Champlain, is more than I can tell; though, of this I am certain, he must equally have returned to Kingston"(Montreal) " after the fleet was beaten, and I am inclined to think he was right. I have told the ministers repeatedly that a naval superiority on the lakes is a *sine qua non* of success in war on the frontier of Canada, even if our object should be wholly defensive."—Wellington to Sir George Murray, 22d Decr, 1814 —*Gurwood*, 12 vol 241.

riod, on the lake—witness their success at York—and thereby put an end, at once, to the struggle in Upper Canada.

The intended surprise having failed, (see *ante* pages 77 to 80) by circumstances beyond the controul of the naval and military commanders, there would really seem to have been more to blame in the attempt to retrieve it, by the attack,(hopeless, after at least the twelve hours fore knowledge of it which the enemy had, and when the militia of the neighbourhood was alarmed and up.) than in any alleged precipitancy of retreat, which, to the contrary was, in fact, too long delayed. The sudden rising of a gale of wind, either on or off the coast, a thing of frequent occurrence at this season, might have proved the total loss of the land and naval forces on the expedition, and with them the immediate fall of Kingston. All things considered, the commander of the forces, feeling the heavy responsibility that weighed upon him, did well to retire when he did, and better it had been if sooner, not only to save a further waste of lives, which could ill be spared, but to avoid the risk of an immediate loss of Kingston and of the whole Upper Province.

A gentleman, who has written on the subject, justly observes—" It is true that gen. Wilkinson," (in his memoirs relating to the late american war,) " adds that if our (the british) troops had persisted twenty minutes longer, the sloop of war then on the stocks, and the whole depot at Sacket's harbour would have fallen into their hands. But this is a mere opinion, springing partly, it would seem, from a jealous wish to disparage general Brown, who commanded the americans ; and partly founded on the supposition of a great superiority of numbers on our side. But be this opinion right or wrong, Sir George Prevost cannot, in fairness, be held responsible for any facts or consequences, but such as were or ought to have been within his knowledge, or reasonably to be anticipated, and he was bound to decide according to present circumstances, as they appeared to him. The hope of a surprise was at an end. His force was reduced by the conflict to less than 400 effectives, while the enemy, after losing 350 had still an unbroken fighting force of 450, besides a strong militia reinforcement estimated at 500 or 600, which it was known had poured into the place during the morning and previous night. The enemy had the shelter of block-houses, stockades and loop-holed buildings, giving them the advantage of a mode of fighting in which they are particularly expert, while our force was exposed.—That force formed the large part of the garrison at Kingston, the military key of Upper Canada, which might, in the mean time, be visited by the hostile fleet and army ; while a prolonged contest, or even a gale of wind forcing the fleet off the land, might seriously endanger the retreat and safety of our troops, and this at a moment when every soldier was of consequence to the safety of Upper Canada."

CHAPTER XX.

Sir Gordon Drummond—army bills called in and redeemed—meeting of the legislature—speech—address in answer—message to the assembly relating to the decision of the home government on the impeachments—resolutions of the assembly on the subject—prorogation and dissolution of the legislature—Sir John Coape Sherbrooke appointed to the government—Sir Gordon Drummond embarks for England—Finances, &c.

LIEUTENANT GENERAL Sir Gordon Drummond, as mentioned, assumed the government on the 5th of April, as administrator in chief. Nothing occurred worthy of notice, until the meeting of the legislature,* except the calling in and redeeming the army bills issued during the war. A proclamation to that effect, appeared on the 14th November, notifying that this paper was to be redeemed in cash, at the army bill office in Quebec, it being also declared, that all interest upon such bills as were in circulation would cease, after the fourteenth day next

---

* A new steamer, "*The Malsham,*" (the third on the St. Lawrence) made its appearance at Quebec, on the opening of the navigation.—It was, as the previous steamers had been, built at Montreal, and belonged to Mr. Molson. To this another, "*The Car of Commerce*" built by an association of Montreal merchants, was soon after put in competition, to the great gratification of the public. From that to the present time, these useful and splendid conveyances have progressively advanced to their present state of perfection, not only on the St. Lawrence, and over the great inland lakes Ontario, Erie, Huron, and Michigan, (which at that time were deemed impracticable by steamers,) but to the Atlantic and Pacific oceans.

thereafter. These were all honorably discharged. A paper of the day remarks,—"they (the army bills) have enriched the country, not so much by the interest they paid, which, of itself, is no inconsiderable addition to its wealth, as by the high prices paid for its commodities, arising from that abundance of the circulating medium, the full nominal value of which could be relied on, equally with the precious metals; and which, for some time past, has even exceeded in value the precious metals, from $2\frac{1}{2}$ to 5 per cent, by their ability to procure government bills of exchange, at a discount so much greater than gold and silver could effect it.—Such was their superior value, notwithstanding some alarm arising from numerous american forgeries of our army bills. What is still more striking is, that Canada paper bore this high value at the period when the paper of the United States was in such a state of depreciation as to create the utmost confusion in the States. Our paper, aided the government. because it operated as a loan, at a moment when the expenditure was of a magnitude not to be paralleled in the history of nations, but which, far from depressing the nation, served to evince not only the immensity of its resources, but the unbounded confidence placed in them."

The provincial parliament met on the 26th January, 1816. This was opened with the speech following:—

" Gentlemen of the legislative council, and gentlemen of

the house of assembly,—His royal highness the Prince Regent, having been pleased to commit to me the administration of this government, I have entered on the duties which that trust prescribes, with a deep sense of their importance, and an earnest desire to discharge them for the general advantage of the province; to which my attachment naturally derives additional strength, from the circumstance of my having been born in its capital.

"It would be to me a source of inexpressible comfort, and I am confident would convey to you sincere satisfaction, if I had it in my power to communicate any favorable account respecting the indisposition of our venerable Sovereign; I regret, however, that I have no such information to impart: yet, under this awful dispensation, it is not an inconsiderable consolation to be assured, that his Majesty has no corporeal suffering, and continues in a state of undisturbed tranquillity.

"The total overthrow and final exile of the usurper, whose insatiable ambition, and remorseless thirst of blood, were permitted so long to afflict the world;—the restoration once more, of the family of Bourbon to the throne of their ancestors;—the general peace which has been given back to Europe, by the magnanimous exertions of the allied powers;—and the high distinction obtained by the british forces, under the conduct of the illustrious duke of Wellington, consummated and crowned by the glorious victory of Waterloo; while they fill our minds with exultation, and open to us the prospect of permanent prosperity, will not fail to awaken a profound and grateful sense of the goodness of Divine Providence, so conspicuously manifested in these great events.

"In adverting to those matters of internal concern, which have been the object of assembling this provincial parliament, I have to direct your early attention to the renewal of the militia act, and such others as with it may be about to expire, and as it may be necessary and expedient to continue.

"I must also, in consequence of many discontented adventurers, and mischievous agitators, from the continent of Europe, having recently thrown themselves into the neighbouring States, strongly recommend the immediate revival of the "Act for establishing regulations respecting aliens," with such modifications as those circumstances may render it proper to adopt.

"You have had the satisfaction of seeing that the executive government has completely redeemed its pledge to the public, by calling in and paying with cash, the army bills which were in circulation.

"Gentlemen of the house of assembly,—I shall order a statement of the provincial revenue of the crown, and of the expenditure of the last year, to be laid before you.

"I have it in command from his royal highness the Prince Regent, to assure you that his royal highness views with much pleasure, the additional proof of patriotism and public spirit, afforded by the sum voted towards the completion of a proposed canal from Montreal to Lachine. His Majesty's government, duly appreciating the many important objects with which that work is connected, are greatly interested in its early execution ; and I await only further instructions upon the subject, to proceed to carry it into effect.

"Gentlemen of the legislative council, and gentlemen of the house of assembly,—I cannot omit to press upon your consideration, the importance of further promoting the internal communications of the province, and of making effectual provision for the full accomplishment of an object of such obvious and general utility.

You will, I doubt not, justify the firm reliance which I place on your loyal attachment to the person and government of your sovereign, and your enlightened zeal for the public service ; nor will you, I trust, disappoint my confident expectation, that this session of the provincial parliament will be distinguished for accordant exertion, and efficient dispatch, in conducting the public business. You may be assured, that on my part, I shall be most cordially disposed to second your laudable endeavours, by a ready co-operation in every measure which may tend to advance the interests, and promote the welfare, of this province."

The address in answer was an echo, though the egotism, in the first paragraph of the speech, did not escape comment in subsequent debates:—

"When circumstances required the presence in England, of his excellency Sir George Prevost, for whom we entertain so grateful a recollection, his royal highness has afforded additional proof of his paternal solicitude for the welfare of this province, in committing the administration of its government to your excellency, whose conspicuous services, during the late contest with the United States of America, bear such honorable testimony to that native patriotism and military talent, of which it is the glory of this province to have produced so brilliant an example in the person of your excellency."

To this address his excellency, in reply, observed:—

" Although you estimate too highly the services I have been fortunate enough to render in the defence of this, my native country, I receive with pride and satisfaction the flattering expression of your honorable opinion of them, and I assure you that the same local attachment by which I have hitherto been animated will increase, if possible, the readiness which, from a sense of duty alone I should feel, to co-operate in every measure tending to the advantage of the province."

The good feeling which, at this moment, prevailed between Sir Gordon Drummond and the parliament of his native country, was but of short duration.

On the 2d February, the following communication from the administrator of the government, came down to the assembly, by the civil secretary, R. R. Loring, esquire, and which being read by him, at the bar, was then delivered to the speaker, and laid on the table:—

" GORDON DRUMMOND, administrator in chief.

" The administrator in chief has received the commands of his royal highness the Prince Regent, to make known to the house of assembly of this province, his pleasure on the subject of certain charges preferred by that house against the chief justice of the province, and the chief justice of the court of king's bench for the district of Montreal.

" With respect to such of the charges as relate to acts done by a former governor of the province, which the assembly, presuming to be improper or illegal, imputed by a similar assumption to advice given by the chief justice to that governor, his royal highness has deemed that no enquiry could be necessary; inasmuch as none could be instituted without the admission of the principle, that the governor of a province might, at his own discretion, divest himself of all responsibility on points of political government.

" With a view, therefore, to the general interests of the province, his royal highness was pleased to refer for consideration, to the lords of the privy council, such only of the charges brought by the assembly as related to the rules of practice established by the judges in their respective courts, those being points upon which, if any impropriety had existed, the judges themselves were solely responsible.

" By the annexed copy of his royal highness's order in council, dated the 29th June, 1815,* the administrator in

---

* " GORDON DRUMMOND, administrator in chief.

" L. S.—(A true copy.)

" *At the Court of Carlton House*, 29*th June*, 1815.

" Present—His royal highness the PRINCE REGENT, in council.

" Whereas there was this day read at the board, a report from a committee of the lords of his Majesty's most honorable Privy Council, dated the 24th of this inst., in the words following, viz:

" Your royal highness having been pleased, by your order in council of the 10th December last, in the name and on the behalf of his Majesty, to refer unto this committee a letter from earl Bathurst, one of his Majesty's principal secretaries of state, to the lord president of the council, transmitting a copy of a letter from Sir George Prevost, dated Quebec, the 18th of March, 1814, forwarding an address of the house of assembly of Lower Canada, to your royal highness, with certain articles of complaint therein referred to, against Jonathan Sewell, esquire, his Majesty's chief justice of the province of Lower Canada, and James Monk, esquire, chief justice of the court of king's Bench for the district of Montreal, and also transmitting a memorial from the executive council, judges in the court of appeals, and of the puisné judges of the court of king's bench for the district of Quebec, and of the court of king's bench for the district of Montreal, in the said province of Lower Canada, praying to be included in the examination and decision of the said articles of complaint, together with a

chief, conveys to the assembly the result of their investigation, which has been conducted with all that attention and solemnity, which the importance of the subject required.

"In making this communication to the assembly, it now becomes the duty of the administrator in chief, in obedience to the commands of his royal highness the Prince Regent, to express the regret with which his royal highness has viewed their late proceedings against two persons who have so long

---

petition from the said Jonathan Sewell, esquire; in which letter the said earl Bathurst requests that so much of the said complaints of the house of assembly, as relate to the rules of practice stated to have been introduced by the said chief justices into their respective courts, may be submitted to your royal highness in council, in order that if such rules shall be found to have been introduced, it may be decided whether, in so doing, the said chief justices have exceeded their authority.

"The lords of the committee, in obedience to your royal highness' said order of reference, have taken the said letter and its inclosures into consideration, and having received the opinion of his Majesty's attorney and solicitor general, and been attended by them thereupon, and having maturely deliberated upon the complaints of the house of assembly, so far as they relate to the said rules of practice, their lordships do agree humbly to report as their opinion to your royal highness, that the rules which are made the subject of such complaint of the said house of assembly of Lower Canada, against the said chief justices Jonathan Sewell, esquire, and James Monk, esquire, which their lordships observe were not made by the said chief justices, respectively, upon their own sole authority, but by them in conjunction with the other judges of the respective courts, are all rules for regulation of the practice of their respective courts, and within the scope of that power and jurisdiction with which, by the rules of law, and by the colonial ordinances and acts of legislation, these courts are invested, and consequently that neither the said chief justices, nor the courts in which they preside, have, in making such rules, exceeded their authority, nor have been guilty of any assumption of legislative power."

"His royal highness the prince regent having taken the said report into consideration, was pleased, in the name and on the behalf of his Majesty, and by and with the advice of his Majesty's privy council, to approve thereof, and to order, as it is hereby ordered, that the said complaints, so far as they relate to the said rules of practice, be, and they are hereby dismissed this board."

(Signed)   "JAS. BULLER."
                         "G. D."

Previous to the convocation of the legislature, a pamphlet was circulated, containing part of the correspondence that had taken place in England, between the colonial minister and Mr. Sewell, in which the following appeared:—

and so ably filled the highest judicial offices in the colony; a circumstance the more to be deplored, as tending to disparage, in the eyes of the inconsiderate and ignorant, their character and services, and thus to diminish the influence to which, from their situation, and their uniform propriety of conduct, they are justly entitled.

"The above communication, embracing so much of the

"DOWNING-STREET, July 23, 1815.

"Sir,—His royal highness the Prince Regent, having been pleased to refer to the consideration of a committee of the most honorable privy council, certain articles of complaint against you and Mr. Monk, so far as related to the rules of practice established by you in the courts in which you respectively preside, it now becomes my duty to communicate to you the result of that inquiry, which having received the entire approbation of his royal highness, is expressed in the order of which the enclosed is a copy.

"The officer at present administering the government of Canada, has received his royal highness's commands to communicate this decision to the house of assembly; and in making this communication to state the grounds upon which his royal highness has declined considering, as articles of complaint against you, the advice which you are at different times stated to have given to the preceding governors of the province. It is highly satisfactory to me to assure you, that although his royal highness felt compelled upon general principles to exclude those particular charges from consideration, and thus to preclude you from entering upon your justification, yet his royal highness entertains no doubt as to the general propriety of your and Mr. Monk's conduct, or as to your being able to offer, with respect to them, a full and satisfactory explanation.

"I am, sir, your obedient humble servant,
(Signed) "BATHURST."
To J. SEWELL, Esq., chief justice of Lower Canada."

"DOWNING STREET, July 27th, 1815.

"Sir,—I had the honor of receiving your letter of the 24th instant, expressing your apprehension, that as the instructions transmitted to the officer administering the government of Canada, do not embrace any other charges brought against you and Mr. Monk, than those which relate to advice given by you to the governor, and the rules of practice established in your respective courts, the house of assembly may be induced to consider you as not free from blame on the other points of charge, not strictly falling within that description.

"As the letter addressed to the officer administering the government of Canada, bears testimony to the uniform propriety of your and Mr. Monk's conduct, I do not conceive that there can be any ground for the house of assembly to doubt that your justification is complete: but, I am glad to have an opportunity of stating that the charges not specifically adverted to in my letter, appeared to be, with one exception, of too little importance to require consideration, and charges preferred against the said chief justices, as relate to the rules of practice, and as are grounded on advice assumed to have been given by the chief justice of the province to the late Sir James Craig, the administrator in chief has been further commanded to signify to the assembly, that the other charges appeared to his Majesty's government, to be, with one exception, too inconsiderable to require investigation, and that (namely the one against the chief justice of the court of king's bench for the district of Montreal, which states him to have refused a writ of *habeas corpus*) was, in common with all the charges which do not relate to the rules of practice, totally unsupported by any evidence whatever.

"G. D."

This communication threw the assembly into a ferment, and a call of the house, on the 14th

---

that (the one against Mr. Monk, which charges him with having refused a writ of *habeas corpus*) was, as well as all the other charges, which are not founded on the rules of practice, totally unsupported by any evidence whatever

" I have the honor to be, sir,
" Your most obedient humble servant,
(Signed) " BATHURST."
" To J. Sewell, Esq., chief justice of Lower Canada."

" Council Office, Whitehall, August 17th, 1815.

" Sir,—Agreeably to the request, signified in your letter of the 30th ultimo, I have the honor to enclose you a copy of the order in council, dismissing the complaints of the house of assembly of Lower Canada, so far as they relate to the rules of practice, &c., with the names of the lords present in council, when the report of the lords of the committee respecting those complaints was approved.

" The report of the lords of the committee is entered at length in the copy of the order; but it is not the practice to insert the names of the lords who make the report; yet, as it is important that it should be known in Canada, by what high legal authority the said report was made, I have it in command from the Lord President to communicate their names to you, and they are as follows:—

The Lord President,	Master of the Rolls,
Earl Bathurst,	Sir John Nichol,
Lord Ellenborough,	Lord Chief Justice Gibbs,
Sir William Scott,	Lord Chief Baron.

" I have the honor to be, sir,
" Your most obedient humble servant,
(Signed) " CHETWYND."
" J. Sewell, esq., chief justice of Lower Canada."

of the month, was immediately ordered. His excellency's message was, at the same time, referred to a committee of the whole, on that day.

This subject was, on the fourteenth, referred to the consideration of a special committee of seven members, to whom two others were afterwards added, with directions " to report their opinion on the most expedient manner of proceeding on the same." On the twenty-third, this committee reported to the house, that having maturely deliberated upon the order of reference, they were of opinion that the matters disclosed in his excellency's message would render necessary an humble representation and petition to his royal highness the Prince Regent, and that the great importance of the matters involved in the said message, made it advisable that the wisdom of the house should be consulted, and its sense taken preparatory to such representation and petition.

On the twenty-fourth, the assembly accordingly adopted resolutions on the subject. By these were expressed, a sense of the public duty under which the house had acted, in impeaching the chief justices;—its opinion of the right of the commons of Lower Canada to be heard, and of having an opportunity of adducing evidence in support of their charges;—the causes which had prevented them from maintaining those charges;—their desire of having an opportunity to do so;—and finally, that an humble representation and petition, on behalf of the commons of Lower Canada, to his royal highness the Prince Regent be prepared, appealing to the justice of his Majesty's government, and praying that an opportunity might be afforded to his Majesty's most dutiful commons of Lower Canada, to be heard upon, and to maintain their complaints.* A special committee was appointed, for preparing an humble

---

* " Resolved, as the opinion of this committee, that this house, acting in the name of the commons of Lower Canada, in its proceedings relative to the impeachments of Jonathan Sewell, esquire, chief justice of the province, and James Monk, esquire, chief justice of the court of king's bench for the district of Montreal, was influenced by a sense of duty, by a desire to maintain the laws and constitution of this province, and by a regard for the public interest, and the honor of his Majesty's government.

" Resolved, as the opinion of this committee, that the commons of Lower Canada were entitled to be heard, and to have an opportunity of adducing evidence in support of their charges against the said Jonathan Sewell and James Monk, esquires.

" Resolved, as the opinion of this committee, that the resistance and opposition of the legislative council, of which the said Jonathan Sewell and James Monk, were and are members, to the right of the commons of Lower Canada, to exhibit the said charges, and the obstructions subsequently interposed to the prosecution of them, prevented this house from being represented by an agent to maintain and support the said charges.

" Resolved, as the opinion of this committee, that this house has always been, and is desirous, of an opportunity of being heard on the said charges, and of supporting them by evidence, and hath reason to lament that no such opportunity hath hitherto been afforded to them.

" Resolved, as the opinion of this committee, that an humble representation and petition, on behalf of the commons of this province, to his royal highness the Prince Regent, be prepared, appealing to the justice of his Majesty's government, and praying that an opportunity may be afforded to his Majesty's dutiful commons of this province, to be heard upon and maintain the said charges."

These were carried by considerable majorities.—The names taken on one divison were as follows :—

" Yeas—Messrs. A. Stuart, Prevost, Déligny, Breux, Gauvreau, Richer, Dénéchau, Huot, Bellet, Bresse, Lagueux, Robitaille, O'Sullivan, Cherrier, Amiot, Blanchet, Lee, Duchesnois, Bruneau, J. Stuart, and Sherwood."

" Nays—Messrs. Browne, Davidson, Ogden, Taschereau, Fraser, Vanfelson, Borgia, Jones, Malhiot, Fournier and Bourdages."

representation and petition, in conformity with the last of these resolutions.

It seems that Sir Gordon Drummond was impelled by his instructions from home, to resort to a dissolution, in the event that the assembly should resume this subject, and consequently had no discretion to exercise on the occasion. On the twenty-sixth, before any of the measures which had been resolved were brought to maturity, his arrival at the council chamber was announced by a discharge of artillery. He prorogued the session with the following speech :—

"Gentlemen of the legislative council, and gentlemen of the house of assembly,—Having indulged the hope, when I met you in the provincial parliament, that your unanimous exertions would have been diligently applied to those objects of public advantage, which I recommended to your particular attention, it has been with extreme concern, that I have found those, my reasonable expectations, disappointed.

"The house of assembly has again entered on the discussion of the subject, on which the decision of his royal highness the Prince Regent, in the name and on the behalf of his Majesty, has already been communicated to them; and while I deeply regret that the assembly should have allowed any consideration to overbear the respect which his royal highness's decision claimed, I feel it my duty to announce to you my determination to prorogue the present parliament, and to resort to the sense of the people by an immediate dissolution."

Several objects of importance were brought before the assembly this session, but no more than a single Act* received the royal sanction.

---

* An act to regulate the trial of controverted elections, &c.

The expediency of having an agent in England, to attend to the interests of the province, whenever it might be requisite, was again considered; but the dissolution prevented a perseverance in the measure. The assembly, in pursuance of a resolution made in the last session, passed a bill " to appropriate a sum of money therein mentioned, to the purchase of a service of plate, to be presented to Sir George Prevost, late governor in chief of the province, as a mark of respect for his character, and of gratitude for the services which he had rendered to the province."† This bill being sent up for the concurrence of the legislative council, was rejected by that body. A committee was named to enquire into the state of the property heretofore appertaining to the late order of jesuits, and it was made an instruction to the committee to prepare and report the draft of an humble address to his royal highness the Prince Regent, exhibiting the rights of the province to possess the said property for the purposes of education, and to pray for its restitution for the purposes to which it was originally destined.

The elections for the new assembly took place in the month of March, and but few alterations in the representation were made. In the meantime, the administrator in chief received notification of the appointment of Sir John Coape Sherbrooke, to the chief command in British North America; and on the twenty-

---

† The sum appropriated by the bill was £5,000.

first day of May, he sailed for England, having, on the day of his departure, received a valedictory address from the citizens of Quebec. The temporary administration of the government devolved upon major general Wilson, until the arrival of Sir John Coape Sherbrooke.

The revenues of the year 1815, amounted to £150,273, currency; the expenditure to £125,218, sterling. In this latter was included the sum of £16,555, for erecting the gaol in the city of Quebec; £26,439, on account of mililia services; £35,325 to Upper Canada, being its proportion of the duties levied in Lower Canada, in the year 1814. From the port of Quebec, there were cleared during the year 1815, one hundred and ninety-four vessels, making 37382 tons, and employing 1847 men, besides ten built thereat, making 1462 tons more.

CHAPTER XXI.

Sir John Coape Sherbrooke, lieut. governor of Nova Scotia, succeeds to the government of Canada—failure in the harvest—relief afforded by the governor to the distressed parishes—submits his view to the colonial minister, with respect to public opinion on the impeachments, and of the state of the province—parliament meets—speech and proceedings—governor announces that the Regent had sanctioned the bill allowing a salary, during the last parliament, to the speaker of the assembly—assembly make good the advances by the governor, for relieving the distressed parishes—vote also a further relief—Mr. justice Foucher impeached—steps thereupon by the legislative council—Petition to the assembly by the family of the late François Corbeil—Petition by S. Sherwood, esq., against Mr. chief justice Monk—Mr. Stuart moves the reconsideration of the impeachments against the chief justice, and is left in a small minority—retires in disgust—elucidation of the means by which he was foiled in this matter, and a salary of £1,000 granted to Mr. Sewell, as speaker of the legislative council—Finances, &c.—judges' salaries increased to £900 sterling—prorogation—miscellanies—parliament again opened—governor authorised to call upon the assembly to vote the necessary sums for the civil expenditure, agreeable to their offer in 1810—despatch and instructions relating to the impeachment of Mr. Foucher—proceedings of the council on the subject—Estimates for the year 1818—voted, but no bill of appropriation passed—bills passed—Sir J. C. Sherbrooke relieved by the duke of Richmond, and departs for England—exhumation of remains of general Montgomery, at the request of his widow.

Chap. XXI.

1816.

Sir John Coape Sherbrooke, landed in Quebec, on the 21st July, on his arrival from

Halifax, having for some time previously administered the government of Nova Scotia, whence he was advanced to that of Canada. One of his first measures, after the assumption of the government, made him a favorite with the people. The failure of the wheat crop, in the lower parts of the district of Quebec, from early frosts, gave cause to apprehend a famine throughout that part of the province. Representations from several of the afflicted parishes, being submitted to him, he threw open the king's stores for the public relief, advancing besides, a very considerable sum of money, upon his own responsibility, from the public treasury, for the purchase of such supplies as were not in those stores. Provisions in abundance were forwarded before the commencement of winter, to the country parts in distress, which, by his seasonable relief, were rescued from famine.

The instructions given Sir Gordon Drummond, with respect to the Prince Regent's decision upon the impeachments, had compelled him to dissolve the assembly, upon its calling in question the course adopted. Sir John Sherbrooke was anxious to avert the necessity of a similar step on his part, and accordingly, he lost no time after his arrival, in requesting further instructions for his guidance in the matter, in case of its revival by the assembly, and in submitting to the colonial minister, his views of the public opinion on the subject, in the province.

He stated, that the late dissolution, by Sir Gordon Drummond, in consequence of the commands he had received, if it were intended to have its effect, by changing for the better the representation of the assembly, had entirely failed; and not only that, but it had augmented the evil, by causing much irritation, both among the representatives and in the country, and by leading to the general election of the same members, or, in the few instances where a change had taken place, the election of others more immoderate than those whom they replaced. He submitted it as his opinion, that in this country, the strong measure of a dissolution, must, in almost all possible circumstances of the country, produce rather evil than advantage, and could never have that effect which might be given to it in England, by the exertion of the different means that might be brought into action there, for the correction of popular opinion, and for securing to the crown a stronger influence in parliament.

Expressing, however, his willingness to carry into full execution, the strongest measures his Majesty's government should think proper to prescribe; he, nevertheless, requested specific instructions as to the course he was to pursue, in case the assembly should recur, as there was scarcely a doubt they would, to the subject which had lately led to a dissolution of that body.

It would seem that, in the determination of the home government to support the chief justice Sewell, against the popular feeling of which he was the object, the governor was advised, in answer to the above, to conciliate the favor of the roman catholic bishop and clergy, as a means of influence over the people. This led his excellency to submit to the minister a clear and correct view of the state of parties in the province, and of the dilemma into which he was thrown by his instructions on the one hand, and the actual state of affairs on the other.

He stated to his lordship, earl Bathurst, the colonial secretary, that of the unpopularity of the chief justice he might have some idea, from the proceedings that had taken place against him, and which he may have supposed originated merely in the hostility of a particular party in the assembly, or among the people. That he had endeavoured to make himself master of the subject, and from information, personal inquiry and observation, in a tour he had lately made through the province, he had found the feeling of hostility against that gentleman, to pervade all classes, and to prevail with violence, even in the obscurest parts of the province. It mattered not that the feeling proceeded from the arts and calumnies of designing demagogues, or was urged by personal dislike. It had long existed, and had derived fresh virulence from the apparent triumph of the chief justice, and that while adopted generally among the inhabitants, the catholic clergy themselves were among the most strenuous asserters of its justice, if not the warmest propagators of it.

That if the influence of the catholic clergy over the laity, on different subjects, were great, his lordship might judge what must be the vigour and effect of its operation, when directed to a point in which the people believed their dearest interests to be involved, and against a man whom they, unfortunately, considered to have outraged their feelings of loyalty and religion. That in such a case as this, the clergy acted with double force, and as they had carried the people with them, by the combined effect of political and religious prejudice, it was to be expected that there would arise, and that there had arisen against this gentleman, throughout both laity and clergy, an infatuated dislike.

That into the original views he (the governor) did not enter. It sufficed to say, that when Mr. Sewell was attorney general, it fell to his lot to maintain doctrines and support measures that clashed with the religious opinions of the canadians. The disposition which was then exerted against him was confirmed after his promotion, by the part he was considered to have taken in the government of the country and in the legislative council, and it grew and strengthened until it produced his impeachment by the assembly.

The governor was persuaded, that had it accorded with the views of the government, to grant a hearing to both parties on the impeachment, even though the decision had been precisely as it was, it would have been conducive to the peace of the province, as it would have deprived the party hostile to him here, of a pretext of complaint, by which, in a free government, the people will always be interested, and which in that case, derived weight and plausibility, from the presence of the chief justice in England,—that is to say, that the decision of government had been formed on an *ex parte* hearing. He was bold to say, that it was the force of this argument, that had produced the resolutions, in consequence of which the late assembly was dissolved.

It had been, he observed, the hope of many well informed persons in this country, that the government would have permitted the chief justice, after his acquittal, to have retired on a pension; a measure which, whether effectual or not, in quieting the country, would have taken from the leaders in the assembly, their chief source of influence over popular opinion, by removing the principal object of popular dislike. The delusive arts of popular leaders had produced a persuasion among both clergy and people, that he was the cause of those public evils which the province was then suffering, by the dissolution of the assembly—the expiration of municipal laws—the suspension of public establishments, and the interruption of projects of public advantage.

He observed, that in pursuance of the minister's directions, he would give the chief justice, however unjustly aspersed, as he was, by the hostility of the bar and the pulpit, every support; although for this, he should forego the conciliation of the clergy, the harmony of the province, and the advancement of its interests. That he would also endeavour to establish a good understanding with the roman catholic bishop, to whom he already had given proofs of his disposition to that effect. But that he would deceive the minister, were he to hold out to him any expectation of a change in the sentiments either of the clergy or people, in the point alluded to. Argument had failed to persuade them,—coercion it was rather feared would fix the feeling deeper. It was the opinion of well-informed and moderate men, that prorogation might succeed to prorogation, and dissolution to dissolution, but that there would sooner be a revolution in the country, than in the feelings of its inhabitants on that point.

In pointing out thus strongly the state of things, it might be expected he should say something of the remedies suggested to him, as applicable to the case.—One of these was the appointment of an agent in England, long an object of popular desire, and which had been effected in almost all the other colonies—it being to the opposition the measure had met with in the legislative council, in which the chief justice was considered by the assembly to have great influence, that they ascribed the loss of it; which, independently of its general advantage, would, as they alleged, have enabled them to support their impeachments against him. The other was to detach Mr. Stuart (the prime mover of the resolutions at the previous session) if possible, by motives of self-interest, from the party with which he had connected himself, and which, it was thought without him, would gradually lose vigour and dwindle into insignificance.

It had, he said, been hinted to him, (the governor) that if the attorney generalship should become vacant, the offer of it would be a powerful temptation to desert those with whom he had hitherto acted. But the delicacy of an attempt of that description was felt, and probably it never was made. The more successful course was pursued of detaching the party from him, adroitly adopted by the governor, favoured as he was by circumstances, at the ensuing session of the legislature, as we shall presently see, and by which the party Mr. Stuart seemed triumphantly to lead, though in truth, like most of those imagining themselves the leaders of a party, but the humble followers of the multitude, was induced to abandon him.

A more faithful representation of matters in the province, at this time, in connection with the subject alluded to, could not be desired than that understood to have been given by Sir John Coape Sherbrooke, to the colonial minister, to whom he also suggested the expedience of giving the speaker of the assembly a seat in the executive council. The great evil of this country, and the most fruitful source of its dissensions had been, he observed, a want of confidence in its executive government, not so much in personal character of the governor as in the executive council, who have come to be considered the governor's advisers, and whose movements were watched with a jealous suspicion that tended to hamper every operation of government. The removal of this distrust, he conceived, would be effected, if the speaker of the assembly, for the time being, were made a member of the executive council.

The new parliament (the ninth of Lower Canada) met on the 15th January, 1817.* Mr. Papineau was again chosen speaker of the assembly, *nem. con.* The governor called the

---

* The members of the assembly were as follows :—
Upper Town of Quebec, Claude Dénéchau and George Vanfelson ; County of Hertford, Louis Turgeon and Ferréol Roy ; County of Orleans, Charles Blouin ; County of Montreal, James Stuart and Augustin Richer ; County of Hampshire, George W. Allsopp and François Huot ; County of Dorchester, John Davidson and J. T. Taschereau ; County of Northumberland, Etienne C. Lagueux and Philippe Panet ; County of Buckinghamshire, François Bellet and Joseph Badeaux ; County of Warwick, Jacques Déligny and Joseph Douaire Bondy ; County of Huntingdon, Austin Cuvillier and Michael O'Sullivan ; Borough of Three Rivers, Charles Rd. Ogden and Pierre Vezina ; Borough of William Henry, Robert Jones ; East Ward of Montreal, Louis Roi Portelance and John Molson ; Lower Town of Quebec, Andrew Stuart and François Languedoc ; County of Quebec, Peter Brehaut and Louis Gauvreau ; County of Kent, Denis B. Viger and Joseph Bresse, senr. ; County of Cornwallis, Joseph L. Borgia and Joseph Robitaille ; County of Leinster, Benjamin Beaupré and Jacques Lacombe ; West Ward of Montreal, L. J. Papineau and F. Vinet, *alias* Souligny ; County of Effingham, Joseph Malhœut and Samuel Sherwood ; County of Bedford, Thomas McCord ; County of Devon, Joseph Couillard Després and Frs. Fournier ; County of St. Maurice, Etienne Mayrand and Louis Gugy ; County of York, Eustache N. L. Dumont and Jean Bte. Ferré ; County of Surrey, Pierre Amiot and Etienne Duchesnois ; County of Richelieu, Jean Dessaulles and Seraphin Cherrier ; County of Gaspé, James Cockburn

immediate attention of the legislature, to the failure of the crops in different parts of the province, but more particularly in the parishes below Quebec, where it had been represented to him that the inhabitants had been reduced to a state of absolute want :—

"Having ascertained,"—said he—" that this evil really did exist to an alarming extent, I lost no time in making such temporary arrangements as would secure the lower orders from the dreadful effects of famine, until the legislature could be convened. The information on which I acted, together with a statement of the steps I have taken in consequence, shall be laid before both houses with as little delay as possible, when I shall leave it to the provincial parliament, to take such further measures, as the nature of the case may appear to require.

" Gentlemen of the house of assembly,—I rely upon your liberality to make the necessary provision for defraying the expenses already incurred for the purpose of supplying the immediate and more pressing wants of the distressed parts of the community, and I feel assured that you will likewise grant such further aid as necessities may require. I shall order a statement of the provincial revenue of the crown, and of expenditures of the last year to be laid before you as usual.

" Gentlemen of the legislative council, gentlemen of the house of assembly,—I feel it my duty to call your early attention to the renewal of the militia act, and of several other acts, which are of the utmost importance to the province, and which have already expired, or will do so very shortly. You are too well acquainted with the advantages which must result from every improvement in the internal communications of this province, and from the encouragement of its agriculture and commerce, to make it necessary for me to do more than recommend these most important subjects to your attention."

To the above, the assembly courteously responded :—

" We have remarked with pleasure that your excellency's

arrival in this province was preceded not only by the fame of your excellency's military life, but also by that of the successful administration of the civil government of a neighbouring province; and we have been led to form the agreeable anticipation, that, under your excellency's wise and impartial government, the advantages produced by your excellency's administration in that province, may be realised in this.

"We are sensible with your excellency of the necessity of early attention to the renewal of the militia act, and several other acts of importance to the province; some of which have already expired, and others of which are about to expire; and we shall be anxiously desirous of accomplishing your excellency's recommendation on this head. In what relates to the militia law, we shall use our zealous efforts to place the militia upon the most respectable footing, as the substantial support of our constitution, and a safeguard against attempts to sever us from the british empire."

The assembly, besides appointing the grand committees of grievances, courts of justice, agriculture and commerce, usually established at the commencement of each parliament, named also a committee of five members to keep up a good correspondence between the two houses—a measure at which the legislative council expressed its satisfaction, naming on its part also a committee for the same purpose.

These preliminaries over, the governor acquainted the assembly by message, that the Prince Regent had been pleased to assent to the bill granting a salary (£1000 a year) to the speaker of that house, during the late parliament, and which bill, in March 1815, had been reserved for the signification of the royal pleasure. There was, however, no provision for the like purpose, during the present parliament, a circumstance which, as we shall soon perceive, the governor turned to account.

The assembly readily discharged by its vote the governor of the responsibility he had assumed in making advances, to the amount of £14,216 currency, to relieve the distressed parishes, voting at the same time an additional sum of £15,500 for their further relief, independently of twenty thousand pounds currency, for the purchase of seed grain for distribution to such industrious husbandmen as could not otherwise procure it, to be repaid in such time and manner as might be the most convenient.

Articles of impeachment were presented by Mr. Cuvillier, against Mr. Justice Foucher, one of the judges of the court of king's bench at Montreal, for alleged " malversation, corrupt practice, and injustice," which were referred to a select committee to enquire into and report upon them. The enquiry resulted in a confirmation of the charges by the committee, and Mr. Foucher was accordingly impeached by the assembly. An address was drawn up on the subject to the Prince Regent, praying he would be pleased to remove Mr. Foucher from his office, and to interpose the authority of his Majesty's government, in such way as in the wisdom of his royal highness should appear necessary for bringing him to justice, which, together with the articles of impeachment, the house requested the governor to transmit to his royal highness. The assembly also requested the governor to suspend the judge while the charges were pending. His Excellency informed the house that he would not fail to transmit their address with the articles of complaint and documents accompanying them to the regent. " Many objections"—he observed—" would have arisen to prevent me from suspending Mr. Justice Foucher, but particularly the precedent furnished by the course pursued on a similar occasion, by the late governor-in-chief, respecting which, as his Majesty's government do not appear to have stated any explicit opinion, I could not but feel some doubt"—but he acquainted them that this difficulty was avoided; for, that having previously perused the evidence adduced in the course of the investigation, he had already communicated to Mr. Foucher his desire that he should abstain from the exercise of his judicial functions, until the determination of the regent, with respect to any further proceedings on the accusations were made known.*

These proceedings of the assembly were resented by the legislative council, who, also, addressed the regent on the subject:—

" In these proceedings,"—said they—" we have had no participation in any shape, the resolutions of the assembly not having been submitted to us for our concurrence, nor has the accused been at all heard in his defence, or had any communication of the charges against him, other than what the public papers or private information may have conveyed;

---

* The charges against Mr. Foucher were, in substance, that he had aided and given advice to certain attornies of his court, to whom he was partial, and to parties pleading therein, in matters wherein he afterwards sat as judge, and gave judgment thereupon—and of acts of insolence and oppression, from the bench, to individuals he disliked.

we, therefore, do not presume to give any opinion upon the guilt or innocence of the accused.

"Under all the circumstances of the case, however, we consider it our bounden duty, humbly to submit to the consideration of your royal highness, the serious consequences which are likely to result, if the claim of the assembly be sustained,—that claim extends to the right of passing articles of accusation, without limitation and without controul, in the province, either when voted after the hearing of *ex parte* testimony, without notification to the accused of complaint against him, or in the absence of all testimony, as hath been already practised.

"If such a right in the assembly shall be established, and that articles of complaint and accusation by that house, neither require any concurrence in the legislative council previously to being submitted to your royal highness, nor can be adjudged upon by this house or any other tribunal constituted or to be constituted in this province,—then every public officer being liable, at his own expense, to go to England before being heard, at an immense distance from the place of residence of his exculpatory witnesses, must henceforth feel himself wholly at the mercy of the assembly, and thereby become disqualified from an independent and faithful discharge of official duty.

"We, therefore, humbly beseech your royal highness not to inflict punishment upon the said Louis Charles Foucher, esquire, one of the judges of his Majesty's court of king's bench for the district of Montreal, in consequence of the articles of complaint exhibited against him by the assembly of this province, until such articles of complaint shall have been submitted to this house, and this house shall have concurred therein, and such articles of complaint, after such submission and concurrence shall have been heard and determined in such tribunal as your royal highness shall be pleased to appoint for that purpose; or until such articles of complaint, without such submission and concurrence, shall have been heard and determined in due course of justice in this house, under such commission as your royal highness shall see fit to issue for that purpose, with such powers and limitations as to your royal highness shall seem meet."

In reply to this, it was resolved by the assembly "that the claims of the legislative council touching the complaints brought by the assembly were not founded on constitutional laws, or any analogy thereto—that they tended to prevent offenders, out of the reach of the ordinary tribunals of the country, from being brought to justice, and to maintain, perpetuate and encourage, an arbitrary, illegal, tyrannical and oppressive power over the people of the province."

A petition was presented by Mr. Sherwood, to the assembly, from the family of the late François Corbeil, who, it was alleged, had died in consequence of his imprisonment, under the administration of Sir J. H. Craig, complaining of Mr. Chief Justice Monk and others, by whom, in their capacity of executive councillors, the warrant had been issued in virtue whereof their father had been imprisoned, on a charge of treasonable practices, which they asserted to be notoriously false." Another petition from Mr. Sherwood himself, against the same functionary, was also presented, representing his conduct on the bench in a case of indictment for libel found against that gentleman, in a most unfavorable light.

It is to be observed, that soon after the acquittal of the chief justices, by decision of the Prince Regent, a pamphlet, in print. containing copies of the order in council absolving those gentlemen, and of the correspondence between chief justice Sewell, and certain functionaries in England on the subject, was circulated in Quebec and Montreal, in order, probably, to inform their friends and the public of the course pursued, and result of the impeachments. This was followed by another pamphlet, in which the order in council, and correspondence were travestied into the most perfect burlesque, and which, though nothing more than risible, sir Gordon Drummond, then administering the government, nevertheless, deemed a libel on the british government, of sufficient gravity and importance to induce him to direct his Majesty's attorney general, Mr. Uniacke, to institute legal proceedings for bringing to punishment the authors and publishers, if they could be ascertained. The attorney general (who was understood to have disapproved of the notice bestowed upon the matter) had no difficulty in fixing the authorship upon Mr. Sherwood, a popular member of the assembly, who was accordingly indicted for it as a libel upon the king's government, at a court of oyer and terminer, held at Montreal.

The petitioner complained that he had been much aggrieved and oppressed by a persecution carried on against him, under the influence of the chief justice of Montreal, James Monk, esquire, acting in the triple capacity of a leading member of the executive government, a prosecutor and a judge. He represented this court to have been held in consequence of the absence of the chief justice Monk, from his duties as judge at Montreal, during the time when by law the criminal term of the court of King's bench there ought to have been held, and which, owing to his absence at Quebec, in attendance upon the council had not taken place, and that the laws of the land had been thereby suspended and dispensed with, contrary to the bill of rights—he alleged the special commission under which the court had been held, to have been unnecessary—that it was to answer the private purposes of Mr. Monk, and the party to which he belonged—that the grand jury instead of being drawn from the body of the district, had been packed from the city of Montreal, "composed of individuals devoted to the said James Monk"—that they hunted up evidence for themselves, sending out bailiffs without any subpœna or process of court to bring before them citizens of Montreal, who were supposed to be in habits of intimacy with the petitioner, and who were lawlessly dragged before the grand jury and examined on matters relating to the private concerns of the petitioner, and wholly irrelevant to the indictment—that a bill of indictment had been found against him merely on suspicion. The pretended libel, it was said, is inserted in the body of the indictment, and principally directed against the said James Monk and against his interest—his name being mentioned upwards of thirty times, although the indictment contains but one count. Yet, (said the petition) he sat upon the bench, and countenanced and encouraged the packed grand jury in their iniquitous conduct. "His whole behaviour manifested"—it continued—" a lively personal interest in the prosecution. When the officer of the court was reading the indictment, the said James Monk perceiving a smile upon the countenance of a gentleman of the bar, interrupted the reading, assailed him with fierce animadversions and threatened that he would remember that smile when he should give a charge to the petty jury against the petitioner— The example of a british judge sitting in a cause in which he was interested, the petitioner believed, was never known before, not even in the days of *Scroggs* and *Jefferies*." The petitioner represented that in consequence of this lawless persecution, he had been falsely imprisoned, and held to excessive bail, his liberties as a british subject violated, and his privileges as a member of the house trampled under foot.—He, therefore, prayed the house would take his grievance into consideration, and use their efforts to prevent any judge of this province, in future, from perverting the administration of justice for party purposes, and converting it into an instrument to gratify personal vengeance.

Although not without strong suspicion that the indecorous conduct here imputed to Mr. Monk, whose character for judicial integrity stood high, and the other excesses complained of are overcharged, it is, nevertheless, well that the reader should see a picture characteristic, to a certain extent, of these times, when those high functionaries and other head officials were the lords of the land, and could with impunity forget themselves. It must also be observed, that since the impeachment of the chief justices, there was a prurient disposition in the assembly, to disparage and pull down the judges, arising partly perhaps, from the unguarded conduct of some of them on the bench, and partly from their interference in politics, and otherwise mixing themselves up in matters foreign to their station.

The petition was referred to a select committee of five members who instituted an inquiry, but which, being continued throughout the session and over to the next, finally ended in smoke, as did also the indictment that provoked it, which never was brought to trial, propably as a matter too ludicrous and absurd for judicial investigation.*

Mr. Stuart preparatory to his stirring in revi-

---

* Shortly after this petition was laid before the assembly and the matter referred to a select committee, the following communications were submitted to the house :—

"Castle of St. Lewis, Quebec, 19th Feby., 1817.

"Sir,—The chief justice of the court of king's bench for the district of Montreal, having addressed to me a letter explanatory of the cause of his absence from Montreal, in March, one thousand eight hundred and sixteen, at the period when the court is by law appointed to sit there, for the trial of criminal causes, for which absence a charge has been brought against him in the house of assembly, I think it proper to transmit you a copy of this communication, and of the enclosure which accompanied it, in order that in any further proceedings of the assembly on this subject, they may be informed of the circumstances represented by the chief justice.

"I have the honor to be, sir,

Your most obedient humble servant,

"J. C. SHERBROOKE, govr. in chief.

L. J. PAPINEAU, esq., speaker of the house of assembly."

val of the impeachments, moved, on the 27th January, that a call of the house should take place on the 21st February. This motion was

The following are the letters above referred to:—
(Copy.) " MONTREAL, Feby. 14th, 1817.

"Sir,—As I find that the house of assembly is proceeding under a committee, upon a petition presented to that house by Samuel Sherwood, one of the members thereof, made early in the session of the present legislature, wherein he has stated, " that I had absented myself from sitting in, and holding a court of king's bench for the district of Montreal, on the first ten days of the month of March last past, whereby the said court was not held, and the law of the land was dispensed with, contrary to the bill of rights;" and as this assertion may improvidently be brought forth as a charge against my official character and duties, in a case where the prerogative of the crown has been legally exercised, and when the conduct of its officer is not culpable, I am impressed with the duty of presenting to your excellency my conduct, and the exercise of the prerogative, in respect to my duties upon holding the said court, in the month of March last.

Your excellency will perceive, by the enclosed letter, the exprsss injunctions of his excellency the administrator in chief, and may be a better judge than I can presume, of the reasons that occasioned his exercise of the rights of the sovereign, in respect to my duties.—And your excellency will justly appreciate how far the assembly should be permitted to proceed, in a formal charge, which, I submit, could not take place, were that house officially apprised of the circumstances attending the conduct that had superinduced a supposed culpability in a servant of the crown.

"I have the honor to be, &c.
(Signed) " J. MONK."
" His Excellency Sir JOHN COAPE SHERBROOKE,
" K. C. B., &c., &c., &c."
" A true copy, ANDW. WM. COCHRAN, secretary."

(Copy.) "CASTLE OF ST. LEWIS, Quebec, 15th Feb., 1816.
"Sir,—With reference to the representation you have made to his excellency the administrator in chief, of your intention of proceeding shortly to Montreal, to attend there the approaching session of the king's bench, for the trial of criminal causes, I am commanded by his excellency to acquaint you, that he conceives your presence here indispensably necessary, to preside as speaker of the legislative council."
" I have the honor to be, &c.
(Signed) " ROBERT R. LORING, secretary."
" The hon. chief justice MONK."
" A true copy of the original letter,
" ANDW. WM. COCHRAN, secretary."

rejected, (yeas 10, nays 23.)* He immediately moved a second time, for a call on the 20th of the same month, but this also was rejected, affording evidence of the reluctance of the assembly, from, as said, the state of the country, to re-enter upon the consideration of the subject. It was, however, resolved on the following day (28th January) that the house would go into committee of the whole on the 22nd February, to take into consideration the message of the late administrator-in-chief, (Sir Gordon Drummond) of the 2nd February last. The matter, nevertheless, lay over to nearly the close of the session, Mr. Stuart having occasion to absent himself in attendance upon his private affairs at Montreal where he resided; but, in the meantime, measures were concerted and a negociation carried on at once to paralize his measures, recompense Mr. Sewell for the ill treatment he had experienced, and relieve the government from the embarrassing dilemma in which it was placed, and which perfectly succeeded. The game was as follows:—

A provision had been made, as previously seen, for a salary to the speaker (Mr. Papineau) of the assembly during the last parliament, but none as yet, for the present. Here was a groundwork to proceed upon, with a prospect of success. Mr. Sewell was speaker of the

---

* " Yeas—Messrs. Gauvreau, Bruneau, Bellet, Huot, Sherwood, Viger, A. Stuart, J. Stuart, Cuvillier, and Dénéchau,—10."

" Nays—Messrs. Borgia, Vanfelson, Panet, Vézina, Giugy, Ogden, Davidson, Taschereau, M‘Cord, Dumont, Allsopp, Cockburn, Déligny, Mayrand, Lacombe, Malhiot, Richer, Cherrier, Lagueux, Dessaulles, Bondy, Fournier and Souligny,—(23.)

legislative council, and enjoyed its confidence to an eminent degree. That body had asserted the claim of its speaker to a salary, as well as that of the lower house, and it was evident that no bill making a provision for the one would pass in the council, unless with a like provision for the other.

The assembly voted on the eleventh of March, addresses to the governor " representing to his excellency that the house being impressed with the propriety and necessity of remunerating the speaker thereof, by an annual salary, for the arduous and important duties of his high office—humbly prayed his excellency would take the same into consideration, and allow him such annual salary as he should deem an adequate and sufficient remuneration therefor, from the commencement of the present parliament to the end thereof, and that he would direct the same to be charged upon and taken from the funds raised under the act for the payment of the salaries of the officers of the legislative council and house of assembly, assuring his excellency that if those funds proved insufficient the house would make good the same,"—and, furthermore. that " his excellency would be graciously pleased to confer some signal mark of the royal favor on Dame Louise Philippe Badelard, widow of the late honourable Jean Antoine Panet, late speaker of the house, in testimony of the great and eminent services performed by him to his country, for the space of twenty years and upwards, during which he had, with such distinguished ability and integrity, presided in the chair of that house without any recompense or remuneration, and to the great detriment of his health and fortune—assuring his excellency that whatever expenses he should think proper to be incurred on that account, the house would make good the same to his Majesty."

In answer to the former of these addresses, his excellency informed the messengers, who waited upon him, with them, that—

" The legislative council having, by their address of the fourth of March, one thousand eight hundred and fifteen, stated, that that house is impressed with the expediency of remunerating their speaker also by an annual salary, for the arduous and important duties attached to his high office, and having prayed that such measures may be adopted for that purpose as may seem meet, he would readily comply with the wishes of the assembly, and make an adequate and proper remuneration for the services and duties of the speaker of that house, from the commencement of the present provincial parliament to the end thereof, upon being enabled to make a similar provision for the speaker of the legislative council, for the same period."

In answer to the latter, he acquainted them, that in compliance with their request, and in consideration of the sense he entertained for the long service and great merit of the late speaker, he had, in his Majesty's behalf, conferred an annuity on his widow of three hundred pounds currency during her life.

Upon receipt of these answers the house of assembly immediately resolved *nem con* :—

" That an humble address be presented to his excellency the governor in chief, stating that, inasmuch as his excellency has taken into consideration the address of the legislative council, of the fourth of March, one thousand eight hundred and fifteen, to the then governor, representing the expediency of remunerating their speaker, by an annual salary, for the arduous and important duties attached to his high office, and praying also the then governor to adopt such measures, as to him might seem meet, and his excellency having been pleased in consequence to allow an annual salary to the speaker of that body, this house assures his excellency, that in making good the sums which his excellency may cause to be expended for the payment of the salary of the speaker of the assembly, this house will also make good the sums which his excellency may cause to be expended for the payment of the salary of the speaker of the legislative council."

This address being presented to the governor, he sent, on the 17th March, a message to the assembly to inform them that, in consequence of their addresses, he had conferred, on each of the speakers, an annual salary of one thousand pounds currency, from the commencement, of that parliament, until the end thereof.

This seasonable communication was decisive of the matter in dispute with respect to the impeachments, which stood for discussion, on the 19th of March. Accordingly, when, on that day, the order was read for going into committee, to take into consideration the message of the administrator in chief to the assembly, dated the second day of February one thousand eight hundred and sixteen, it was first moved, by Mr. Sherwood, that the order of the day be postponed till the 27th March instant, and that a call of the house be made on that day. But it was then moved by Mr. Ogden in amendment, " that the said order of the day be discharged, and that the subject matter thereof be taken into consideration at the next session of the provincial parliament." Long and warm debates ensued which continued until the following morning, when, upon a division of the house, the motion in amendment prevailed, (22 against 10*) disposing of the matter by postponement; in other words, virtually retracting the impeachments which a former assembly had brought against the chief justices, and absolving them both, after having recompensed Mr. Sewell for the trouble and anxiety to which they had put him; his income now, in his double capacity, of chief justice of the province and speaker of the legislative council, exceeding £2,500, sterling, a year.

Never was cause more powerfully advocated, nor a more brilliant display of oratory and talents exhibited, than by Mr. Stuart on this occasion, who must have felt that he was contending against the current, and that there was a preconcerted and foregone conclusion on the subject, which it was in vain to struggle against. Abandoned by the party whom he hitherto led, or had imagined himself to lead, this put an end to his connection with it, and he finally took his leave of them in disgust, returning on the morrow of their desertion of

---

* " Yeas—Messrs. Huot, Bellet, Bruneau, Viger, Badeaux, Taschereau, Languedoc, Allsopp, Panet, Vézina, Després, Gauvreau, Roy, Duchesnois, Jones, Cockburn, Vanfelson, Turgeon, M'Cord, Ogden, Gugy, and Dessaulles.

" Nays—Messrs. James Stuart, A. Stuart, Sherwood, Davidson, Borgia, Cuvillier, Brehaut, Dénéchau, Lagueux, and O'Sullivan."

him and his defeat, to Montreal, in pursuit of his private avocations, appearing no more in parliament, until afterwards, towards the conclusion of lord Dalhousie's administration, when appointed attorney general, and then but for a session.

Besides the appropriations of relief previously mentioned, fifty-five thousand pounds were voted for the improvement of internal communications, and upwards of two thousand pounds for the encouragement of vaccine inoculation. The revenue of the year ending, on the 1st January, 1817, amounted to £138,791 currency, (exclusive of the expenses of collection, £5,834,) and the expenditure to £75,638 sterling, including £24,495, paid as the proportion of duties to Upper Canada, for the year 1815,

The expenses of the legislature, for the same period, were £3.203, currency; the salaries of the judges which had been, heretofore, £750, sterling—it now appeared by the public accounts were increased, since the 10th May, 1816, to £900 sterling, (£1000 currency,) but by what authority is not stated, though probably by order from home, upon their application. The balance of monies, according to those accounts, remaining unappropriated and at the disposal of the legislature, was £140,153, currency. The revenue was in fact productive and the country flourishing.

The governor closed this long and important session on the 22d March, with a brief speech, thanking the legislature for the readiness with which the supplies required for relieving the distressed parishes and other public services had been granted; and impressing upon their minds the necessity of using their influence to cherish and encourage that spirit of loyalty, industry and harmony, so essential to the prosperity and happiness of the people.

Chap. XXI.
1817.

The Montreal bank, the first institution of the kind in Canada, was set on foot this summer by an association of merchants in that city, whose example was followed, soon after, by those of Quebec, in the establishment of the Quebec bank, the intended utility of both of which, to the trade and general interests of the country, has been fully realized by those and other banks subsequently formed with the view of facilitating commerce. The appearance of the first steamer on the St. Lawrence, between Quebec and Montreal, has been mentioned in the first volume. The following quotation from the Upper Canada Gazette of the 17th July, 1817, announces the expected appearance of the first steamer on the waters of that province, and the great lakes of Canada. The anticipations of the writer have been more than realized in the splendid conveyances which the traveller now finds from Quebec to Kingston, and thence daily traversing those magnificent expanses of inland fresh water seas, to Cleveland, Detroit, and onward to Chicago, on lake Michigan :—

" A small steamboat is now building at Prescott, intending to pass between that port and Kingston, and another at Ernest Town, for the bay of Quinte. It is said that some steamboats are building on lake Erie. We may confidently expect that the period is not far distant when there will be a continued chain of steamboats from Quebec to Queenston, and thence (except the Portage by the falls of Niagara,) to Drummond Island, on lake Huron. The impediments to the navigation of the St. Lawrence, may, and we hope will shortly be removed, at a comparatively small expense, when the transport of merchandise and produce may be effected at so moderate a price, and in so short a time, as to bid defiance to any efforts the americans can make, by means of their long projected canal, to divert the natural channel of commerce of the whole of the country bordering on the lakes: that portion of the States, situated nearest the Mohawk River, will, of course, find the canal the cheapest mode of conveying their produce to market; but those more distant, will prefer, for the same reason, the old channel.

From the prorogation of parliament to the following session we meet with no incident of any public moment. The legislature met on the 7th January, 1818. The governor informed them that the liberal provision made at the previous meeting, not only for the immediate relief of the sufferers, but also for furnishing the husbandmen with seed wheat and other grain, for the season, had been attended with the happiest consequences:—

"I have received the commands of his royal highness the Prince Regent, to call upon the provincial legislature to vote the sums necessary for the ordinary annual expenditure of the province.—These commands will, I am persuaded, receive from you that weighty consideration, which their importance deserves.

"Gentlemen of the house of assembly,—In pursuance of these directions, which I have received from his Majesty's government, I shall order to be laid before you, an estimate of the sums which will be required to defray the expenses of the civil government of the province, during the year one thousand eight hundred and eighteen; and I desire you in his Majesty's name to provide, in a constitutional manner, the supplies which will be necessary for this purpose. I shall also order to be laid before you the accounts of the public revenue and expenditure for the last twelve months, by which you will be enabled to ascertain the means of supply that are at your disposal; and I anticipate, with confidence, a continuance of that loyalty and zeal for his Majesty's service, on your part, which I have hitherto experienced, and a ready execution of the offer which you made on a former occasion, to defray the expenses of his Majesty's government, with a liberality that did you honor."

The assembly, in answer to his excellency's speech, observed:—

"Your excellency has done us justice in expressing your confidence in our loyalty and zeal for his Majesty's service, and expressing your hope of our fulfilling, during the present session, those offers which a sense of duty and gratitude heretofore impelled the commons of this province to make, of defraying the civil expenditure of his Majesty's provincial government."

This call of the regent, was received by the public with satisfaction. The settlement of a provincial civil list, and controul of the public expenditure by the assembly, had been long desired, and given rise, as we have seen, to much heat and some trouble, and it was now hoped that a provision, once for all, on the subject, would set it at rest. But the matter was not contemplated in the same point of view by all who looked towards it. Instead of tranquilising it helped, as the sequel will shew, to bring on, after some years of agitation on that and other subjects, still greater difficulties than before, ending unhappily, in disaster and blood. Some saw in it, indeed, but the means of giving efficiency to the government, for its ordinary indispensable action, by a permanent provision for the purpose, and of a salutary and constitutional check upon the executive government annually, as to the extraordinaries, which, in the rising and improving state of the colony, it necessarily must recur for, year after year to the assembly. Others seem to have viewed it as the means of establishing an undue sway on the part of the commons of the province over the government, at variance with the form and spirit of the british constitution and subversive of it, by insisting upon the right of subjecting each department of the government to an annual vote for the supply necessary to carry it on, and every individual thereof, to an annual dependence upon the assembly, for the salary attached to his office, a pretension, if realised, that must at once change the constitution into a republic.*

---

* The civil list and financial difficulties, as they were termed, connected with it, being the prolific source whence all the other questions that agitated Lower Canada sprung, and which the reader will, no doubt, follow through their various phases, with much interest, he may read with advantage, the following letters that passed between Sir John C. Sherbrooke and Earl Bathurst, the colonial minister, giving rise to the " call" upon the legislature, " annually to vote all the sums required for the ordinary annual expenditure of the province."

" QUEBEC, 18th March, 1817.

" My Lord,—In my despatch, No. 19, of the 23d August last, I had the honor of transmitting to your lordship a general statement of the permanent revenue of the province for the year ending 5th January 1816 and of the ordinary and extraordinary charges upon it, by which your lordship would see that the permanent expenditure in that year exceeded the revenue appropriated to its discharge, by the sum of nearly £19,000.—I now beg leave to call your lordship's attention to the debt which, by this excess has, from year to year, become due by government to the province.

" The amount which had accumulated to the end of the year 1812, was repaid into the provincial chest by sir George Prevost, from the

It being understood that the governor had Chap.
received despatches relating to the articles of XXI.
impeachment against Mr. justice Foucher, by 1818.

extraordinaries of the army; but in the three years following, the excess of the permanent civil expenditure, amounting annually to £20,000, more or less, was taken out of the unappropriated monies of the province, and may, therefore, be now considered as a debt which government may be obliged to repay into the civil chest, whenever the province shall choose to call for it.

" To this there is also to be added the deficiency in the year ending 5th January, 1817. which will appear to your lordship, from the summary statement which I have the honor herewith to enclose.— This account states the balance at the disposal of the legislature, on the 5th January last, to be £140,151—but to make up this sum in the hands of the receiver general, a deficiency remained to be supplied of £7,472, and it also appears that in the above balance there are included three sums amounting altogether to £35,463, which as they have been charged against the province and considered as actual appropriations, though not called for, cannot be considered as part of the balance at the disposal of the legislature. These, therefore, being added to the actual deficit of £7,172, form a total of £42,935, as the deficiency for this year, which, with the amount of the annual excess in the three preceding years of the permanent expenditure over the permanent appropriated revenue, at the rate of £20,000, more or less, in each year, makes the debt now due to the province to be about £120,000.

" Your lordship will, I think, agree with me that the practice of expending the provincial revenue for services for which the legislature has not provided, has been, from the first, irregular, and that it would have been better if the annual deficiency of the permanent appropriated revenue to meet the charges upon it had been, in each year, made up from the extraordinaries of the army, instead of allowing a debt to grow up which may create confusion, embarrassment and misunderstanding.

" It is true, that an account of the greater part of this unauthorised expenditure has, in each year, been laid before the legislature, and that no notice has been taken of it, nor objection made. But this does not render that expenditure the less irregular in the first instance, nor does it ensue that the legislature may not, at some future day, consider it as an unauthorised temporary expedient, and may assert the right of the province to the repayment of the sum so expended in each year, without a regular appropriation. And it is further to be considered, that the whole accounts are not laid before the legislature, there being a class of warrants to the amount of £6,000, on an average, yearly, (including principally the salary of the clergy and pensioners) authorised by his Majesty's government, which are thrown into a separate list, and have generally, hitherto, been provided for out of the extraordinaries of the army, though paid, in the first instance, out of the civil chest. Of these warrants I enclose your lordship an abstract of the last year.

Chap. XXI.
1818.

which their adjudication, it was said, was to be left to the legislative council, an address to his excellency on the subject, was proposed, and

"Your lordship will concur with me as to the necessity of rescuing the finances of the province from the confusion into which they have fallen, by the expenditure, from year to year, of its unappropriated monies; and the questions that, upon the whole matter, appear to me to arise for your lordship's consideration, are these:—with respect to the past, whether the large debt which I have above stated to have accumulated shall be repaid from the extraordinaries of the army, or whether it would be advisable to call on the legislature to cover it by a general appropriation:—and with respect to the future, whether the annual deficiency created by the excess of the annual permanent expenditure over the permanent revenue appropriated to its discharge, shall, in each year, be made up from the extraordinaries of the army, or whether it will be adviseable to submit to the legislature at the commencement of each session, (as the practice is in Nova Scotia and other colonies) an estimate of the sums that will be required for the civil list, and to call on them to make provision accordingly. On these several points, I earnestly entreat your lordship will favour me with particular instructions.

"I have the honor to be, &c.,
(Signed) "J. C. SHERBROOKE."

Answers to the above from lord Bathurst to Sir J.C. Sherbrooke:—

"DOWNING STREET, 31st August, 1817.

"Sir,—I have not failed to take into my serious consideration that part of your despatch, No. 19, which relates to the debt which has become due to the province, in consequence of an accumulation, during the last four years, of the annual excess of the actual expenditure beyond the appropriated revenue of each year. I entirely concur with you in the opinion which you have expressed, that the annual settlement of the accounts of each year, between government and the province, would have been at once the most expedient course, and most likely to prevent any interruption of a mutual good understanding. Under existing circumstances, however, the only point for consideration, as far as relates to the past, is, whether the legislature may not fairly be considered as having sanctioned this appropriation of the funds, by not objecting to it, when submitted to their notice, or whether any further measures are required either for legalising the appropriation itself, or for repaying the debt, which, under other circumstances, may be considered due to the province.

"With respect to some part of the expenditure, the silence of the legislature must be interpreted into an approbation of it, for they could not but think themselves bound to make good the deficiency of the funds appropriated by them to specific objects,—such, for instance, as the charge for the Trinity House, and the payment of the officers of the legislature, which have, I believe, uniformly exceeded the amount of the funds raised under the 33d, 45th, and 51st of the king; and I,

after some debates, carried in that house.—
It prayed his excellency to inform the
house, whether his royal highness the Prince

therefore, see no objection to considering the silent admission of the accounts submitted to them as an implied approbation of the accounts themselves, and of the manner in which they have been discharged. With respect to the future, I consider it certainly more advisable, that the legislature should be annually called upon to vote all the sums required for the ordinary annual expenditure of the province. No rational ground can be assigned why the salaries of the pensioners for provincial services, and of the clergy, should not be paid by those who benefit by their labours ; and there is every reason against charging them on the extraordinaries of the army of this country, as has hitherto been the practice, nor indeed with respect to other charges usually defrayed out of the extraordinaries, do I see any reason except in very special instances, for adhering to a practice which, as it had its origin in the inadequacy of the colonial revenue to meet the annual expenditure, ought not to survive the state of things in which it originated.

" I have the honor to be, &c..
  (Signed) " BATHURST."
" His excellency lieut. gen. Sir JOHN C. SHERBROOKE."

" DOWNING STREET, 8th September, 1817.
" Sir,—With reference to that part of my despatch, No. —, of the 31st ult., which instructs you to call upon the legislature of the province to provide annually, for that part of the provincial expenditure which has heretofore been defrayed out of the army extraordinaries, it appears to me necessary to prepare you for the possible, though I trust, not probable contingency of the house of assembly voting that part of the pension list which provides the stipends of the roman catholic clergy, and omitting the other part which has reference to the maintenance of the protestant establishment. You will be careful, in such case, to use every means in your power, for procuring the rejection of such a partial vote in the legislative council ; or in the event of its being carried there also, you will not consider yourself authorised to give your assent to any vote, unless it shall make the usual provision for the protestant as well as the roman catholic establishment. If it should be proposed in the assembly to vote the stipends of each clergy separately, you will guard against the probability of a partial provision, by taking care that no proceeding be had in the council, on the provision for the roman catholic church, until that for the protestant church shall have been duly made by the assembly.

" I take this opportunity of calling your particular attention to the necessity of vigilantly guarding against any assumption, on the part of the legislative assembly, of a power to dispose of public money, without the concurrence of the other branch of the legislature. A claim to such a privilege has been formerly advanced by them, but has hitherto been successfully resisted ; and, as the necessity of the

Regent had signified his pleasure upon the address presented by the legislative council to his excellency last session, to be laid at the foot of the throne, relative to the articles of complaint against the honorable Louis Charles Foucher; and in case his royal highness had signified his pleasure thereupon, that his excellency would be pleased to communicate to them the same, or such part thereof, as in his wisdom, he might think proper.

In answer to this, a message came down to both houses from the governor, informing them that having transmitted their addresses of the previous session to the Prince Regent, he had it in command from his royal highness to signify his decision that, in this and all similar cases of impeachment by the assembly, the adjudication of the charges preferred against the party accused, should be left to the legislative council. He further informed them, that not having received from his royal highness any instructions as to the manner in which this his decision was to be carried into execution, he had been under the necessity of recurring to his royal highness for his pleasure in this respect, and for such instructions as he might see fit to give thereupon, and which when

---

whole legislature concurring, in order to give validity to a grant of public money, is almost the only substantial check upon the proceedings of the assembly, you will, I am sure, concur with me in opinion that it is more than ever necessary that it should not be relaxed or abandoned.

" I have the honor to be, &c.,

(Signed) " BATHURST."

" His excellency lieut. general Sir JOHN C. SHERBROOKE."

received he would not fail to communicate, as soon thereafter, as might be practicable.

An address of thanks by the legislative council to the Prince Regent, was drawn up and forwarded through the governor to his royal highness, for the signification of his most gracious pleasure in answer to the address from that house, of the previous session, " that in the case of Mr. justice Foucher, and in all cases of impeachment by the assembly of this province, the adjudication of the charges preferred against the party accused, shall be left to the legislative council"—" We at the same time"—they said,—" humbly beg leave to assure your royal highness, that the great and important parliamentary privilege conferred upon the legislative council, is considered by this house as the highest mark of confidence that the crown can bestow upon it, and that it will ever be the earnest wish and endeavour of this house so to discharge the important duties which, under this arrangement will devolve upon the legislative council, as to give complete satisfaction to your royal highness, and to all classes of his Majesty's subjects in this province."

This decision of the regent raised the legislative council, which had recently been increased in numbers by the introduction of some new members, on the recommendation of the governor, much in its own estimation, and several of the body were for immediately taking cognizance of the articles of impeachment against Mr.

Foucher. No movement to that purpose, however, was made in the assembly, where an opinion prevailed that, to give effect to the views of the Regent in the matter, an act of the provincial legislature was necessary. It was, nevertheless, moved in the legislative council, to resolve " that the declaration of the royal pleasure contained in his excellency's message, doth vest in the legislative council full and complete authority to enter on the immediate exercise, if necessary, of the constitutional and parliamentary privilege thereby granted to this house." The chief justice and others in the council, were of opinion that the declaration of itself was not sufficient to authorise the house to form itself into a judicial body, and that a special commission for the purpose was requisite. This opinion prevailing, the proposed resolution was lost, after some long and warm debates upon it, during the greater part of two days. The governor, by referring the matter to to the government at home, probably acted upon the advice of the chief justice, but no definite answer on the point has ever been communicated to the legislature, and to the present time, (1848) it remains undetermined.*

---

* The only further communication on this matter, to the legislature, was made at the following session, by the duke of Richmond. to the assembly, being in terms as follows :—

" The governor in chief acquaints the house of assembly, that he has received the instructions of his royal highness the Prince Regent. as to the manner in which his royal highness' commands respecting the proceedings of the house of assembly against Mr. justice Foucher. which were communicated to the assembly by message, upon the second day of March last, are to be carried into execution.

" His royal highness the Prince Regent, considers it most advisea-

The estimates for the civil expenditure were sent down late in the session. They amounted to £73,646, currency. To meet this, the funds already by law provided for the purpose, would amount, it was stated, to £33,383, upon an average of the last three years, leaving a balance to be provided for, of £40,263, for the current year.—This was voted after long debates on the subject, during nearly a week, and by an address of the house to the governor, the amount was placed at his disposition, the further consideration of the matter being postponed to the next session, when it was proposed that the civil list should be provided for by bill, to put it upon a proper constitutional footing.

Some important acts were passed this session; among them one incorporating a company, with authority to open a navigable canal from Chambly to St. John's, to avoid the rapids, between those places.—The company did not, however, take effect, and the work

---

ble, and has accordingly been pleased to direct, that the assembly, previous to any ulterior proceedings, do adduce without delay, and do deliver to his grace the governor in chief, such documentary evidence as they may consider adequate to support the charges which they have brought against Mr. justice Foucher, and that copies of such charges, of such documentary evidence, and of the examinations already taken and annexed to the charges, be then transmitted by his grace the governor in chief, to Mr. justice Foucher, for his answer and defence.

" And his royal highness has been further pleased to direct, that the answer and defence of Mr. justice Foucher, be by his grace the governor in chief, communicated to the assembly, for their reply, and that the whole of the documents, as soon as the reply of the assembly shall be received, shall be by him transmitted to his royal highness the Prince Regent, for such further course as the case may require."

was subsequently undertaken and accomplished at the expense of the province.—Another was passed for establishing a watch and night lights, in each of the cities of Quebec and Montreal. An act to encourage agriculture, and another authorising the appointment of commissioners for improving the communication by water with Upper Canada, were also passed. An effort was made towards obtaining an indemnity to the members of the assembly, for their attendance at the session, but failed.

The revenues for 1817, amounted in the total to £108,925, currency, and expenditure to £116,920, sterling, including £19,426 to Upper Canada, for its proportion of the duties levied in Lower Canada, in 1816. The expenses of the legislature were £16,173, including the salaries to the two speakers, £3,665 for contingencies from 1st May, 1815—and £3,945 for books purchased for the library of the assembly. Three hundred and thirty-four vessels, containing in all 76,559 tons, including one built at Quebec, and employing 3,950 men, were cleared out from Quebec, during this summer. The merchandize imported, upon which the duty of $2\frac{1}{2}$ per cent. was levied, amounted to £672,876, currency.

The governor being, from illness, unable to go down to the council chamber, to prorogue the legislature, the members of the two houses waited upon him at the castle, for the purpose, on the 1st of April, and were dismissed with his best acknowledgments for the assiduity with which they had despatched the public business.

Sir John C. Sherbrooke's ill health, had induced him to request his recall from the government; but, indeed, he made no scruple in expressing frequently his dislike of the "dirty work," as he expressed it, expected of him, in the position he occupied, and his determination to withdraw from it as soon as possible. He was relieved by the duke of Richmond, and sailed on the 12th of August, for England, in the Iphigenia frigate, receiving, on the eve of his departure, from all classes and from various quarters, the most satisfactory addresses, and retiring from the government, evidently with much more gratification than he had come to it.

The remains of the late general Montgomery which had reposed within the walls of Quebec, since his fall before it, in the night of the 31st December, 1775, were, this year, at the request of his widow, Mrs. Montgomery, one of the Livingston family of the state of New York, to sir John C. Sherbrooke, exhumed by his excellency's orders, and given up to major Livingston, a relation of that lady, to be conveyed by him for reinterment in the country in whose cause he had fallen. The exhumation was made, on the 16th June, 1818, in the presence of captain Freer, one of his excellency's personal staff—major Livingston, and a few other spectators, under the direction of the late Mr. James Thompson of the engineer department, who forty-two years before, had laid the remains of the general in the ground with the bodies of his two aides de camp, Cheeseman and McPherson, one on each side of him. The place of interment (the bastion south of St. Lewis gate, and immediately adjoining it,) had changed its appearance very considerably since 1775, owing to the demolition of an old powder magazine which stood there, and the erection of new buildings near it. Mr. Thompson, however, retained a sufficient recollection of the whereabout he lay, to dig for the coffin, and on removing the earth it was immediatly found where he stated it to be. Mr. Thompson one of the followers of general Wolfe, and present with him on the plains of Abraham where he so gloriously fell;

Chap. XXI.
1818.

a man as all who knew him can vouch, of the highest moral character and respectability, gave the following certificate of facts, in order to satisfy the surviving, relatives and connections, of the late general Montgomery, of the identity of the relics of which they were anxious to be possessed, and whereof there cannot be a doubt:—

"I James Thompson of the city of Quebec, in the province of Lower Canada, do testify and declare that I served in the capacity of an assistant engineer, during the siege of this city—invested during the years 1775 and 1776 by the american forces, under the command of the late major general Montgomery. That in an attack made by the american troops, under the immediate command of general Montgomery, in the night of the 31st December, 1775, on a british post, at the southernmost extremity of the city, near *Pres de Ville*, the General received a mortal wound, and with him were killed his two aides de camp. McPherson and Cheeseman, who were found in the morning of the 1st January, 1776, almost covered over with snow.—That Mrs. Prentice who kept an Hotel at Quebec, and with whom general Montgomery had previously boarded, was brought to view the body, after it was placed in the guard room, and which she recognised by a particular mark which he had on the side of his head, to be the general's. That the body was then conveyed to a house (Gobert's) immediately opposite to the president's residence, by order of Mr. Cramahé, (who was president in the absence of the lieutenant governor) who provided a genteel coffin for the general's body, which was lined inside with flannel and outside of it with black cloth.—That in the night of the 4th January, it was conveyed by me from Gobert's house, and was interred six feet in front of the gate in a wall that surrounded a powder magazine, near the ramparts bounding on Louis gate.— That the funeral service was performed at the grave by the reverend Mr. de Montmollin, then chaplain of the garrison. That his two aides de camps were buried in their clothes, without any coffins; and that no person was buried within twenty-five yards of the general.— That I am positive and can testify and declare that the coffin of the late general Mongomery taken up on the morning of the 16th of the present month of June, 1818, is the identical coffin deposited by me, on the day of his burial, and that the present coffin contains the remains of the late general. I do further testify, and declare, that subsequent to the finding of general Montgomery's body I wore his sword, being lighter than my own, and on going to the seminary where the american officers were lodged, they recognised the sword, which affected them so much that numbers of them wept, in consequence of which I have never worn the sword since.

"Given under my hand at the city of Quebec, province of Lower Canada, 19th June, 1818.   JAMES THOMPSON."

ERRATUM.—For " different," in the fourth line of page 269, read—*indifferent*—and for " views," in the nineteenth line of same page, read—*causes*.

CHAPTER XXII.

Arrival of the duke of Richmond—assumes the government—meeting of the legislature—speech—estimates of the expenses of the civil government—proceedings thereupon—bill passed making provision by *items*, for the expenses of the year—rejected in the legislative council—reasons of rejection—various proceedings during the session—Mr. justice Bedard impeached—impeachment not sustained by the assembly—Mr. justice Foucher directed to resume his duties—proceedings relating to the revenue, and monies in the receiver general's hands—Eastern Townships—message by the governor in chief relating to them—prorogation with expressions of the governor's displeasure—miscellaneous remarks on the public improvement and progress of internal communications, trade, &c.—revenue and expenditure of 1818—Rideau canal commenced (1819)—Mr. Plessis, roman catholic bishop visits Europe—lord bishop of Quebec, Mr. Mountain, returns from England—immigration—duke of Richmond visits Upper Canada—his death—Mr. Monk administers the government—is superseded by Sir P. Maitland—dissolution of parliament—new assembly—declines entering upon business, the returns of members not being completed—dissolution by the demise of his Majesty George the third—George the fourth proclaimed—earl of Dalhousie governor in chief—arrives and relieves sir P. Maitland—general election—admirable speech of Mr. Papineau at the hustings.

THE appointment of the duke of Richmond, to the chief command in british North America, was received in Lower Canada with universal satisfaction. The country, it was hoped, could not but thrive under a nobleman who had administered, with success, the important government of Ireland, and whose rank and influence entitled him to the consideration of the imperial government. He assumed the administration of affairs in this province, on the 29th July, 1818. He was accompanied, on his arrival from England, by sir Peregrine Maitland, (his son in law) appointed lieutenant governor of Upper Canada.

The legislature met on the 12th January, 1819, but accounts of the death of the queen having arrived, his excellency informed the two houses that although the fact had not reached him officially, yet he had no doubt the event had taken place on the sixteenth of November last. He, therefore, conceived it to be incumbent on them all, to adjourn the public business for such a space of time as should shew their respect to the memory of her Majesty, and he consequently prorogued them to the 22d day of the month.

On their reassembling, he opened the session with the following speech:—

"Gentlemen of the legislative council, and gentlemen of the house of assembly,—The respect which we owed to the memory of her Majesty, our late revered queen, having been so far publicly manifested by your short prorogation, I now meet you with the assurance of my confidence in your zeal and assiduity, and on your union and loyalty, to promote by your labours, the best interests of this favoured province, inseparably connected with those of the mother country, and the honor of his Majesty's crown and government; in the progress of which, you may rely on my most cordial support and assistance.

"Gentlemen of the house of assembly,—His Majesty

having been pleased to accept the voluntary offer made by the representatives of the commons of this province, to provide for the expenses of the civil government, measures were adopted by your late governor in chief, Sir J. C. Sherbrooke, during your last session, to carry the same into effect, which you cheerfully supported; but having, by his illness, been prevented from completing the appropriations required, I consider it necessary to call your immediate attention to this subject, by which his administration, so honorably conducted, may be in this respect closed: and for this purpose I shall order the accounts of the actual expense of the civil government for the last year, and of the revenue collected during the same period, to be forthwith laid before you, in order that your course may be open to proceed on other financial objects.

"In like manner, the estimates of the expense for the present year, and of the amount of the revenue to be expected from the existing laws, will be prepared to be laid before you, that you may be able to attend to the whole of those measures which more peculiarly originate with your branch of the legislature.

"Gentlemen of the legislative council, and gentlemen of the house of assembly,—Your joint experience of the public affairs of this province, and your intimate acquaintance with the wants and interests of your fellow subjects, render it unnecessary for me, at this early period after my arrival, to call your attention to any particular objects of legislation; I shall, in the course of the session, communicate to you by messages, such matters as circumstances which may arise shall require.

"My earnest desire is to promote, to the utmost of my power, the prosperity of this rising colony; and I have no doubt of experiencing, from the union of your proceedings, the most satisfactory results to the interests of his Majesty's people and government."

The address of the assembly, in answer to the speech, was very complimentary to the governor personally, promising also that they would bestow their immediate attention on the

Chap. XXII.
1819.

Chap. XXII

1819.

expenses of the civil government, with a view to fulfilling their engagements on that head.

The estimate of the expenses of the civil government for the year 1819, was £81,432, sterling, being upwards of £15,000 over that of the previous year. This sudden increase, without any ostensible necessity, created dissatisfaction, and indisposed the generality of the assembly, who disapproved of the advice that had induced the governor to make so large a demand upon the country upon his advent. The estimate was referred to a select committee, by which, after being particularly examined, a report recommending in strong terms retrenchment and economy was made. " Your committee"—they observed in conclusion—" are of opinion that this house, on making a suitable provision for such offices as are indispensably necessary, will also act in conformity with the desire and interest of the province at large, by making an unqualified reduction of those sinecures and pensions, which, in all countries, have been considered as the reward of iniquities, and the encouragement of vice ; which, in the mother country have been, and still are a subject of complaint, and which, in this province, will lead to corruption."—A provision of £8,000, sterling, a year, for pensions, was unwisely proposed in the estimate as " the pension list at the disposal of his Majesty's representative, for rewarding provincial services, and providing for old and reduced servants of the government and others."

A small party, in the assembly, was for making, as in England, a permanent provision for the civil list, during the king's reign. Others were for granting an aid annually, for the purpose, in addition to the fund already by law provided, which although as yet inadequate, was on the increase, and might in time suffice. The latter was the prevailing opinion. The former party also insisted that if a supply were annually to be voted, it should be in a round sum, without specification of the particular *items* or salaries, to each functionary, or department, as the apportionment, it was said, constitutionally belonged to the crown. The assumption of such a right, by the assembly, as fixing to each officer his salary, and that annually, would, it was contended, establish a direct controul, by that body, over every individual functionary of the civil government, subvert the authority of the executive, and virtually establish a democracy. The majority, nevertheless, were determined not only to apportion by items the supply in aid of the civil list, and expenditure which, as their own free gift or grant, they maintained they had an undoubted right to do; but, also, to apportion the fund previously by law appropriated and vested for the purpose, in the crown, as a preliminary and condition of their grant in aid of it, in order to preserve a controul upon the total annual outlay. It was said that the quantum of aid annually to be supplied, depending much upon the frugality with which the excecutive applied the revenue, already at its disposal, an application of the whole by items under a vote of the assembly and act of the legislature, was the only pledge the country could have to be depended upon, of a faithful apportionment and outlay of that fund. It is clear from the above that the assembly had no confidence in the executive government.

The house of assembly, in committee of the whole, accordingly went through the civil list; fixing by its votes the several salaries to the various public functionaries, from the governor's, (then 4,500 sterling) downwards to the humblest on the list. Several offices were passed over and omitted as unnecessary or sinecures, and no provision made, by vote of the house for their salaries, in order that they might be abolished. A bill, in conformity to the votes, specifying them *item* by *item* was introduced, passed, and sent up to the legislative council, where it was roughly received and immediately rejected. The following resolution passed in the council on the subject, exhibits their views of it :—

" That the mode adopted by this bill, for granting a supply to his Majesty, to defray the expenses of the civil list, is unprecedented and unconstitutional, and a direct assumption on the part of the assembly, of the most important rights and prerogatives of the crown. That were the bill to be passed into a law, it would give to the commons of this province, not merely the constitutional privilege of providing the supplies, but the power also of prescribing to the crown the number and description of its servants, and of regulating and rewarding their services individually, as the assembly should, from time to time, judge meet or expedient, by which means they would be rendered dependant on an elective body instead of being dependent on the crown, and might eventually be made instrumental to the overthrow of that authority, which, by their allegiance, they are bound to support.

"That this house will proceed no further in the consideration of this bill."

Among the occurrences of the session the following deserve to be noted. A bill for making a navigable canal from Montreal to Lachine, by a company incorporated for the purpose, was passed, but like that of the previous session, for the intended Chambly canal, never being acted upon, was superseded by a subsequent enactment, making a provision from the funds of the province to effect that object. An appropriation of £3,000, was made to enable the government to lay out lands for the officers of militia, militiamen, and others, who had served in Canada, during the late war with the United States. The militia laws underwent revision and some alterations (disapproved of by the governor) were made in it, in particular to prevent the appointment of any person as an officer to a battalion, who should not be resident within the limits it occupied, and who was not an owner, or the son of an owner of real estate therein. Pierre Bédard, esquire, the provincial judge for the district of Three Rivers, was impeached by C. R. Ogden, esquire, a barrister practising in his court, for divers alleged high crimes and misdemeanors. The articles of impeachment were referred to a select committee, who after an inquiry reported against them, and they accordingly fell to the ground.* The impeachment against Mr. Justice Foucher not being persisted in, although the house resolved itself, several times, into committee, to consider the message sent to it on the subject ;† that gentleman was

---

* The articles of accusation against Mr. Bedard, were seven in all :

" *First*—That he had totally disregarded the high and important functions of his office—prostrated his judicial authority to the gratification of personal malice—infringed the personal liberty of divers subjects of his Majesty, and by tyrannical conduct disgraced the elevated judicial position in which he was placed.

" *Second*—That he had abused his powers as a judge, for pretended offences towards himself, in declaring the supposed aggressors guilty of the crime of contempt, in certain cases unauthorised by law, and by imposing upon them fines and disabilities, to which they were not by the laws of the land liable.

" *Third*—That he had uttered expressions derogatory to the honor, ability, and integrity of the other judges of the court in which he sat, and of the barristers therein, tending to reflect odium upon them, and brought the administration of justice, particularly in the district of Three Rivers, into disrepute and contempt.

" *Fourth*—That he had conducted himself, in the discharge of his duties, in a violent and abusive manner, towards the barristers, having accused them at divers times of high breaches of moral and professional rectitude, in a manner tending to subvert their characters and to destroy the confidence of their clients and the public, in their professional knowledge and exertions.

" *Fifth*—That he had, on the 3d July, 1816, falsely, wickedly, and maliciously, contrary to his own knowledge and to law, caused to be imprisoned in the common gaol of the district of Three Rivers, Chas. Richard Ogden, esquire, then and still being his Majesty's counsel for the said district, for an alleged libel and contempt against the provincial court in which Mr. Bedard was the judge.

" *Sixth*—That he had, on the 10th October, 1816, condemned, illegally and in contempt of the laws of the province, and without any reasonable cause, Pierre Vézina, esquire, an advocate practising in his court, to pay a fine of ten shillings, for pretended contemptuous conduct, and to be imprisoned until the fine was paid.

" *Seventh*—That he had, while presiding in the court, on the sixth and seventh days of April, 1818, and at divers other times, grossly and unjustifiably attacked the character of Joseph de Tonnancour, esquire, a barrister in his court, charging him with dishonorable practices, &c., derogatory to his professional character, &c., and in gross violation of his own dignity as a judge."

† See note *ante* page 300.

directed, shortly after the prorogation, to resume his functions as judge of the court of King's bench at Montreal.

The vices in the judicature had long been a subject of complaint in Lower Canada; yet no measure of reform had as yet been proposed.* The duke of Richmond now recom-

---

* In the session of 1815, a series of resolutions was passed explanatory of the reforms which, in the view of the assembly, it was proper should be made in the judicature, and upon them an address was voted to the regent, in which we find the following:—

" The experience of more than twenty years, has proved to his Majesty's faithful commons, that the constitution of the court of appeals, in this province, is not adapted to the attainment of the great objects of justice, uniformity and certainty, in legal decisions; as the chief justices who respectively preside in the courts of original jurisdiction for the districts of Quebec and Montreal, in like manner usually preside alternately in the court of appeals; and assisted by four of his Majesty's executive council, alternately revise the judgments rendered in the courts of original jurisdiction; and thus the chief justice of the district of Quebec, revises judgments rendered in the court over which presides the chief justice of the district of Montreal; and the chief justice of the district of Montreal revises the judgments rendered in the court, over which presides the chief justice of the district of Quebec; and this inconvenience is by no means alleviated by the composition of this court, as to its other members; for the judgments of the courts of original jurisdiction, in which sit four judges educated in the law, are thus revised by a court composed of members of his Majesty's executive council, whose rank in society, and whose attainments in other branches of learning, can but ill supply the want of legal knowledge

" His Majesty's faithful commons most humbly beg leave to represent also, that the constitution of his Majesty's courts of criminal jurisdiction for this province, is ill adapted to produce uniformity and certainty in the administration of the criminal law of England in this province; and that his Majesty's loyal subjects resident therein, do not, therefore, enjoy the full benefit of that wise and humane system of laws.

" His Majesty's faithful commons also most humbly represent, that the district of Three Rivers, according to the present constitution of his Majesty's courts of original jurisdiction in this province, as also the more remote parts of the districts of Quebec and Montreal, are subject to great and peculiar inconveniences in the obtaining of justice.

" His Majesty's faithful commons beg leave to lay before your Royal Highness, certain resolutions of the house of assembly, expres-

mended the subject to the consideration of the assembly. It remained, however, unattended to, the executive having in that house no

sive of the inconveniences which result from the present constitution, of the courts of justice, and indicating the means which they humbly conceive adapted to remedy them; and they do most humbly beseech your Royal Highness graciously to take the whole into your consideration, and to give instructions to the governor of this province, to sanction a bill, to be passed by the provincial legislature, upon the principles of those resolutions; or to give such directions and commands upon the subject of the present prayer of his Majesty's faithful commons of this province, as your Royal Highness shall deem meet."

Among the resolutions alluded to above, the following deserve quotation, as being the first decided expression, by the assembly, of the propriety of withdrawing the judges from all participation in the political concerns of the province:—

" Resolved—That it is expedient, in order to secure the independence, and the undivided attention of the judges to the administration of justice, that they should not be withdrawn from their judicial duties by any other offices in the civil administration of the government of this province."

In addition to the foregoing, the following resolutions, on the same subject, were passed during the present session:—

* " Resolved—That it it is the opinion of this committee, that the existing constitution of the courts established in this province, by virtue of the provincial statute of the thirty-fourth Geo. III., are not adapted to produce uniformity or certainty in the administration of justice, either in civil or in criminal matters.

" Resolved—That it is the opinion of this committee, that it is expedient to alter the constitution of the provincial court of appeals.

" Resolved—That it is the opinion of this committee, that it is expedient to alter the constitution of the court of king's bench now established in this province.

" Resolved—That it is the opinion of this committee, that it is expedient and necessary to establish a superior and permanent tribunal, both for the administration of justice in civil matters, and for the administration of justice in criminal matters, having jurisdiction coextensive with the limits of the province, and that such superior and permanent tribunal be called the superior court of king's bench.

" Resolved—That it is the opinion of this committee, that it is expedient and necessary that a court of law, to be called the court of common or civil pleas in this province, be constituted and erected, composed of puisné justices, who within the districts of Quebec, Montreal and Three Rivers, shall have original jurisdiction, and may take cognizance of, hear, try, and determine, all causes of a civil nature, and wherein the king is a party, (those purely of admiralty jurisdiction excepted) according to the laws of this province."

ministry or members of the executive council, or others in its confidence sufficiently influential, in the body, to take up and carry into effect the governor's views, which were but in accordance with and pursuant to the suggestions of a former assembly.

A committee of five members was named to draw up, *first*—a general statement of the receipts of the provincial revenue of the crown, and of the disbursements by the receiver general, from the date of the constitution to the present time. *Secondly*—a detailed statement of all the appropriations made by the legislature, and of the amount paid upon each of them, by the receiver general, for the same period; and to state the balance and count the monies in the hands of the receiver general, belonging to the province, and to report the whole with all convenient despatch, which, however, was never done, for what reason does not appear. A recommendation had been made to the assembly, at the previous session, by the governor, to make some provision for the relief of the eastern townships, already grown into importance, and feeling great inconvenience from the want of a local judicature; the seat of the jurisdiction to which the inhabitants, scattered over a large tract of newly settled country, were subjected, being either at Montreal or Three Rivers, and so remote as to place justice almost beyond the reach of those who sought it, and exceedingly expensive and oppressive to those amenable to it. The consideration of their situation, nothing having then been done for them, was accordingly recommended anew by the duke of Richmond, who, by a message, called the attention of the assembly to the general state of that part of the province, denominated the eastern townships, observing that the peculiar disadvantages under which this newly settled and thriving part of the province was placed, rendered it highly expedient that efficient legislative provision should be made, in order to afford them a full enjoyment of those benefits which his Majesty's government desired should be had by all his subjects in the province. No legislative measure took place for their relief, however, until 1823, when the district of St. François was erected, by act of the provincial parliament, and a provincial judge appointed to it, in virtue thereof.

Business being despatched, or so much of it, at least, as was intended by the assembly should be; the governor prorogued the session on the 24th of April, with expressions of dissatisfaction at the proceedings of this branch:—

"You, gentlemen of the legislative council, have not disappointed my hopes,"—said his grace,—" and I beg to return you my thanks for the zeal and alacrity you have shewn in all that more immediately belongs to your body.

"It is with much concern I feel myself compelled to say, that I cannot express to you, gentlemen of the assembly, the same satisfaction, nor my approbation at the general result of your labours, (at the expense of so much valuable time) and of the principles upon which they rest, as recorded on your journals.

" You proceeded upon the documents which I laid before

you, to vote a part of the sum required for the expenses of the year one thousand eight hundred and nineteen, but the bill of appropriation which you passed, was founded upon such principles, that it appears from the journals of the upper house, to have been most constitutionally rejected: his Majesty's government has been thus left without the necessary supplies for supporting the civil administration of the province for the ensuing year, notwithstanding the voluntary offer and pledge given to his Majesty, by the resolve of your house, of the thirteenth of February, one thousand eight hundred and ten.

"Gentlemen of the legislative council, and gentlemen of the legislative assembly,—I recommended to you, by special message, the consideration of the judicature act, for such amendments as should appear necessary to remedy any inconvenience which time and experience, in the course of the administration of justice, may have pointed out as expedient: and I much regret, that this important object has not been brought so far to an issue, as would have enabled me to transmit the result of your proceedings to his Majesty's ministers, that the opinion and assistance of the law officers of the crown in England, might have been obtained, in aid of the local knowledge and practical experience of those characters, in this province, who have had the best opportunity of studying and understanding the subject. I trust, however, that you will be prepared to proceed effectually thereon, at an early day of the next session.

"It is with some reluctance I have given the royal assent to the militia bill, from a principle being introduced into it of which I do not approve. The information given me of the inconvenience which would arise from losing certain services specially reposed in them, for which no other provision is made by law, has induced me to assent to it, in confidence that it will be amended in the next session of the legislature. The necessity of placing this local and constitutional military force, under proper and efficient regulations by law, is strongly impressed on my mind, and no impediment should be in the way of assisting it, whether embodied or sedentary, with the services of half-pay officers settled in the province, or others from the regular forces, as well as those of enterprising young men, drawn from the cities or towns on any emergency.

"The population of this province affords excellent materials for a defensive army; but a general and proper selection of officers is necessary, to make it formidable to an active and enterprising enemy, and that selection must, in all cases, belong to the executive power only.

"The present time affords you an opportunity of maturely deliberating on these important objects, and on others essentially necessary to be better considered. I recommend particularly to your attention, as individuals, the value of your constitution of government, which affords the most complete and ample protection and freedom of person and property, that can possibly be desired, and superior to every system of government enjoyed by any colony that has heretofore existed, your sister colony of Upper Canada excepted. And as branches of the legislature, it is of the first importance that you should fully understand your constitutional rights; that privilege may not come into question with prerogative, and that while you maintain those rights, which respectively belong to you by the constitution, you may be equally careful of encroaching on each other, and respectively pay a due regard to the rights of the crown."

This assumption of haranguing *en maitre*, and of schooling the assembly, indulged in by the duke of Richmond as well as by Sir J. Craig, was very offensive and produced much ill blood. It was thought unbecoming in the representative of a constitutional king to the representatives in parliament, of a people enjoying a free constitution, to whom it could not be otherwise than irritating. What, it was asked, would be said of a sovereign of the united kingdom, who should take upon himself so to rule his trusty and well beloved commons in parliament assembled? Nothing could be more adapted to wound the self respect of the native colonists, and to alienate their affections than the tone pervading those harangues, savouring rather of the language and spirit of an indignant lord and master, to his serfs, than of those from a wise and prudent governor of a british province, to a co-ordinate branch of the legislature of it.

In proof of the progressive march of improvement, in the communications by steamers on the lakes, a Montreal paper of the 15th May, makes the following remark. "The swift steamboat *Walk in the Water*, is intended to make a voyage early in the summer, from Buffalo on lake Erie to Michillimackinac, on lake Huron, for the conveyance of company. The trip has so near a resemblance to the famous argonautic expedition in the heroic, that expectation is quite alive on the subject." This trip is now, (1848) and for several years past, in the summer, of almost every day occurrence. The first steamer between Lachine and the Ottawa was also established in 1819. Four hundred and nine vessels, in all, 94,675 tons, employing 4,343 men, were during the last summer cleared out at Quebec, four of which were new and built there, the preceding winter. The amount of merchandise imported for the same year, paying the two and a half per cent duty, was £772,373, sterling. The gross revenue of the year was £89,673, currency: but, of this, after paying Upper Canada its proportion (18,673, stg.)

and deducting expenses of collection, and other incidents, there remained but the net amount of £56,332, sterling. The expenditure of the year was £127,379, sterling, included in which were £9,720 for the relief of parishes in distress, in 1817; £45,270, on account of army bills and towards the interest thereupon; £14,988, to Upper Canada, in payment of its *fifth* of duties collected during 1817, in Lower Canada—over and above all these are to be mentioned the salaries to officers of the legislature, including speakers and contingencies £13,420, currency. An article in the Quebec Mercury, (March 9, 1819) apparently from a well informed source, makes the population of Quebec, at this period, 15,257 souls.* The Rideau canal opening a communication between the river Ottawa and Kingston, in Upper Canada, was commenced this summer, an undertaking of great importance, and at the expense of the imperial government.

Mr. Plesis, the roman catholic bishop of Quebec, sailed for England in the beginning of July, this year, on a tour, intending to pass thence to the continent, visiting France and Italy

Division.	Catholics.	Protestants.	Total of Souls.	Dwelling Houses.
*Upper Town,	2100	1375	3475	424
Lower Town,	2223	1020	3243	400
Suburbs { St. John's	3340	428	3768	545
St. Roch's,	4178	433	4611	609
St. Vallier's,	150	10	160	30
	11991	3266	15257	2008

previous to his return. The prelate was accompanied on his voyage, by his secretary Mr. Turgeon and by Mr. Lartigue, of the seminary of Montreal. The lord bishop of Quebec, doctor Mountain, who had been some time absent from his diocese, on a visit to England, arrived at Quebec in H. M. ship Active, a few days after the departure of his confrère of the other church. In August an authentic report reached Quebec, that the pope had erected Canada into an archbishopric. "There is"—remarks the editor of the Quebec Mercury—"something in the reading of this power of the pope, within a british colony, that is not altogether pleasing to an english palate."

A considerable emigration from the united kingdom, (Ireland chiefly) into Canada, took place this season, the number of emigrants landed at Quebec, during the summer, being 12,434, many of them in very destitute circumstances. A society was formed, and liberal subscriptions made for their relief; but this, besides being a public burden at the moment, had a bad effect in holding out inducements to the advent of others, year after year, in the same miserable condition, and perpetuating the tax which for their relief the inhabitants thus imposed upon themselves.— The trade of the province was, however, rapidly increasing—the number of arrivals during 1819, at the port of Quebec, to the 12th October, being 612.

Chap. XXII.
1819.

The duke of Richmond visited, in 1818, soon after his arrival in the country from England, the upper province, to which he again paid a visit this summer, on a tour of inspection, contemplating, it is said, important improvements in the internal communications and military defences in the two provinces. He had nearly finished his tour, being on his way back to the lower province from Kingston to Montreal via the new military settlements between the St. Lawrence and Ottawa, when he took ill, and after a few hours excruciating suffering, died. His decease took place at Richmond, on the Ottawa, the 28th August, 1819. His remains were brought to Quebec, and deposited, with great pomp and ceremony, in the protestant cathedral church, on the 4th September; the civil and military authorities attending, and a vast concourse of citizens of all denominations, much affected by the premature loss of this excellent nobleman.

The government devolved, by the decease of the duke of Richmond upon Mr. Monk, the senior member of the executive council, who accordingly issued his proclamation, on the 20th September, notifying his assumption of the government. He was, however, shortly after superseded by sir Peregrine Maitland, the lieut. governor of Upper Canada, who, as the military officer commanding the forces in the Canadas, was directed by orders from England, to assume, as administrator in chief, the government of Lower Canada, until the

Earl of Dalhousie, promoted from the government of Nova Scotia, to the chief command of the british north american colonies, should relieve him, He, accordingly, repaired to Quebec, with his family, where he arrived on the 7th February, 1820, but immediately departed for Upper Canada, again to meet the legislature of that province, which was summoned for the 21st of the same month, leaving Mr. Monk in charge of affairs in the lower province. This gentleman previous to his knowledge of the appointment of sir Peregrine Maitland, had, by a proclamation, appointed the 29th February for the meeting of the legislature. This resolution was changed after the arrival of the administrator in chief, and on the day of his departure for Upper Canada, (9th Feb.) Mr. Monk issued a proclamation dissolving the parliament, and appointing the 11th April, ensuing, as the day upon which the writs for the new elections were to be returnable, except the writ for the county of Gaspé, the return whereof (one hundred days being then by law allowed for returns to writs of election for that county, owing to its remote situation and want of roads to connect it with the seat of government) was, by the same proclamation, extended to the 1st June next ensuing. This unexpected and impolitic measure, which the experience of former administrations had shewn to be prejudicial to the executive, by weakening its influence in the assembly, could not be otherwise explained, than by the difficulties which had arisen last session, with respect to the civil list. The elections, as on former occasions, were decisively unfavorable to those, who, in accordance with the views of the executive, had sided with it and combated the bill as passed by the assembly, providing for the civil list by items, and accordingly few of them were returned.

Sir Peregrine Maitland, having, after a short session, prorogued the parliament of Upper Canada, returned to Quebec, and on the 17th March, relieved Mr. Monk of the government.

The members, returned at the late elections, attended at Quebec, on the 11th April, in expectation of a session at the return of the writs, and the administrator in chief accordingly went down to the council chamber, and opened the session with a short speech. After the assembly had reelected their late speaker, Mr. Papineau, the first subject to which they turned their attention was an inquiry into their competence to proceed to the despatch of business, no member for the county of Gaspé having as yet been returned. In the meantime the governor sent a message to the house, recommending the renewal of certain acts of the legislature, to which no attention was paid. It being made apparent by returns ordered by the house to be produced and laid before it, by the clerk of the crown in chancery, that the number of fifty members, of which, by law, the assembly must consist, was not completed, it was, therefore, unanimously resolved, that the representation of the province being incomplete, no member having as yet been returned for Gaspé, "this house is incompetent, and cannot proceed to the despatch of business." The twelve months, within which the assembly ought by law to sit, were to expire on the 24th April, (the day twelvemonth from that on which the preceding session had closed last year) and unless a member were returned for Gaspé, on or before that day, so as to render the assembly competent for the dispatch of business within the year, it would become a question whether the late dissolution were not, in its consequences, a violation of the act of the imperial parliament, creating the constitution. These proceedings were formally communicated by address of the assembly, to the governor on the 20th April, who briefly expressed to the house his regret that the public business should be obstructed by its resolutions, which he observed, his duty constrained him to say, he did not admit to be in any respect well founded. The assembly, notwithstanding, persevered in their resolution, and refused to receive a message from the legislative council, by a master in chancery, against whom the door remained closed, although he was the bearer of a bill passed by that body, and sent down for the concurrence of the assembly. In this state of self-alleged incompetency the assembly remained until the 24th April, when the arrival of official news of his Majesty's death, of which unofficial accounts by way of New York, had previously reached Quebec, removed the dilemma, by affording the administrator a constitutional ground for dissolving the legislature. Going down, therefore, with the usual formalities, and summoning the attendance of the assembly, at the bar of the legislative council, he, without the least allusion to their proceedings, announced the King's demise, by which the crown of the united kingdom of Great Britain and Ireland, was rightfully come to his present most gracious Majesty George the fourth. The speaker of the legislative council, by command of the administrator in chief, then declared the provincial parliament, in consequence of the decease of our late sovereign lord, King George the third, to be dissolved. Minute guns were fired, accompanied with the tolling of bells during this ceremony, after which a royal salute, of one hundred guns, in honor of his Majesty's accession took place, at the conclusion, whereof, the new King was solemnly proclaimed, on the Place d'Armes and other public places at Quebec, by the sheriff of the district and his deputy, in presence of the administrator in chief, attended by the civil and military heads of departments, the troops of the garrison under arms, and a vast concourse of citizens. The same formalities were observed at Montreal, Three-Rivers, and in other towns and villages throughout the province.

The Earl of Dalhousie, relieved Sir P. Maitland of the government of Lower Canada, on the 18th of June, 1820, the day of his arrival from Halifax, in H. M. S. Newcastle.

The general election, consequent on the king's demise, took place in June and July. A speech, at the hustings, by Mr. Papineau, late speaker of the assembly, on his reelection, conjointly with Mr. Garden, for the west ward of the city of Montreal, much spoken of at the time, and going, with great applause, the rounds of the journals, is, in all respects so faithful, as to deserve notice and a place in the annals of his native country. The testimony, on a subject of this nature, of one occupying the eminent public position which Mr. P. so long did, in the councils of the province, whose private life, whatever may be said of his political career, is unblemished and exemplary, and who then stood, and possibly, notwithstanding all that has occurred, still stands higher in the estimation of his compatriots than any other man living, will, in all time to come, be read with interest, whatever vicissitudes may still await the political course he has reentered upon:—

"Not many days have elapsed since we assembled on this spot for the same purpose as that which now calls us together—the choice of representatives. The opportunity of that choice being caused by a great national calamity, the decease of that beloved sovereign who had reigned over the inhabitants of this country since the day they became british subjects, it is impossible not to express the feelings of gratitude for the many benefits received from him, and those of sorrow for his loss, so deeply felt in this, as in every other portion of his extensive dominions. And how could it be otherwise, when each year of his long reign has been marked by new favours bestowed upon the country?

Chap. XXII.
1820.

To enumerate these, and to detail the history of this country for so many years, would occupy more time than can be spared by those whom I have the honor to address. Suffice it, then, at a glance, to compare our present happy situation with that of our forefathers, on the eve of the day, when George the third became their legitimate monarch. Suffice it to recollect, that under the french government (internally and externally, abitrary and oppressive) the interests of this country had been more frequently neglected and mal-administered than any other part of its dependencies. In its estimation, Canada seems not to have been considered as a country which, from fertility of soil, salubrity of climate, and extent of territory, might then have been the peaceful abode of a numerous and happy population; but as a military post, whose feeble garrison was condemned to live in a state of perpetual warfare and insecurity—frequently suffering from famine—without trade, or with a trade monopolized by privileged companies—public and private property often pillaged, and personal liberty daily violated—when year after year the handful of inhabitants settled in this province were dragged from their homes and families, to shed their blood, and carry murder and havoc from the shores of the great lakes, the Mississippi and the Ohio, to those of Nova Scotia, Newfoundland, and Hudson's bay. Such was the situation of our fathers: behold the change. George the third, a sovereign revered for his moral character, attention to his kingly duties, and love of his subjects, succeeds to Louis 15th, a prince then deservedly despised for his debauchery, his inattention to the wants of the people, and his lavish profusion of his public monies upon favorites and mistresses. From that day, the reign of the law succeeded to that of violence; from that day, the treasures, the navy and the armies of Great Britain, are mustered to afford us an invincible protection against external danger; from that day, the better part of her laws became ours, while our religion, property, and the laws by which they were governed, remained unaltered; soon after, are granted to us the privileges of its free constitution—an infallible pledge, when acted upon, of our internal prosperity. Now, religious toleration; trial by jury—that wisest of safeguards ever devised for the protection of innocence;—security against arbitrary imprisonment, by the privileges attached to the writ of Habeas Corpus; legal and equal security afforded to all, in their person, honor and property; the right to obey no other law than those of our own making and choice, expressed through our representatives;—all these advantages have become our birthright, and shall, I hope, be the lasting inheritance of our posterity. To secure them let us only act as british subjects and free men."*

Mr. Papineau's just appreciation, at this period of his political life, of the paternal treatment and protection Canada had ever experienced, since it became part of the british empire, at the hands of its government, found a hearty approval in every truly british bosom, and rendered him not less popular with his fellow subjects of british, than with those of his own origin; a distinction, which unhappily, had now come fully into vogue between the two classes. But the really patriotic views he then entertained, have since, it seems, undergone a total change, and others of a different character been adopted in their stead, unprofitable to his country and himself, the more to be regretted, as the quiet redress of all real grievances and abuses of which the province may have had just cause to complain was within his reach. A man of his acknowledged talents and standing, mediating between the people and the government, confided in as he might have been by both, could not have failed, by a prudent and pacific course, to reconcile all jarring interests, and to secure, without an effort, the

---

* Extract from the speech of Mr. Papineau, to the electors of the west ward of Montreal, in July, 1820, when he was returned with Mr. Garden, without opposition.—(*Quebec Gazette.*)

repose and prosperity of his country, and with them its gratitude. At all events, it is more than probable that the affliction it has experienced, and the position in which we find it to-day—a false one, as many will have it, but the necessary consequence of its own erroneous policy, stimulated by the virulence and intolerant politics of that gentleman—might have been avoided—Happy, however, if he does not again succeed in plunging it into still deeper trouble, by a perseverance in his former agitation and another hegira.—No man in Canada at the present hour is so esteemed by his countrymen, the canadians of french origin, as Mr. Papineau—none so influential throughout the masses, for good or for evil to them, as all those observant of the times must perceive, as he. But their true interests cannot possibly lie in the direction he seems determined, at the time we are writing, to pursue, but the opposite.—Will he see it so, and have the wisdom to follow it?

The arrivals at Quebec this season, (1820) were in all 585 vessels, making 147,754 tons, and employing 6767 men, and the number cleared out 596, seven of which were built at Quebec the same year. The value of merchandise imported, paying the duty of two and a half per cent. was £674,556.

CHAPTER XXIII.

Opening of the new parliament by lord Dalhousie—speech—Mr. Papineau again speaker—address in answer to the speech—estimates of civil list and expenditure for the year—divided into chapters or classes—votes of the assembly and bill on the subject—rejected by the legislative council—arguments *pro* and *con*—assembly tender the supply by a vote and address—governor's answer—various proceedings of the assembly during the session—vote the duke of Richmond's speech in proroguing the legislature a breach of privileges—proposed indemnity to members—Mr. Jas. Stuart proposed agent—salary voted—a bill passed for the purpose—rejected in the legislative council—address to the governor representing divers grievances—retrospect of the last twenty years—prorogation—miscellaneous matters—population of Canada since the commencement—parliament assembled—speech and address in answer—estimates for the year—assembly refuse to vote a permanent civil list—reasons of refusal and address to his Majesty—Mr. Marryat, M. P., named agent of the province, by resolution of the assembly—legislative council protest against it—Mr. Marryat declines in consequence of the disagreement—assembly allow a revenue act to expire—no supply voted for the year—assembly resolve to hold receiver general responsible for all monies he should pay without legal authority—quorum of assembly increased from twelve to twenty-six members—Mr. Richardson a member of the legislative council in debates in that house makes certain remarks, which being reported to the assembly are deemed offensive—resolutions of the assembly and address on the subject to the governor—his excellency's answer—resolution of the legislative council on the matter—message of the governor to the assembly on financial matters—address in answer to it—financial difficulties with Upper Canada—

Chap. XXIII.
1820.

prorogation—union of the Canadas proposed by bill in parliament—great stir in Lower Canada in consequence of it—deputations to England for and against the proposed union.

The Earl of Dalhousie, shortly after his arrival, visited the upper districts, to which, however, he was not a stranger, having the preceding summer, while lieutenant governor of Nova Scotia, paid a visit to the duke of Richmond, making with him a tour through the Canadas.

The legislature met on the 14th December, and Mr. Papineau was again chosen speaker by the assembly.* The governor, in his speech, after paying a tribute of respect to the

---

* The following were the names of the members returned at the late general election:—

Upper Town of Quebec, A. Stuart and J. R. Vallières de St. Réal; Lower Town of Quebec, John Bélanger and Jas. McCallum; County of Quebec, John Neilson and Louis Gauvreau; County of Cornwallis, Joseph Robitaille and Jean Bte. Taché; County of Dorchester, John Davidson and Louis Lagueux; County of Devon, Frs. Fournier and J. Bte. Fortin; County of Hertford, François Blanchet and François X. Paré; County of Hampshire, François Huot and Charles Langevin; County of Northumberland, Etienne C. Lagueux and Philippe Panet; County of Orleans, François Quirouet; Borough of Three Rivers, Charles Richard Ogden and Joseph Badeaux; County of St. Maurice, Louis Picotte and Pierre Bruneau; County of Buckinghamshire, Jean Bte. Proulx and Louis Bourdages; East Ward of Montreal, Hugues Heney and Thomas Thain; West Ward of Montreal, L. J. Papineau and George Garden; County of Montreal, Joseph Perrault and Joseph Valois; County of Bedford, John Jones, junior; County of Effingham, Jacob Oldham and François Tassé; County of Huntingdon, Austin Cuvillier and Michael O'Sullivan; County of Kent, Denis B. Viger and Frederic A. Quesnel; County of Leinster, Jacques Lacombe and Michel Prévost; County of Richelieu, Jean Dessaulles and François St. Onge; County of Surrey, Etienne Duchesnois and Pierre Amiot; County of Warwick, Jacq. Déligny and Alexis Mousseau; County of York, Eustache N. L. Dumont and Augustin Perreault; Borough of William Henry, Robert Jones; County of Gaspé, John Thomas Taschereau.

memory of the late king, adverted also in the strongest terms of regard to that of his deceased predecessor, the late duke of Richmond :—

"When the british empire expressed its unfeigned sorrow upon the loss of a monarch, in whom the whole world acknowledged every public and private virtue, I believe,"—said his excellency—"that no part of his Majesty's subjects lamented that loss more deeply than you did in Canada."

"The manly character of the late duke of Richmond, his liberal mind, his experience in public affairs, his amiable disposition in private life, all qualified him in an eminent degree to fill the high station to which he was appointed; and it is deeply to be regretted that his grace has been lost to this province, before he had time to render it the services he had contemplated. It is"—said he—" pleasing to me to offer this tribute to the memory of a friend, whom I have known and honoured during thirty years."

He called the attention of the assembly to the accounts of the general expenditure in the administration of the government for the last two years. He informed them that he would lay before them accounts of the expense annually incurred, in payment of the salaries and contingencies of the civil officers permanently established for the service and support of his Majesty's government in the province, including such occasional payments as were unavoidable under it; and to this, he would add a statement of the annual product of the permanent taxes, and hereditary territorial revenue of the crown. That from these documents formed upon an average of the last six years, the assembly would perceive that the annual permanent revenue was not equal to the amount of annual permanent charges upon the provincial civil list, by a deficency of twenty-two thousand pounds ;* and that he had it in command from his Majesty to say, that having from past experience the fullest confidence in their loyalty, sense of duty, and attachment to the principles of the constitution, his Majesty did not doubt they would make a proper and permanent provision to supply the deficiency, and thereby enable him to sustain the civil government of the province, with honour and with advantage to his subjects.

He observed, that immediately after his arrival he had made it his duty to visit as much of the country as the regular despatch of business had permitted him to reach, in the course of the last summer;—that although he had derived some local information by so doing, he did not presume to speak to the legislature with confidence, of the various measures which might be suggested for the improvement of the province, and therefore should confine himself to those points he considered most immediately important.

Of these, the first was the constitution of the courts of law in the province. He concurred in all that had been expressed on this subject in a message from the late duke of Richmond, to both houses in March, 1819, and he therefore again recommended it to their consideration.

The permanent enactment of the revenue laws, or at least for such a period as would

---

* Charge, £15,000—revenue, £23,000—deficiency, £22,000.

give confidence to those whose interest in a great measure depended upon the stability of the commercial regulations, he deemed a subject highly worthy of their attention, convinced as he was, that great advantage would result from it to the province in general, and in particular to the mercantile classes.

The improvement of agriculture and the interior communications, he considered objects of great moment; and as they had already extended a liberal hand to encourage these, he trusted they would continue the support necessary to their success.

He also recommended to early attention, the laws which had recently expired, or that were about to expire, and among these, the the militia laws. That system of constitutional defence, he said, was peculiarly adapted to the state of the province; and the events of the late war, had shewn how justly the confidence of his Majesty's government might rest upon it in the day of danger :—that the knowledge of what the canadian militia was capable, taught them also the wisdom of watching over it in a state of readiness, complete in formation, and respectable in officers.

The settlement of the waste lands was a subject to which he also called their particular attention. He observed that the great tide of emigration to the province, promised to continue, and that the experience of several years had shewn the want of some measures to regulate and give effect to this growing strength

Chap. XXIII. 1820.
—many of these people arrived, he observed, in poverty and in sickness; many also with abundant means; but, the settlement of both descriptions, is impeded by the want of legislative aid.

In acknowledging the advantages which these provinces might derive from the acquisition of so many thousand british subjects, he knew, however, that Lower Canada possessed in itself an abundant population to settle these waste lands, and the yet unconceded seignioral territories—that he was aware there were strong prejudices to be overcome; and, therefore, that inducements must be held out to make the people spread more widely, such as the erection of parochial churches, and the laying out of roads of access to the distant woodlands:—that the subject was of difficult and distant accomplishment, but in his idea, of the utmost importance to Canada.

In conclusion, he expressed his sense of the great trust his Majesty had been pleased to commit to him, and that it should be the object of his highest ambition to render himself worthy of such distinguished honor:—that it should be his constant study to administer the government according to the laws, and in equal justice to all classes of his Majesty's subjects. "A stranger among you"—said he—"I have no partialities—no object but the good of the country.—All my exertions, and all my attempts must, however, be vain, unless I have the support of the provincial parliament; and, it is exactly to the extent of that confidence which shall be placed in me, that I can hope to render myself useful to the country."

The assembly, in their address, observed that they should—

"Hold themselves wanting in that sincerity which was due to the frankness of his Excellency's character; in their duty and the respect which they owed to their sovereign by whose command he had submitted the proposal of an additional and permanent appropriation, which with that already made, would exceed half the usual amount of the whole provincial revenue, were they not even at that early stage of the proceeding, most humbly to represent that the declared sense of their constituents, the duty which they owed to their posterity, and to that constitution of government which the wisdom and beneficence of the mother country had conferred on this province, together with the variable and uncertain future amount of that revenue, which, as well as their resources depended on a trade at that moment peculiarly uncertain, would preclude them from making any other than an annual appropriation for the general expenditure of the province, conformably to the recommendation of his Majesty's government, as signified to the parliament of this province, by his Excellency Sir John Coape Sherbrooke, late Governor in chief—in his speech delivered from the throne at the opening of the session, on the 7th of January, 1818.

They prayed,—"his Excellency would accept their humble assurance of the unalterable disposition of that house to vote annually in a constitutional manner according to that recommendation, and to the voluntary offer of the assembly in the year 1810, all the necessary expenses of his Majesty's civil government in this colony, in the honorable and permanent support of which, none were more deeply and sincerely interested, than his Majesty's loyal subjects whom they had the honour to represent; or more anxious to merit the continuance of the confidence which his Majesty was graciously pleased to express of their loyalty and duty."

To that part of the speech recommending a permanent enactment of the revenue laws, the house observed—

"That the establishment of permanent taxes being impracticable, they would carefully investigate the effects which might result to the province, and to the commercial classes in particular, from the duration of the revenue laws, and that they would endeavour to adopt every means in their power to inspire confidence into all his Majesty's subjects, and especially the mercantile classes, by applying to this important subject all that consideration which it merited."

The other topics, in the governor's speech, were answered in a way affording hope for a fair understanding between the assembly and the executive.

The estimate of the civil list, divided into classes, was laid before the assembly early in the session. The first class consisted of the governor in chief and officers immediately attached to him. The second, of the legislature and the officers appertaining thereto. The third, of the executive council, and officers immediately appertaining to it. The fourth, of the judges and officers concerned in the administration of justice. The fifth, of the secretary and registrar of the province and his allowance for office rent; the receiver general and allowance for a clerk; the surveyor general and allowance for his clerks; the surveyor of woods; the auditor of land patents; the inspector of provincial accounts and allowance for a clerk, and a variety of other subordinate officers. The sixth consisted altogether of contingencies, relative as well to the legislature, as to the administration of justice, and other departments of government, and different objects of public charge, amounting in all to £5,375.—The total of the estimate amounted to £44,877 5s., sterling.

The assembly having entered upon the subject, and discussed the civil expenditure *item by item*, voted the supply with some reductions; and in the hope of reconciling the other branch to the doctrine of an annual appropriation of the supply, and the assumption of the assembly to apply, by an annual vote, the fund previously appropriated in support of the civil government, waved the form adopted in the last session, and passed a bill providing, by chapters or classes, instead of *items* as before, a sum total, (including the appropriated revenue to be levied for the current year) of £46,060 10s. 2d., sterling, for the expenses of the year. This sum was to include the charge upon the pension list £3083 12s. 8d., sterling, and that of the militia staff £1543 16s. 3d., sterling, neither of which, however, had been comprehended in the estimate laid before the house. But this spontaneous provision of the assembly, in matters of public expense not regularly before them by message from the Governor, gave umbrage. The legislative council threw out the bill, as well because it interfered with the appropriated funds permanently appertaining to the crown in support of the civil government,* as because it had not in conformity with his Majesty's desire signified by the governor's speech, made a permanent provision to cover the annual sum required to supply the deficiency called for in aid of those funds.

The assumption of the assembly in applying the appropriated fund was said to be justifiable, by the reason and equity of the thing itself, for upon economy in the application of that fund, must necessarily depend the quantum to be supplied in aid of it: and that unless the assembly should have the controul of it, the amount to be supplied might be annually increased at the will of the executive.

In behalf of the executive, the inviolability of the funds vested in the crown and applicable by it, towards the support of the government, by act of the imperial parliament, was insisted upon. The assembly were accused of seeking rather their own aggrandizement than the stability of the government, which if it were to depend upon an annual vote of the assembly, for its necessary expenses, far from being stable,

---

* The bill was intituled " A bill to appropriate certain sums of money therein mentioned, to defray the expense of the civil government of Lower Canada, for the year 1821."—The following proviso was asserted,—" provided always, and be it further enacted, that the monies by law heretofore appropriated for the support of the civil government which now are or that hereafter shall come into the hands of the receiver general of this province, shall be applied in part payment, for the purposes of this act, and the remainder shall be made up and be taken from and out of any unappropriated monies which now are or that hereafter may come into the hands of the receiver general of the province."

might be paralized at the caprice of the popular branch of the legislature.

Their right of limiting, directing and appointing their own money grants, was not denied, but that of interfering with grants already made, whether by act of the imperial parliament, or of the provincial legislature, was contested. The pretensions set up with respect to the supply were such, it was said, as to render the proffered aid wholly inadmissible, since it could not under the conditions attached to it, unwarranted by precedent in the like cases in the parent state, be accepted by the executive without a dereliction of principle, a sacrifice of its legal rights, and placing itself in a state of annual and precarious dependence on the assembly.

While the bill of supply was in progress in the assembly, the legislative council entered into certain resolutions, to remain as standing orders, indicative of their predetermination with respect to it.*

---

* Of these resolutions the following will suffice for the information of the reader:—

" Resolved—That the legislative council will not proceed upon any bill of aid or supply, which shall not, within the knowledge of this house, have been applied for by the king's representative in this province."

" Resolved—That the legislative council will not proceed upon any bill appropriating public money that shall not, within the knowledge of this house, have been recommended by the king's representative."

" Resolved—That the legislative council will not proceed upon any bill of appropriation, for money issued in consequence of an address of the assembly to the king's representative (addresses of the assembly for the expenses of that house excepted)unless upon some extraordinary emergency, unforeseen at the commencement of a session, and which unforeseen emergency will not allow of time for passing a bill of ap-

Chap. XXIII. 1821.

The rejection of the supply bill, by the legislative council, leaving the executive without the necessary means of defraying the civil expenditure for the year, the assembly willing as far as depended upon them, to avert the inconvenience, placed by vote at the disposition of the executive, a sum sufficient to defray the expenses of the current year. Upon this vote an address was presented to his excellency, stating that from peculiar and unforeseen circumstances, it had not been in the power of the assembly to lay before him a bill of appropriation, but tendering out of the unappropriated funds of the province, such sum as with the funds already appropriated, might make up the sum of £46060 10s. 2d., sterling, for the expenses of the civil government during the year, the assembly pledging itself to make good the amount by bill, at the ensuing session.

To this he briefly answered, that the question out of which the address had sprung had been considered with the utmost attention of which he was capable, and his opinion was, that the grant now proposed was wholly ineffectual,

---

propriation for the same, in the session, when the address shall have been voted."

" Resolved—That the legislative council will not proceed upon any appropriation of public money, for any salary or pension hereafter to be created, or any augmentation thereof, unless the *quantum* of such salary, pension or augmentation shall have been recommended by the king's representative."

Resolved—That the legislative council will not proceed upon any bill of appropriation for the civil list, which shall contain specifications therein, by chapters or *items*, nor unless the same shall be granted during the life of his Majesty the king."

without the concurrence of the legislative council.

Here the matter rested until the ensuing session, neither house evincing a disposition to relinquish the ground taken up. The one would entertain no bill of appropriation for the civil list containing specifications by chapters or items, nor unless provision were made for it during the King's life. The other would pass no bill without such specifications, nor for a longer period than a year, nor even for this, unless the right of applying and apportioning by vote, the monies previously appropriated towards supporting the civil government, were also conceded them.

The consideration of that part of the speech which related to the settlement of the crown lands, was early in the session referred to a special committee, and an inquiry instituted by it, pursuant to the reference was continued through several successive sessions. This inquiry was conducted by Mr. Andrew Stuart, through whose perseverance and ability, the enormous abuses that had prevailed in the improvident and prodigal grants of the crown lands, in the province, were brought to light and exposed to public view—a large mass of evidence on the subject is recorded in the journals of the assembly.

A bill for more effectually ascertaining the state of the public funds in the hands of the receiver general, was brought forward in the assembly. By it the receiver general was annually to account to the legislature, and tell over the balance remaining in hand, and at its disposal. It was proposed instead of a salary to allow him a commission on the monies paid into his hands. He was to be debarred from commerce, and to be in no wise concerned in trade of any kind. The bill was referred to a special committee, where it underwent revision, but, afterwards, being submitted to a committee of the whole—the committee rose without reporting, and the measure was thus lost, rather from a want of diligence in the member who had taken it up, than from any opposition to it in the house. The receiver general was largely concerned in the lumber trade of the province; and the possession of the provincial monies by a person engaged in commerce, was the subject of uneasiness to the assembly, and of much dissatisfaction among the merchants.

A bill " for the trial of impeachments in this province" was also introduced this session. By it the legislative council were to take cognizance of impeachments by the assembly, and to be styled the " provincial high court of parliament," while in the exercise of this authority. The bill was declaratory, the promoters of it pretending the right of judging in cases of impeachment to be already inherent in the legislative council, by the analogies of the constitution of the province with Great Britain. The bill was committed, but, on discussion in committee of the whole was relinquished. The legislative council was not, in fact, constituted of members enjoying the confidence of the country: its dependent character, from the over proportion of officials in it, being such as to render it rather unpopular than otherwise, and it probably was on this account that the measure failed.

The resolution adopted by the legislative council last session, in rejecting the supply bill, and the duke of Richmond's speech, at the prorogation were, at an advanced stage of the present session, on motion of Mr. Neilson, taken into consideration by the assembly. After some discussion on them, it was resolved by it, with only two dissentient votes—that " the speech of his grace the Governor in chief, of the 24th April, 1819, contained a censure of the proceedings of this branch of the legislature,"—and

" That all censure of any proceeding of this branch of the legislature, by either of the other branches thereof, is an assumption and exercise of power contrary to law, a breach of the undoubted rights and privileges of this house, and subversive of the constitution of government, as by law established in this province.

" That it is the undoubted right of this house, in voting aids or supplies, or offering money bills for the consent of the other branches of the legislature, (as well as in all other proceedings under the afore recited act of the parliament of Great Britain,) to adopt such order or mode of proceedings, as it may find to be conformable to its rules, and to propound such matter as in its judgment shall seem fittest, and most conducive to the peace, welfare and good government of this province."

Amidst other concerns, the representatives of the people were not unmindful of themselves, and an effort was again made to obtain a vote of indemnity for their attendance during the session. The subject was brought forward and discussed in committee of the whole house, but the proposition was negatived.

The appointment of an agent for the province, in England, again as in former sessions, engaged the attention of the assembly. James Stuart, esquire, was named as such, and a sum voted by the house, not exceeding two thousand pounds per annum for the purpose. A bill was accordingly passed and sent to the legislative council, where it was thrown out. A gentleman (Mr. Gordon) holding an under situation in the colonial office in England, already, as it appeared, held by nomination of the provincial executive, the appointment of agent for the province, in consequence, it would seem, of a vote some years ago, previously mentioned, with a salary of two hundred pounds sterling per annum, but this the assembly refused to recognise, considering him merely an agent of the executive. Various messages had been sent down by the governor during the session, recommending divers objects of public moment, but little attention, however, was paid to them. The house, towards the close of the session, presented an address apologising for the apparent backwardness of the matters recommended. It stated " that the house had taken into its serious consideration the several objects recommended in his speech at the opening of the session, and the divers messages since transmitted for the attention of the legislature, but that the great importance of most of those objects and the multiplicity of business before the house, had prevented it from terminating several of them; and that as they were now in a state of forwardness, the house would, at an early period of the ensuing session, resume their consideration, so as to bring them to a speedy conclusion, equally advantageous to his Majesty's government and the general welfare of the province."

The governor, in answer, said he was "perfectly aware that many objects of great importance had been brought under the consideration of the house of assembly during the session, and was fully satisfied that the delay in terminating some of them might be unavoidable: that still he could not but express his regret that several of them had been deferred to a period so late as to make this delay necessary."

Just before the close of the session, an address was presented to the governor, representing a variety of anomalous matters which the house thought proper to submit for his consideration. The salary of £1,500, sterling, a year, to a lieut. governor, residing in England, and who had never even visited the province, was the first point submitted. The governor in chief was requested " to suspend the payment of his salary until he shall actually reside in the province, and perform the duties of his office therein." The situation of lieut. governor of Gaspé, was declared an unnecessary charge (£300) upon the province, that officer also being a non-resident. The secretary of the province, (a Mr. Amyot,) also absent, but receiving £400 a year, his deputy receiving the fees of his office, it was requested, should only be paid his salary on residing in the province and performing the duties of his office therein.* The agent of the province in London, at £200 a year, was represented as appointed, in a manner different from the agents of most other colonies and that he had no services to perform ;—his office was, therefore, declared an unnecessary burden on the people of this province, and his excellency was requested to relieve the province of it.—It was also the opinion of the house that " no salary should be allowed to any of the members of his Majesty's executive council, non-resident in the province," and his excellency was humbly requested to withhold payment from such as did not actually reside therein. That the offices of judge of the vice-admiralty and judge of the court of king's bench, in the same person, were incompatible, as was also the combination of the offices of judge of the king's bench and of french translator, and those of a judge of the said court, and of auditor of public accounts in the same person—" subversive of

---

* This gentleman, who never once set foot in the province, not only retained his office, however, as a *sinecure*, (his duty being done by deputy) but to make room for his deputy, Mr. Daly, he was translated finally to the pension list, at £400 sterling, a year, which it appears, by the public accounts, was paid him down to 1845, inclusively. His name disappears since then, from the list, owing probably to his decease.

the dignity of the judicial offices, and of the estimation and respect due to those important trusts—that much public inconvenience and discontent had resulted from such anomalies." His excellency was accordingly requested to take the subject into consideration, and require the gentlemen in whose persons those offices were combined, to make their election of one or the other of them. The exaction of fees, since 1810, by the judge of the vice-admiralty, from suitors in court, while receiving a salary of £200 for the duties of his office, in lieu of fees, was complained of as contrary to law—" a manifest obstacle to the administration of public justice, prejudicial to the industry of the province," and the cause of " much public discontent."—To these, one or two other matters, of minor importance, were also added.

This was intended as a statement or petition of public grievances. His excellency received it in a manner gratifying to the house, answering that he would not fail to transmit the resolutions of the assembly for his Majesty's most gracious consideration ; but that he could take no steps in regard to the purport of them, until he had received his Majesty's commands upon them. These were afterwards signified to the assembly, and will be noticed in their proper place.

On the 17th of March, his excellency prorogued the parliament, addressing them as follows:—

"Although I cannot, by any means, express my satisfaction in the general result of your deliberations, yet it is with great pleasure I acknowledge your assiduous and zealous attendance in the discharge of your public duties, during the long and laborious session, which I am now to close.

"Gentlemen of the house of assembly,—I thank you in his Majesty's name, for those supplies which have been granted by bills of appropriation, and assure you of my best attention in the application of them to the purposes for which they are intended.

"I exceedingly regret that the expectations of his Majesty, which by his command, I had the honour to express to you on the opening of the session, have not been realized.

"Gentlemen of the legislative council, and gentlemen of the house of assembly,—When this parliament met for the despatch of public business, I did entertain a hope that the experience of the last few years would have led you to a mature and serious consideration of the consequences that would inevitably follow, if the then state of things should not be remedied; you cannot therefore be surprised that I should now express not only my disappointment, but great concern, that the same question of constitutional principle, should have again disturbed the unanimity of your legislative proceedings.

"Upon this occasion, I think it a duty which I owe to you and to your country, to call upon you to consider during this summer, the result of the discussions of the session in all its bearings.

"You will see the administration of the civil government left without any pecuniary means, but, what I shall advance upon my own personal responsibility; you will see individuals suffering under severe and unmerited hardships, caused by the want of that constitutional authority, that is necessary for the payment of the expenses of the civil government; you will see the interior improvements of the country nearly at a stand; you will see, in short, the executive government, in a manner, palsied and powerless.

"When I shall again summon you to meet here in parliament, you will come to decide the important question, whether the government shall be restored to its constitutional energy, or whether you are to deplore the prospect of lasting misfortune, by a continuance in the present state of things. Important as the question is, there can be no difficulty in the decision.—When the blessings of the british constitution were granted to this province, you received with it the recorded experience of centuries of practice ; there is no question of doubt or of difficulty that may not find its precedent in the records of the imperial parliament, and I cannot think that any wiser guide need be desired."

Most of the members of the assembly were rather gratified than otherwise, to learn the crippled state in which it was probable they should find the government at the ensuing session. The more it were paralized and dependent, the sooner their views were likely to be realized, and their power over it established.

Several bills of importance were passed during the session, and among them one for opening the Lachine canal at the expense of the province, in the event that the company which previously had been incorporated for the purpose, should be unable to carry it into effect, or should relinquish their right. This the company thought proper to do, and accordingly the canal was commenced with great ceremony and demonstrations of public satisfaction on the 7th July.*

---

* This canal, now open and in operation, for several years, has, of late, been considerably enlarged, so as to admit the passage of large steamers, from sea to the lakes, but the improvements are not yet quite finished. By a return laid before the assembly last session, the whole expense of this important work, to 1st January 1848, is stated at £327,016, currency. That of the Beauharnois canal, at £303,847. This part of the line of canal communication with Upper Canada, which, being on the south, instead of the north side of the St. Lawrence, as many think it ought to have been, is liable, in case of a war with the United States, by a sudden irruption of the enemy, to be laid

Mr. Papineau, speaker of the assembly, was shortly after the beginning of the session, called to a seat in the executive council, as were also Mr. Hale, a member of the legislative council, and lieut. col. Ready, civil secretary to the governor in chief, a gentleman who had come to the province with the duke of Richmond, and served in that capacity, under him.

The governor visited in the course of the summer the military posts in Upper Canada, including Drummond island, returning by the river Ottawa to Quebec, where he arrived after completing his tour, towards the end of August.

We may here, to advantage, take a retrospect of the last twenty years. The state of the

---

hold of or rendered useless, was most injudiciously determined upon and commenced during the administration of sir Charles Bagot, at the instance, it seems, of Mr. E. G. Wakefield, at that time in Canada, and who is said to have received for his " influence", in bringing about this job, £12,500, from the proprietors of the Beauharnois seigniory, for whom he was agent, in the transaction, besides £7,500 previously, from Mr. Ellice, for his agency in the sale of that seigniory to the company now holding it.

Mr W. was one of those patriots, in England, who, sympathising during the so called " financial troubles," with the *oppressed* in Canada. philanthropically followed, with other speculators, lord Durham hither, and was confidentially employed by him. He returned to England, shortly after his lordship's departure hence, but came back to Canada, upon Mr. Poulett Thompson's advent, procured a seat as representative of Beauharnois in the legislature, and finally managed, by his *agiotage*, to secure himself £20,000, as above, relieving the distressed canadians, in this manner! He was influential, it was thought, with sir Charles Bagot, in the making, in 1842, of the Lafontaine-Baldwin administration, as he no doubt was, in 1843, with sir Charles Metcalfe, in the unmaking of it, in consequence, it was said, of some disappointment he had experienced at the hands of those gentlemen.—He certainly played a game in the government and concerns of this province, which his standing in it did not entitle him to.—*Quebec, May* 1848.

country, at the beginning of the present century, has been noticed. That part of it known as "the Eastern Townships," then a wilderness, in which there scarcely was a settler, had now become a populous and thriving district, equal in population nearly to Canada at the time of the conquest. The distance from the canadian settlements, in the seigniories along the St. Lawrence, and total want of roads thence into this new country, were serious impediments to their colonization, and few or no canadians, of french origin, were found to venture in and avail themselves of the superior advantages of soil and climate, independently of their free tenure, which the fertile lands in these townships presented over those of the seigniories. The descendent of the briton and the celt, however, pushed in, and had set to work, and in the twenty short years we have been tracing, had studded with promising, and already, in some parts, populous settlements, a territory unsurpassed, if, in fact matched, in fertility, salubrity and beauty, by any tract of equal extent in North America.

The increase of population in the other parts of Lower Canada, during the same period, we have no means certain of determining, no act for taking a census of the province having as yet been passed by the legislature; but it must have been very considerable, probably doubled, or nearly so.*

---

* The following sketch of the population of Canada, at the different periods specified in it, is, perhaps, as near to the truth, as we can

Chap. XXIII. 1821.

The province had sustained a war declared against Great Britain, avowedly with a view to the conquest of her canadian possessions, and had come from the ordeal not only unscathed, but with honor, evincing most decisively, its ability for self-defence, as well as the loyalty and determination of the inhabitants, of both origins, to maintain its connexion with Great Britain and the integrity of the empire in this quarter.

Steamers had been introduced, upon the St. Lawrence and great lakes, and the internal communications, by means of them, prodigiously accelerated, and extended to all quarters. The trade with Britain, also had vastly

---

now get. We are indebted for it to our friend, G. B. Faribault, esq., whose researches into and knowledge of the early history of the country are well understood, and such as will entitle it to some credit. The statements from 1825 inclusively, excepting 1848, being founded upon statistical and official returns, pursuant to acts of the legislature, may be taken as correct, or nearly so, being, probably, rather under, than over the mark :—

Census of the population of Canada, at different epochs.
In 1617, there were but 52 souls in Quebec.

	souls.		souls.
1666 the population of Canada, was	3418	In 1790 the population of Canada, was	123000
1667 Ditto,	4312	1806 Upper Canada,	80000
1668 "	5870	1808 " "	100000
1677 "	8500	1811 " "	95000
1679 "	9400	1816 both Provinces,	350000
1680 "	9719	1821 Upper Canada,	122716
1688 "	11249	1823 " "	150000
1714 "	20000	1825 " "	157000
1719 "	22530	1825 Lower Canada,	423630
1720 "	24434	1828 Upper Canada,	190000
1721 "	24511	1831 Lower Canada,	511917
1734 "	37252	1842 Upper Canada,	486000
1760 "	60000	1841 Lower Canada,	691000
1763 "	76275	1848 { U.C. 650000 / L.C. 800000 }	1450000
1783 "	113112		

increased, the article of lumber alone exported to Great Britain, employing annually, several hundreds of british ships—the lumber trade, as it is termed, being a branch of commerce not commenced in 1800, but now established to a great extent, increasing the demand for british manufactures, and laying the foundation of the many flourishing settlements on the Ottawa and in other remote parts, which, without this trade, might have remained still for many years unsettled, and perhaps unexplored. The revenue, which previous to 1800, did not reach £25,000, had now more than quadrupled, exceeding in some years £150,000, and without the least inconvenience to the trade, upon which it was nearly altogether levied. The Lachine and Rideau canals had been commenced and were in progress—great and important works in a military and commercial point of view—and the army, military and naval establishments which the mother country kept up in the province, together with the sums expended annually in improving the fortifications of Quebec, and at Montreal, as well as in other parts of Canada, were sources of wealth to it.

But this progress had also its attendant evils, in the growth of luxury and its vices. Crime was then scarcely known; it was now fearfully on the increase, as the gaol calendar, and business of the assizes clearly evinced. But this, it is also to be observed, was owing, in a measure, to the tide of immigration now setting in. The concord characteristic of the two races in Canada, previous to, and for a few years after 1800, had altogether passed away and was replaced by far different feelings. —Party spirit, springing chiefly from distinctions of national origin, and fomented by appeals to prejudices from it, had started and risen to an alarming degree, and faction also was at work to undermine and paralize the government. The notion of a speedy nationality or national existence, and independency of Great Britain, by the inhabitants of french descent in Canada, had taken possession of almost every mind; its achievement, as they deemed it, being of easy and early accomplishment, depending but upon their own pleasure, and a simultaneous effort by the masses; an unhappy delusion, encouraged by the demagogues and speculative politicians of the hour, and in which they universally indulged. The government openly maligned and reviled with impunity in all quarters, as it had become fashionable to do in quest of popularity with the multitude, had fallen in their estimation, and was no longer contemplated with the respect and veneration it had been twenty years ago, being now publicly spoken of as tolerated only, and on the eve of dissolution. The native population of british descent, as well as immigrants from the United Kingdom, were held up as strangers and intruders upon the " *enfants du sol*," whose exclusive right to the country was a doctrine currently asserted, and the expedience of superseding the british authorities by those of "*la nation canadienne*," and the sooner the better, boldly maintained, as a policy and aspiration, at once praiseworthy and patriotic, in every canadian of french origin. Their success, during the late war, in a good cause, backed by the empire, had not only inspired them with a confidence in their own prowess; but it also had fallaciously emboldened many of them, in the very different one on which they seemed now bent. Sedition, in the inverted spirit of the times, had become a virtue and loyalty anything but that; and, indeed, the government, itself, has since sanctioned the doctrine, rewarding, as the better cause, agitation and disloyalty, with the richest gifts at its disposal, treating with neglect, and ingratitude, those who, in the time of its need, stood to their allegiance and defended it,—casting off old and faithful servants, to make room for others formerly hostile to and in open array against it, with a faithlessness, injustice, and, in some instances, cruelty, which no political expedience or conciliatory policy can possibly justify or palliate—a reproach to which the british government, in Canada, has subjected itself, and whereof, in time to come, it will, perhaps, feel the evil effects. It has itself indeed done more, by its own false and suicidal policy, to destroy all confidence in it, by the well affected of both races, than all its enemies have done or could do to its prejudice. The loyal and independent press of the day will correct us if we are in error, and to it we appeal, if necessary, in confirmation of this statement.

The governor again opened the legislature, on the 11th December :—

"I now again,"—said he,—"bring under your consideration the state of the province; and as a part of the subject above all others the most important, I recommend to your immediate attention the financial affairs, with the view to making a suitable provision for the support of the civil government.

"Gentlemen of the assembly,—under the difficulties in which I found myself placed at the termination of the last session of the legislature, it became my duty to adopt a course for the payment of the current expenses of government, as nearly consistent as possible with the existing laws, or to the practice hitherto observed.

"I have ordered that the estimate for the ensuing year, should be laid before you without delay, and I have it again in command from his Majesty, to acquaint you that his Majesty still has the fullest confidence in your loyalty and affection towards his person and government: that he rests assured of your disposition to provide for the necessary expenses of his civil government, and those also equally necessary for the honour of his crown. And I am further commanded by his Majesty to recommend, that such provision as shall appear necessary for these purposes, should be granted permanently, during his Majesty's life.

"Gentlemen of the legislative council, and gentlemen of the assembly,—It has been established in the british parliament, as a principle of the constitution, that the civil list should be granted during the life of the King, and I am commanded to impress upon this occasion his Majesty's recommendation that such principle of the constitution should be adopted and observed in future as the practice in this province.

"It would be presumption in me to add any words to what is thus stated to you by his Majesty's authority; it is a fresh instance of his Majesty's paternal care, and of the interest he takes in the welfare of his american provinces.

"I confidently rely on your well known loyalty and attachment to the principles of the british constitution, and cannot doubt, that this, his Majesty's recommendation of the measure, will have its due weight with you.

"I shall not advert to any of the various topics of great public interest, which in the course of the session I may have to submit to you; I consider them of far inferior importance to the subject now communicated to you, by the royal command, and I have therefore thought it proper to postpone them for the present."

It was inferred from the concluding part of this speech, that the royal sanction would be withheld from all legislative proceedings of the assembly, until a bill providing for the civil list in a manner satisfactory to the executive were passed.

The legislative council, in answer to the speech, observed—that distinguished as the Canadas had been above all other provinces of the british empire, by a constitution perfectly analogous to that of the parent state, they could not but feel it their paramount duty, as far as in them lay, to adopt what had been established in the british parliament as a constitutional principle; the granting of the civil list during the life of the king.

The assembly entertained a very different opinion.—They requested the governor to convey to his Majesty:—

"Their most humble thanks for the gracious expression of his Majesty's fullest confidence in their loyalty and affection towards his royal person and government, and their assurance that his Majesty might always place the fullest reliance on the invariable disposition of that house to provide for the necessary expenses of his civil government, and those also necessary to the honor of his crown." They received, they said,—"with all due humility, the communication of his Majesty's present recommendation, that such provision as should appear necessary for those purposes,

Chap. XXIII.
1821.

should be granted permanently, during his Majesty's life; as well as the information, that it had been established in the british parliament, that the civil list should be granted during the king's life; and the recommendation which his excellency was commanded to impress upon their minds, that such principle of the british constitution should be adopted and observed in this province.

" We are"—continued they—"fully thankful for the confidence which your excellency is pleased to repose in our well known loyalty and attachment to the principles of the british constitution, and we most respectfully assure your excellency that in the conscientious discharge of our duty to our constituents, under the act of the british parliament in virtue of which we are constituted and assembled, the recommendation of his Majesty will have due weight."

In concluding, they humbly begged his excellency to be assured that whatever topics he might be pleased to submit to them, in the course of the session, in addition to the subject already communicated by the royal command, would receive their ready and respectful consideration.

The governor, in reply, told the assembly that in the prospect, and hope also, of a calm and dispassionate discussion, he availed himself of that opportunity to express his own opinion, that the measure proposed was in itself essential to the well being of the province. That until the expenses of the government were provided for in this manner, he could entertain no hopes of harmony, in the proceedings of the three branches of the legislature; and that until harmony and union and cordial co-operation in these branches were established, he considered the real prosperity of the province decidedly arrested. How correctly he viewed this matter will be but too apparent in the sequel.

These preliminaries being over, a faint hope was entertained, as well from the solicitude of the governor, to bring about harmony in the legislature, as from the professed spirit of humility, with which the assembly received the King's recommendation, that the present would prove a prosperous and satisfactory session. Never was prospect more delusive. Disregard for almost every subject, recommended to their attention by the Governor, and above all a spirit of intolerance and tyranny over those whose opinions were opposed to the prevailing party, were its most prominent characteristics.

The governor sent down on the 21st of December, the "estimate of the probable amount of the sum required in future for the support of his Majesty's civil government in this province, and the honour and dignity of the crown."

In submitting the estimate he thought proper to remark, that he sent it in the form in which it had been sent for some years past; but, at the same time, he informed the assembly that his Majesty did not expect that the provision which it might be deemed expedient to make for defraying such civil contingences as were purely casual, should be otherwise than annually voted.

The assembly, shortly after this message addressed the governor, requesting he would cause to be laid before the assembly, a statement of the proper provision for the support of the civil government of the province of Quebec as fixed by the royal instructions, previous to the 17th December, 1792—also a statement of the same for the province of Lower Canada, as fixed by the royal instructions, at the latest period previous to the 31st December, 1797—also a statement of the same, as fixed by the royal instructions at the latest period, before the 10th February, 1810, and finally a statement of the same as fixed by the royal instructions, at the latest period before the 7th January, 1818.

The governor, in answer to this application, a few days afterwards acquainted them, by message, that he "felt it his duty to decline to lay the royal instructions or any part of them, before the house for public discussion, considering them to be confidential instructions, from his Majesty to his representative, for the time being."

The assembly proceeded to business, but the civil list, which the executive considered an object of the first importance, and as such entitled to the immediate attention of the house, was not, however, viewed by it in the same light. They entered upon it with reluctance, determined not to comply with the royal recommendation, nor yet, if it could be avoided, pointedly refuse compliance. The member, however, who conducted the measure (Mr Taschereau) was resolved to leave no room for doubt in the matter, and took the necessary step to bring the question to a close, by putting it at once in proper shape before the house. Accordingly, upon motion, in committee of the whole house, to resolve " that a permanent provision be made, for the support of the civil government of the province, and of the honour and dignity of the crown, during the life of his present most gracious Majesty,"—it was negatived; thirty-one being against, and but five for the motion."

To soften the refusal, several resolutions were passed explanatory of the reasons which had influenced the house in its determination. These were made chiefly to rest upon the disparity in circumstances between the mother country and the province, from which it was deduced, " that in the situation in which this province is, this house can only, and ought to provide for the expenses of his Majesty's civil government annually, and not otherwise." This was followed up by an " opinion of the committee, that according to the offer of the assembly of this province, made in the year 1810, and accepted by his Majesty in 1818, and to the terms of the speeches of the Governors of this province, at the opening of the sessions of the provincial legislature in the years 1818 and 1819, the sums necessary for the support of his Majesty's civil government in this province, ought to be voted and appropriated annually, and not otherwise."—An address to his Majesty, expressing great respect for the principles of the constitution and government followed, in which the substance of the resolutions, were embodied, the whole being intended as an apology for not acceding to the demand of a permanent appropriation for the civil list.

The house went up to the governor with the address, requesting he would be pleased to transmit the same to his Majesty's ministers; to which his lordship answered, that he should always think it a duty incumbent upon him to convey to the foot of the throne the sentiments of the house of assembly, whatever they might be, provided they were suitably expressed; and that such being the case at present, he willingly complied with their request.

The expedience of appointing an agent for the province, near the government at home, was again considered. The effort of the assembly in the preceding session, to appoint as such Mr. James Stuart, having failed, they now fell upon another plan. This was, to request, by resolution of the assembly, some popular member of the british house of commons, to act in that capacity, which it was maintained would suffice. It was hoped that the government at home would, if their choice fell upon some influential member, virtually if not formally recognize him, and that, by this means, the assembly might effect their purpose.

The assembly, therefore, after expressing their "unabated confidence in the talents, integrity and devotion to the interests of the province, of James Stuart, esquire, whom it had twice nominated as agent, to reside in the united kingdom, but that under the circumstances in which the house was placed, it was expedient to request a member of the honorable, the house of commons, to act as an authorised agent, to attend to the interests of the colony, and communicate with his Majesty's ministers, on all points relating thereto. as he might be instructed, or as occasion might require"—resolved, " that Joseph Marryat, esq., a member of the honorable the house of commons, be requested to act as such agent."

Copies of the resolutions of the assembly, on the subject, were ordered to be transmitted to Mr. Marryat, and that gentleman was requested to correspond with their speaker. Entries of the correspondence were directed to be made in a register, to be kept for the purpose by the clerk of the assembly, and of these, copies were to be laid before the governor for the time being, within fifteen days after the opening of every session of the legislature. Voluminous instructions, principally relating to the civil list matter, were digested by a special committee, with a view of putting the agent in full possession of the subject, from its origin to the present time; the whole of which after receiving the concurrence of the house were transmitted to Mr. Marryat.

The legislative council not having been consulted in this measure, resented the course pursued by the assembly, and in turn resolved, that "the resolutions of the assembly, requesting Joseph Marryat, esquire, to act as an authorised agent for the province, to attend to the interests of this colony, and communicate with his Majesty's ministers on all points relating thereto, as he might be instructed by the assembly, or as occasion might require, were a dangerous assumption of legislative power by the assembly alone, without the concurrence of the other branches of the legislature, and an attempt at appointment to office, in direct breach and violation of the constitution,—of the king's prerogative,—and of the rights and privileges of that house (the legislative council) and tended to subvert the constitution of the province."

A copy of the resolutions passed in the legislative council on the occasion, was laid before the governor, with an address assuring his excellency of the fixed determination of that branch to support the constitution of the province, as by law established, the prerogative of the crown, and the independence of the legislative council; and requesting that his Excellency would be pleased to lay their resolutions and assurances at the foot of the throne, in such way as he might see fit.

Mr. Marryat, in a letter to the speaker, declined the charge which he had been requested by the assembly to take upon himself. His reason for declining it, was the misunderstanding which existed on the subject, between the assembly and the legislative council, without the concurrence of which, he gave it as his opinion, such appointment could not constitutionally exist, nor be acknowledged by the government in England. Thus terminated that matter for the present.

The exhaustion of the public chest, as already mentioned, was looked upon in the assembly as the most speedy and effectual method towards bringing the executive under its subjection; and, accordingly, one of the temporary revenue acts, which had previously been renewed, for short periods, from time to time, and then stood limited to the first of May ensuing, was allowed to expire, although the governor, by a special message to the assembly, called their attention to those laws, considering it a subject, he said, of the highest importance to the interests of the province.—Another which was limited to the same day of the following year, it was also determined should share the same fate.*

No appropriation for the service of the current year was voted, under pretext that it was needless to tender an aid for that period, cir-

---

* One of the acts alluded to was the provincial statute 53 G. III., ch. 11, as amended by the 55th Geo. III., ch. 2. The other was the 55th Geo. III., ch. 3. The former yielded for the year ending 1st November, 1821, the sum of £12384, currency; the latter £26,222 currency. The timely interference of the imperial parliament, at the instance of Upper Canada, as subsequently noticed, revived the one, and prevented the expiration of the other, making both permanent.

cumstanced as matters were in consequence of the call for a permanent provision, which had been made by the governor in his Majesty's name, and refusal. It was said that the remonstrance to his Majesty on the subject, might probably induce a change of opinion, and that in the mean time, the governor, as he had previously done, was, if he chose, still free to advance, upon his own responsibility, out of the unappropriated funds, in the public coffers, such monies as were necessary to defray the expenses of the year, or until an answer to the address of the assembly should be signified by the ministers; though liable, in the opinion of this body, to be treated, if he did so, as a public dilapidator.

While, however, this alternative was spoken of as open to the executive, resolutions at variance with it were adopted by the assembly, expressive of their determination, to debar the government of the use of any monies, even for its temporary support, unless particularly authorised by act. It was resolved that the house would "hold personally responsible his Majesty's receiver general of the province, and every other person or persons concerned, for all monies levied on his Majesty's subjects, which may have legally come into his or their hands, and been paid over by him or them under any authority whatever, unless such payments be, or should be authorised by an express provision of law."

The quorum which previously stood at fifteen, was early in this session increased to twenty-six members, including the speaker, constituting a majority of the whole house.

The governor acquainted the assembly by message, that he had forwarded their address of the previous session respecting certain matters to the king, and that he had it in command to inform them, that the subjects upon which they had remonstrated should receive all due attention. That, in the mean time, the lieut. governor had been ordered to repair to Quebec, and to continue resident in the province. That the residence of an efficient officer in the district of Gaspé, was deemed by his Majesty, in the highest degree expedient; instead, therefore, of sanctioning the abolition of lieut. governor, he recommended rather, that the assembly should make such adequate provision for a resident lieut. governor, as would ensure the services of a respectable and efficient officer. With regard to the secretary of the province, the assembly were assured that, whenever a vacancy should occur in the office, care would be taken that the successor should be a resident officer. The absent incumbent, in the mean time, was not to be dispossessed, " considering"—it was said,—" that having now held the place for many years, and that his duties in the province had been adequately discharged, it did not appear to his Majesty necessary or just, to dispossess him without some adequate compensation for the loss of his office."

The appointment of colonial agent had existed, it was stated, for many years, and till of late had never been objected to in the province—that there was no charge of misconduct against him, and that as the utility of the office had, it appeared, been experienced very recently, in bringing under consideration of the government, a very intricate case, affecting materially the colonial interests; his Majesty, for these reasons, was not disposed to encourage the expectation that the office could be properly abolished. That his Majesty was not aware of any circumstance which required the payment of salaries to the absent members of the executive council. The other matters were reserved for further consideration.

An unsuccessful effort was made in the legislative council, by the opposition members in it, to rescind the resolutions passed, relating to the civil list, during the last session. These, it was argued, interfered with the privileges of the assembly, as dictating to it the terms upon which only, the legislative council would accede and give effect to any grant of the assembly, towards the support of the civil government, pursuant to the call of his Majesty; whereas by the privileges of the commons, it appertained to them exclusively to dictate their own terms and conditions, relatively to all aids to the crown, for whatever purpose they might be.

In the debate which arose in the legislative council on this matter, Mr. Richardson expressed himself with his usual independence on the course of the assembly, which he considered as unconstitutional and overbearing. He thought their pretensions subversive of the prerogatives of the crown; and indicative of a desire to govern that ought to be curbed in time. He spoke of the proceedings of the ruling party in the lower house as revolutionary, intimating that secret committees, from which certain members were excluded, assembled from day to day, to concert schemes in furtherance of a disorganizing system, acted upon by the body. He compared their measures with those characteristic of the times of Charles I. in England, and of the french revolution, observing that it would be no matter of surprise, if at the moment he was speaking, a committee of the assembly were in consultation about replacing the personage at the castle, by another of their own choice. These comparisons gave serious offence to certain members of the assembly, present at those debates, and it was determined, after two or three days private consultation among themselves, to make it the subject of complaint to, and consideration in the assembly.

Accordingly, on the 29th of January, Mr. Quirouet, a member of the assembly rising in his place informed the house, " that on friday the 25th inst., he heard the honorable John Richardson, one of the members of the legislative council of this province, express himself in his speech, in english, in reply to the honorable P. D. Debartzch,* in the debate of the council, as follows:—

"How can we rescind our resolutions when there is a secret committee sitting in the house of assembly, which is, perhaps, deliberating on the appointment of a governor of their choice, and on the removal of the person now in the castle, and putting their own in his place. The committee even sits without the knowledge of several members of the house, of which there is no example in England, except in the time of Charles the first. The committee is, perhaps, a committee of public safety."

This piece of information was referred to a select committee of five, who after taking such ex-parte information relative to it, as they could get from bye-standers during the debates in the legislative council, reported the whole to the assembly. Long debates ensued, abounding generally, with abuse against all those who presuming to disapprove of the proceedings in the assembly, arraigned, as they said, by implication, the whole french canadian population. The language complained of was exaggerated into atrocity, and the council treated as criminals for not having censured the member who had dared to allude in such terms before that body, to the assembly. The offence was said to be the more heinous, as it came from one who being at the same time senior member of the executive council, might, on a contingency, be invested with the temporary administration of the government, but,

---

* It was Mr. Debartzch who moved in the legislative council, for he rescision of the rules relating to the civil list, already noticed, and which, it was contended by that gentleman in debate, intrenched upon the rights and privileges of the assembly.

who, it was observed, now, by this his illiberal opinion of the representatives of the people had rendered himself unworthy of ever being allowed to take charge of it, for a single moment. That for this reason, it behoved them to endeavour to accomplish his removal from every situation of confidence, honour or profit he held under the crown, and, as far as in them lay, to fix upon the offender an indelible mark of public opprobrium and disgrace, by stigmatizing him as an enemy to the country, and recording it on their journals.

It was accordingly resolved by the assembly—

"That the discourse and language of the honorable John Richardson, a member of the legislative council, in the said council, as proved before a committee of this house, are false, scandalous, malicious—are a high contempt of this house—an odious attempt to destroy his Majesty's confidence in the fidelity and loyalty of this house, and of the people of this province, and a breach of the rights and privileges of this house.

"That the information given to the house on the 29th instant, of the discourse and language used and held by the honorable John Richardson, a member of the said council, against the honor and loyalty of this house—the proofs and evidence before a committee of this house, on the said information—and also the resolutions adopted by this committee, be communicated by message to the legislative council, that the said discourse and language be laid to the charge of the said honorable John Richardson, before the said legislative council—and that the legislative council be desired to proceed in justice upon the said charge, and to inflict upon the said honorable John Richardson, a punishment adequate to so high an offence against this house.

"That the information given to this house on the 29th instant, of the language and discourse used and held on the

Chap. XXIII. 1822.

25th inst., in the legislative council, by the honorable John Richardson, a member of the said council, against the honor and loyalty of this house, and also the proofs or evidence received before a committee of this house on the said information, and the resolutions adopted by the house, be communicated, by an humble address, to his excellency the governor in chief, praying his excellency would be pleased, for the reasons contained in the said address, to remove and dismiss the said John Richardson, from all offices and places of honor, trust, or profit, which he may hold during pleasure, under his Majesty's government in this province."

Messengers were appointed, who went up to the castle with the address. The governor answered, that " the address involved consequences of the highest importance. That the resolutions appeared to him to be expressed in language inconsistent with the calm dignity of a legislative body—that they affected the privileges of the legislative council, and especially in that of freedom of debate—and that he must, for these reasons, distinctly refuse the request of the house of assembly in this matter."

This firm and becoming answer cooled the ardour of those who had urged the hasty step which the assembly had taken. They felt that the freedom of debate ought last of all to be assailed by a popular body, and that in respecting it, the governor had taken a position that must tell to his credit, and which they had unwarily relinquished, in the pursuit of a vindictive and unworthy purpose. They finally edged off by an awkward resolution on their journals, reprobating all attempts in any member of the council, to destroy the confidence of the King's representative in their honor and loyalty,—as a contempt of the house, and a breach of its rights and privileges:—as tending to destroy harmony, and to render useless the endeavours of the assembly for the general welfare—adding, as an apology for their proceedings, that, "it is the incontestable right of this house to repress such attempts by every constitutional means in their power."

The messengers who had taken up the humble address on this matter to the castle, immediately afterwards, also laid the complaint of the assembly before the legislative council ; which, viewing the steps that body had adopted with respect to one of its members, for language used in debate, within its own walls, as a flagrant breach of its privileges, refused to compromise its own honour, or the rights of its members, by any measures on the subject, until reparation were made by the assembly, for the actual breach by them, of the privileges of the legislative council in the same matter.*

---

* Mr. Richardson, when the subject was taken up before the legislative council repeated the substance of his observations in the debate which had given such offence. There was some unimportant variance between his statement and the reports given of them, arising probably from imperfect recollection or misunderstanding by the persons examined before the committee. He did not repeat his observations for the purpose of retracting them, he said, but rather to show more clearly than ever his meaning, if there could have been any doubt about it, intending fully to confirm, on further reflection, all he had then said, and which the assembly, by their proceedings in this matter, had strikingly justified.

There were no debates in the legislative council on the subject.—Mr. Richardson, after these observations withdrew, when the following resolution was unanimously adopted:—" That an answer should be sent to inform the assembly, that the legislative council were extremely desirous to preserve a good understanding between the two houses, and were willing to inquire into the subject matter of the message of the assembly and do right therein; but that the house

Chap. XXIII.
1822.

After the assembly had refused to provide for the civil list during the King's life, and the resolution already noticed, of holding the receiver general and all others concerned, responsible for all payments made from the public chest, without the authority of an express provision of law, the Governor sent a message to the assembly, acquainting them of the course he intended to adopt in consequence of their determination.

He had, he said, at the close of the last session, pointed out the difficulties which would follow from the want of the usual appropriations of public monies, to meet the public expenditure, and particularly stated that the government would be left without the pecuniary means which its exigences would indispen-

---

conceived it was not consistent with its honor or with the rights of its members to proceed upon a presumed breach of the privileges of the assembly, which the said message alleged, until the legislative council should have received reparation from the assembly, for the actual breach of the privileges of the legislative council by the assembly, in the same matter, by their address to his excellency the governor in chief, praying him to remove the honorable John Richardson from all his offices and places of honor, trust or profit, which he might hold during pleasure under his Majesty's government in this province, and thereby censure and punish him for words used by him in debate in that house, where only, a member thereof, for words so used, can be questioned. The said address being a proceeding on the part of the assembly, which inasmuch as it sought, upon the application of the assembly, to subject the members of the legislative council, without hearing or enquiry, to censure and punishment by another branch of the legislature for their conduct in that house, restrains the freedom of debate, and deeply affects the constitutional independence of the legislative council." Mr. Richardson never held, nor would hold any post of profit under the crown. As an executive councillor he received a £100 a year, which, however, was not an indemnity for the expense to which he must actually have been put, in attending upon the court of appeals at Quebec, as a member of the executive council, and as such, one of the judges in appeal.

sably require, if he did not advance them on his own personal responsibility.

That accordingly he did so advance the difference between the amount of the royal revenue which was placed at his disposal,* and the total amount of the civil expenditure of the province, and had called upon the assembly by message of the 8th January last, to make good this difference.†

That he therefore had not put in question the constitutional principle, which directs the application of the public monies to the purposes for which they are appropriated. He had relied with confidence upon the faith of the assembly, which was pledged to pay the civil expenditure of the province, and in the firm belief that he should act in conformity to the wishes of the legislature, he had taken upon himself this great responsibility in order to prevent consequences equally distressing to individuals, and ruinous to the general interests of the province.

That by the proceedings of the present session, circumstances were materially changed. It would not now be in his power to make

---

* That is to say, the proceeds of the 14th Geo. III., ch. 88, together with the casual and territorial revenue of the crown, in the province, and other specific appropriations.

† By this message he had called " the attention of the assembly to the enactment of a law to reimburse and make good to his Majesty's government the various advances in money for which provision had not been made by the legislature, but which had been found indispensably necessary for the support of his Majesty's provincial government, as also for certain public institutions heretofore sanctioned and assisted by the beneficence of the legislature, as detailed in the accounts before the assembly."

further advances, nor would it be consistent with his duty to venture a greater stretch of responsibility. He, therefore, would apply the territorial and casual revenues, fines, rents and profits, which were reserved to and belonged to his most christian Majesty at the conquest, and surrender of Canada to his late Majesty the King of Great Britain; the monies raised by statutes of the imperial parliament, and the sum of £5000 sterling, raised by the provincial statute 35th Geo. 3, ch. 9, towards defraying the expenses in support of his Majesty's civil government, and of the administration of justice in the province, according to the appropriations of those statutes.

That should there be any surplus remaining after the payment of these expenses, he would then apply that surplus towards defraying the expenses of such local establishments and objects of public charge, as form no part of his Majesty's civil government, and are not connected with the administration of justice.

He did not, however, flatter himself that there would be any such surplus: he therefore called upon the assembly for the supply necessary for defraying the several expenses of those different local establishments, and objects of public charge to which he had referred, and which, as appeared by the expenditure of last year, laid before the assembly in this session, would amount to about £30,000, including the expenses of the legislature, and the collection of the public revenue—that he deemed it his indispensable duty to add, that if these supplies were not granted, he would have no means to defray the expenses of these local establishments and objects of public charge, except where payment had been provided by specific appropriations.

The assembly by an address to the Governor, thanked him for his message, assuring him that they had received with the greatest satisfaction his declaration, that he had not put in question the constitutional principles, that the public money should be applied only conformably to law: and expressing—" deep regret that the standing rules adopted by the legislative council, in the preceding month of March, and still acted upon by that body, in manifest violation of the constitutional rights of the assembly, of advising his Majesty by bill, in such manner as they might judge best and most conducive to the peace, welfare and good government of the province, and particularly with regard to money bills, prevented the house from entertaining at present, any hope that its invariable disposition to provide for the necessary expenses of his Majesty's civil government in this province, could have its proper and legal effect." They concluded by assuring his excellency, " that the house, as soon as it should have been left in the full enjoyment of its rights and privileges, and his excellency have communicated to the house his Majesty's gracious acceptance of the renewed offer of the house to vote annually all the expenses of of his civil government in this province, would not fail, in the faithful discharge of its obligations, having regard to that just economy which the present circumstances of the province imperiously demand."

The governor, in reply to the address, simply expressed his " most sincere regret that the house of assembly should have thus resolved to grant no supply, nor means by which the expenses of the local establishments or objects of public charge in the province could be paid that year."

The assembly wound up the business of the session by a series of resolutions declaratory of their views, with respect to the financial misunderstanding with Upper Canada. A negotiation had, in the course of the previous summer, been carried on at Montreal, by commissioners on the part of both provinces, which was broken off; those of Lower Canada considering the claims of the upper province for the proportion of drawbacks on dutiable goods imported into Lower, and passing thence into Upper Canada, inordinate: while those of Upper Canada complained of the evasion and injustice done that province, by the commissioners on the part of Lower Canada. By the last agreement that had been entered into,* one fifth of the whole duties raised in Lower Canada was allowed the upper province, the expenses of collection first deducted. A

---

* 1st May, 1817. This was ratified in the session of 1818, and expired on the 1st July, 1819.

greater proportion was now claimed, besides certain arrears to the amount of £30,000. which the commissioners of Lower Canada refused.

The legislature of Upper Canada, thinking that province aggrieved, in the result of the negotiations with the commissioners of this province,* took early measures to bring the subject under consideration of the imperial government. An agent was appointed, pursuant to an act passed for the purpose, and a suitable appropriation made to defray the expenses of his voyage to England. Notice of this measure was officially forwarded to the government of Lower Canada, but came too late for the session, which was prorogued on the 18th of February. The governor observed:—

" That on a full consideration of the situation of affairs, and of the peculiar circumstances which had led to it, he was satisfied that no benefit to the public could be expected from a continuance of the session, and he had therefore determined to prorogue the provincial parliament."

He expressed his " regret that it should have been thought proper to have recourse to the unusual practice of withholding the necessary supplies," but observed (sarcastically:)— that whatever might have been the intention of that measure, he was happy to state that it would not at all affect the administration of his Majesty's civil government, or of justice, or the officers employed in either of those departments —That the effects would fall entirely on the local establishments, and he felt highly injurious to the interests of his Majesty's loyal and faithful subjects in this province."

* These were Mr. Papineau, Mr. Cuvillier, Mr. Neilson, Mr. Davidson, and Mr. Garden, all members of the assembly, and named by it in the act under which they were to negotiate. The commissioners for Upper Canada, were appointed by the executive government, under an act of the legislature of that province.

"The proceedings which have led to this measure,"—said his lordship,—"have afforded me the greatest satisfaction of knowing that the legislative council of this province, duly appreciate the important duties of their elevated station. Their conduct has assured me that his Majesty may rest confident of their firm support, in maintaining the true principles of the constitution and the just rights of the crown; so also it will be the object of my constant study to maintain these, and to employ the powers entrusted to me by his Majesty to the only end for which they were given;—the good of his subjects."

The lieutenant governor of the province, sir Francis N. Burton, arrived at Quebec early in July, from England; in consequence of the remonstrances of the assembly, at the previous session, and on the fifth of the month was sworn into office.

The state in which the proceedings of the last session had left the affairs of the province, and the disputed claims of Upper Canada on the lower province, urged the government at home to take steps as well of coercion, as for adjustment of the financial difficulties between them. A legislative union of the two provinces was also resolved upon, as a measure of necessity, and a bill accordingly was introduced in the house of commons for that purpose, and the settlement of the other matters.

That part of the bill which related to the union being warmly opposed in the house of commons, as unnecessarily interfering with both provinces, was relinquished by the minister until the sense of their inhabitants could be ascertained. The bill divested of this measure, was passed in parliament, and became a law, afterwards known as "the Canada trade act." By it every essential claim of Upper Canada was awarded, and with a view of securing it in future against the caprice of, and sustaining wrong from the assembly of Lower Canada, all the duties which, at the time of the expiration of the last agreement* between the two provinces, were payable under acts of the legislature of Lower Canada, on the importation of goods into it, were permanently continued. The two temporary provincial acts previously noticed, (including that which the assembly had previously suffered to expire, being also revived by the imperial act,) consequently became permanent laws, liable always to be repealed or altered by act of the legislature of Lower Canada, in case such repeal or alteration should meet with the concurrence and sanction of the legislature of Upper Canada.

Nor did the act stop here. It disabled the legislature of Lower Canada, from imposing new duties on articles imported by sea into this province, unless with the sanction of the legislature of Upper Canada, or unless the bill passed for the purpose should have been laid before the imperial parliament and the royal assent obtained. Thus were the schemes for impoverishing the treasury and reducing the executive to dependence on the assembly, not only frustrated, but the assembly itself, in jus-

---
* 1st July, 1819.

tice to the adjoining province, restrained in the exercise of its legislative powers in matters of finance.

One very important provision of the act was the power it gave of commuting, by transaction with the crown, the seigniorial or feudal tenure into that of free and common soccage. This, the first blow to the prostration of that servile and unenglish tenure in Lower Canada, was, however, far from being satisfactory to the most of those, the canadians of french origin, supposed to be oppressed by it, being held up to them as an undue interference by the imperial parliament, an encroachment on the rights of the local legislature, and consequently a grievance. This enactment was said to have been at the instance of Mr. Ellice, proprietor of the seigniory of Beauharnois, a member of the house of commons.

The intended union, when made known in Lower Canada, produced great excitement, as a project interfering with the *national* rights of the people, particularly those of french origin. The Canada trade act was considered of little or no importance contrasted with the mischief anticipated from the extinguishment of the influence and ascendency which the population of french descent maintained under the existing constitution, in the legislature of the province, and of which, those of british birth and descent in it, now began loudly to complain, as opposed to and prejudicial to improvement, and to the introduction of british enterprise and capital.

It was proposed by the union bill, to unite the legislatures of both Canadas, under the style or denomination of "*The Legislative Council and Assembly of the Canadas.*" The governor was to have been authorised to erect the townships hitherto unrepresented, into counties, each to consist of not less than six townships, and to return a member to the assembly. The whole number of representatives for each province, was not to exceed sixty. As a qualification, each member was to be possessed of a freehold in *fief* or in *roture*, of the clear value of £500 sterling, over and above all incumbrances. Two members of each of the executive councils of either province, were, in virtue of an appointment under the hand and seal of the governor, to take seats in the assembly, with the right of taking part in the debates, but not to vote. The assembly was to be quinquennial. Neither of the two houses was to be capable of imprisoning for breach of privilege, any of his Majesty's subjects not being members, or officers, or servants of the house, until an act were passed by the legislature, declaratory of the privileges of those bodies in this respect. All written proceedings of the legislative council and assembly were to be in the english language only, and at the expiration of fifteen years after the union, all debates in those bodies were to be carried on solely in english. The free exercise of the roman catholic religion, was respected, subject to the king's supremacy, and to the collation or induction into cures, a privilege of which the bishop superintending the catholic church in this province, had been heretofore, (as he still is,) left in the enjoyment. This circumstance seeming to the clergy a grievous interference with their church, gave umbrage to the body, who accordingly declaimed against the bill.

Resolutions, for and against the union, were adopted at public meetings held for the purpose. The canadians of french descent, were almost to a man anti-unionists; those of british origin were, for the greatest part, unionists.— Party spirit ran high, and all other political animosities seemed confounded in this matter, in which the attention of both parties was, for the present, wholly engrossed. The unionists in their petitions complained in strong terms of the grievances under which the inhabitants of british birth and descent laboured, by reason of the inveterate prejudices and systematic opposition of the french canadians, having the ascendency in the legislature of the province, to all improvements of a nature to encourage the introduction of british capital and enterprise.— That instead of using their ascendency to assimilate the province with the parent state, they abused it in checking every thing of a tendency in that direction, recommended by the government or solicited by petition; and that they only desired to maintain their power, that they might the more effectually retard the assimilation of the laws, language, institutions and feelings of the province, with those of England.—They were represented as anti-british and french at core, and the strong policy of prostrating at a single and determined blow, the ascendency complained of, and thereby of altering the gallic and foreign aspect of the province, was recommended and solicited.

That from Montreal, excelled all others in asperity. It condemned the policy that prompted the british government to divide the province of Quebec into two provinces, whereby " the english population in Lower Canada, was rendered inefficient, from the comparative smallness of their numbers, and the whole power of the representative branch of the government was given to the french canadians." —It represented that " the french canadian population, for a short period of time after the adoption of the present constitution, partly from incapacity to exercise the political powers with which they had become invested, and partly from some remaining deference for their english fellow subjects, used their ascendency with moderation, but this disposition was not of long continuance, and soon yielded to inveterate anti-british, and anti-commercial prejudices, by which they have not ceased to be actuated."

It was represented that " all commercial enterprise and improvement had been crippled and obstructed, and that the country remained with all the foreign characteristics which it possessed at the time of the conquest, that is, in all particulars, french."

"Without a union",—it was said,—" this population must retain its present ascendency in the government of the country, and will not of course, of its own accord, cease to be french.—Its progressive increase under the fostering protection of Great Britain, will, therefore, necessarily lead to a result, which, without a union, is anticipated." They added that they " could not omit to notice that the unreasonable extent of political rights which had been conceded to this population, to the prejudice of their fellow subjects of british origin, together with a sense of their growing strength, has already had the effect of realising, in the imagination of many of them, their fancied existence as a separate nation, under the name of the " *nation canadienne,*" implying pretensions not more irreconcilable with the rights of their fellow subjects, than with a just subordination to the parent state." They therefore " respectfully submitted, whether a system of government which had had such effects, and which in its ulterior consequences must expose Great Britain to the mortification and disgrace of having, at immense expense, reared to the maturity of independence, a foreign conquered colony, to become the ally of a foreign nation, and the scourge of its native subjects and their dependants, ought to be persisted in."

Almost every township and settlement, as well as the cities and towns, in which there were inhabitants of british birth or descent, prepared separate petitions to the king and parliament on the subject; but the anti-unionists proceeded with greater unity and system than their adversaries, and indeed, with a moderation of language at least, in their petition, which, in some instances the latter, in the heat of party spirit, lost sight of altogether. A public meeting was held at Montreal, on the 7th October, and at Quebec another on the 14th of the same month, by the anti-unionists. At the former, a committee of seventeen, and at the latter place another committee of thirty members were appointed to prepare petitions against the union. That of Montreal consisted wholly of french canadians; in that of Quebec there was a sprinkling of anglo-canadians, and persons of british birth.

These committees, styling themselves "*constitutional committees*," corresponded together, and concluded upon an address to the king and parliament, in the name of the inhabitants of the province, deprecating the intended legislative union of the Canadas. Messengers were dispatched throughout the country parishes for the purpose of obtaining subscribers. The signatures and *crosses* obtained from the various parts of the province amounted, as it was stated, to about sixty thousand in all. Mr. John Neilson, of Quebec, was deputed, on the part of the Quebec committee, and Mr. Papineau, speaker of the assembly, on the part of that of Montreal, to take home the address. Mr.

<small>Chap. XXIII. 1822.</small>

James Stuart was appointed by the unionists to carry home their petitions. These gentlemen accordingly proceeded to England, by way of New York, early in the winter, so as to be in time for the opening of parliament. The committee of anti-unionists at Quebec, while the petitions were in progress, addressed printed circulars to several members of the british house of commons, requesting that all proceedings with respect to the intended union might be stayed, until their petition should reach England, and be laid before parliament.

The governor, in this matter, kept aloof, patronising neither of the parties, but giving to those who went to England, with their respective petitions, letters of introduction to the colonial minister.

The Eastern Townships, hitherto unrepresented in the legislature and virtually excluded from it, very generally expressed themselves in favor of the union. The following are instances of their views of the subject:—

At a meeting of the inhabitants of St. Armand, it was resolved,—

" That this meeting has observed with the greatest satisfaction, the disposition that prevails in his Majesty's government, to apply an effectual remedy to existing political evils in the provinces of Canada, by uniting them under one legislature.

" That in the opinion of this meeting, the proposed measure of a union, is not more imperiously demanded, by the respective interests of the two provinces, which, from local situation and other circumstances, are interwoven, than by those of the mother country, which, without this salutary measure, must continue to be counteracted by national prejudices, habits and dispositions, proceeding from the foreign origin of a part of the population..

" That the inhabitants of the townships of Lower Canada, composed of loyalists and the descendants of native british subjects, under the existing constitution of the legislature of the province, have not only been debarred from the exercise of the political rights belonging to british subjects, but have been in a great measure excluded from the benefits of civil government, in consequence of the utter disregard of their wants, as well as their rights, by the majority of that legislature.

" That this meeting are of opinion that, without the benefit of the proposed union, the industry and enterprise of the inhabitants of the townships will continue to be crippled and rendered unavailing and unproductive to this province, and to the mother country, with the humiliating and painful prospect, in the view of the present inhabitants, that their posterity may be doomed to acquire the language and assume the manners and character of a foreign people.

That it is the opinion of this meeting, that the proposed union would, in its consequences, gradually remove the prejudices and distinctive marks which now divide the population of Lower Canada, and render its inhabitants one people, united by their principles, institutions and manners, as they are by their interest.

" That it is the anxious wish of the inhabitants of the townships, when admitted by their representatives to a fair participation in the colonial government, to coalesce with the rest of the population of this province, without distinctions of any kind; and as they have done in time past, demonstrate, not in words, but by their conduct, the invariable loyalty and attachment to his Majesty's government, by which they have never ceased to be actuated.

At a meeting of the inhabitants of Grantham, it was resolved,—

" That in the opinion of this meeting, the union of the legislatures of Upper and Lower Canada, proposed by his Majesty's ministers, during the last session of the imperial parliament, is highly expedient not only for the security, improvement and extensive settlement of both provinces, as british colonies, but likewise as the mildest remedy for the intolerable political evils, which, during thirty years, have prevailed in this province.

" That in the opinion of this meeting, the said measure will produce a salutary change in the composition of the house of assembly, which body, under the present constitution, chiefly consists of members of french origin, who, founding their political power as well as their expectations of private interest on the national prejudices of their uneducated countrymen, have studiously discouraged the settlement of Lower Canada, by emigrants of a different origin, possessing the enterprise, perseverance and knowledge which qualify them for the improvement of the country, developing its commercial resources, and rendering it a useful and creditable appendage to the british empire.

" That the Eastern Townships, containing a numerous, educated, and increasing population, are, nevertheless, without a single voice in the provincial legislature, and have likewise, in a great degree, been debarred from the benefits of the civil government; and their wants and their rights have been utterly neglected by the french canadian majority, who have treated their complaints and humble petitions, with opprobrious ridicule or silent contempt.

" That besides regarding the proposed union as the means of speedily relieving these townships from the intolerable privations and political evils under which they labour, this meeting consider it as a proof of

Chap.
XXIII.
1822.

the liberal policy and enlightened wisdom of the british government, being eminently calculated to remove national prejudices derived from difference of origin, and to consolidate the whole population of both provinces into one homogeneous mass, animated by the same views for the public interest, and the same sentiments of loyalty towards their common sovereign."

These may be taken as expressive of the views of the universality of the inhabitants of british origin in those townships. Meetings in support of the intended union were also held in the townships of Hatley, Shefford, Farnham, Stukely, Granby, and West Bolton, Odelltown, and Caldwell Manor, and at various places in Upper Canada. The unionists in Quebec, more reasonable and just in their views perhaps, than those in any other part of the province, in petitioning parliament, expressed themselves as follows :—

" As the re-union of the two provinces has been proposed in the imperial parliament, they beg leave to express their entire acquiescence in the adoption of that measure, upon such principles as shall secure to all classes of his Majesty's subjects in these provinces, their just rights, and protect the whole in the enjoyment of existing laws and their religion as guaranteed—such a union would, in the opinion of your petitioners, afford the most effectual remedy for existing evils, as it would tend gradually to assimilate the whole population in opinions, habits and feelings, and afford a reasonable hope that the wisdom of the united legislature would devise a system of government of more consistency and unity, and of greater liberality to all classes than has hitherto been experienced.

" A union on the equitable principles humbly suggested by his Majesty's petitioners, will necessarily include a representation proportionate, as near as possible, to the numbers, wealth, and resources of the different classes of inhabitants of these provinces ;—will require no innovation in the laws or religion of the country, nor proscription in debate or motion in the legislature, of the language of any portion of the inhabitants, in every class of whom, bravery and loyalty have been evinced as fellow soldiers in defence of the province."

The petition from the town and district of Three Rivers, contained the following passages :—

" Your petitioners are impressed with a firm conviction that the present organization of the province of Lower Canada, and that of its house of assembly, are of a nature and composition too heterogeneous ever to assimilate its population in manners, customs, language, or feeling. That invidious distinctions, and asperities are the natural consequences which must arise, and ever continue to flow, from these causes. That no fair and equal portion of british feeling, or interest is ever likely to be created, or maintained in the popular branch of the legislature, during the continuance of the present state of things.

" That it is our firm conviction that these and many other evils of vital detriment to the growing prosperity of both provinces, originate primarily from the injudicious sub-division of the late province of

Quebec, into two provinces, with distinct and separate governments.

"To enable your Majesty to form a correct opinion of the truth and justice of the foregoing facts, the consequence of which we, your Majesty's loyal subjects of this district, in common with all the british part of the province, so oppressively feel; it may, perhaps, be in itself sufficient and conclusive to point out, that out of fifty members constituting the house of assembly of Lower Canada, one-fifth part only are of british origin or language, and that this branch of the legislature is almost exclusively returned by uneducated farmers and peasantry, always actuated upon by a few of the influencing leaders among their countrymen, thus forming a mass of influence, rarely, if ever exercised in unison with the wishes of the government, or of the british part of the community, insomuch that the progress of improvement and amelioration is greatly retarded ;—the benefits of an immense and valuable emigration from the mother country altogether lost by discouragement, and commerce languid and unimportant.

"A further conviction of the necessity of a reunion must, we presume, occur to your Majesty, from the utter impracticability of deriving any adequate means for an equable subdivision and participation of the revenue, to be derived from the import and transit of of goods (for which Quebec alone can ever be the port of entry from the sea) capable of reconciling the interests of the divided provinces, in a satisfactory manner."

Besides the passages quoted above, from the petition of the unionists at Montreal, were the following :—

"In adverting to the injurious consequences arising from the division of the late province of Quebec, your petitioners cannot omit to notice more particularly the effect that measure has had in preventing the increase of the british population in Lower Canada, and the development of its resources. The predominance of the french population in the legislature has occasioned obstacles to the settlement of british emigrants that have not been surmounted; so that the vast increase of british population to have been expected, from this cause has been, in a great degree, prevented. The injury sustained in this particular, may be easily appreciated, when it is observed that, since the late american war, upwards of 80,000 souls (that is, a number equal to one-fourth of the actual french population) have found their way to this province from Great Britain and Ireland; and of those scarcely one-twentieth part remain within its limits, the rest, with the exception of a small number who have settled in Upper Canada, having been induced, by the foreign character of the country in which they had sought an asylum, and the discouragements they experienced, to try their fortune in the United States. The loss thus sustained is not confined to those who left the country, but comprises their connexions and friends who would have followed them.

"In the same proportion as the increase of british population has been prevented, has the agricultural and commercial prosperity of the country been retarded and obstructed; as it is to the enterprise, intelligence, and persevering industry of that population, that both agriculture and commerce must be principally indebted for their advancement. On this head it may be fairly advanced that, had not the impolitic division of the late province of Quebec taken place, and had a fit plan of representation been adopted, the british population would now exceed the french, and the imports and exports of the country be greatly beyond their present amount."

The petition drawn up by the committees of the districts of Quebec and Montreal, against the union, was temperate and well reasoned. The following are extracts from it:—

" That your petitioners have learnt, with the most profound grief and the greatest alarm, that a bill was introduced, with the sanction of your Majesty's servants, in the honorable house of commons, at the last session of the parliament of the United Kingdom, for making changes in the constitution of the government in this province, as by the statute 31st Geo. III., chap. 31st, happily established therein.

" That inasmuch as by reason of the near approach of the time when parliament may be assembled, the legislature of this province may be deprived of the opportunity which the commons, in their wisdom and justice, proposed to afford to the people of this province, of submitting to your Majesty and to the two houses of parliament, their sentiments on this momentous subject, your petitioners conceive it to be their duty to your Majesty and to themselves, most humbly and with the least possible delay, to lay their representations on the subject of the same bill at the foot of your Majesty's throne.

" That no alteration in the aforesaid statute had, at any time, been, publicly, prayed for, by any of the authorities constituted under it, or by any portion of your Majesty's subjects residing in this province; but on the contrary, all classes and descriptions of people therein, have uniformly expressed their inviolable attachment to the said constitution, and have but recently, cheerfully hazarded their lives and fortunes in defence of your Majesty's government, as established by the said statute in this province.

" That the said statute was granted to your Majesty's subjects in this province, conformably to the royal promise contained in the proclamation of the 7th October, 1763, after various petitions for, and against the proposed measure, from the different descriptions of persons whose interests were to be affected thereby, after a royal message to parliament recommending the division of the province, and after a hearing at the bar of the honorable the house of commons, whereby the said act was received and justly regarded by all your Majesty's subjects in these parts of your dominions, as a solemn compact, forming, by the highest authority in the british empire, the legal and permanent guarantee of their liberty, their property and dearest rights.

" That the said statute, modelled upon the constitution of the parent state, by some of the best and wisest of her statesmen, provides sufficient powers for the remedying of abuses, redressing of grievances, allaying discontents and promoting the general welfare of the province, without the necessity of those legislative interferences on the part of the supreme government, which, in similar cases, have been found so pernicious, by transforming discontents, purely local and temporary, into dangerous misunderstandings between the colonies and the mother country.

"That notwithstanding various obstacles and difficulties, which the powers and operation of the constitution, established by the said statute, are gradually removing, the population of this province has been progressive in a ratio fully equal to that of the United States of America, without a proportionate increase from emigration; the public revenue has proved nearly sufficient to cover all the necessary colonial expenditure, and trade and agriculture, notwithstanding the extraordinary pressure of the times have, in the aggregate, greatly improved.

P. S.—The following letter, hitherto unpublished, from sir George Prevost, to earl Bathurst, will be read with interest. Its proper place would have been in page 249, while on the subject of the expedition to Plattsburgh; but we were not possessed of it when that matter was put to press. It feelingly expresses sir George Prevost's conviction of the necessity of the course he adopted after the loss of the fleet, and may, in some sort, be considered as his vindication on the occasion:—

"Head Quarters, Montreal, 6th October, 1814.
"No. 20.

"My lord,—On my return to Montreal, I met a messenger bringing your lordship's despatch, No. 75, of the 22d August.

"I read with deep concern, and was particularly sensible to that part of it which apprises me that the expectations of his royal highness the Prince Regent, and of the country, would be seriously disappointed should I allow the present campaign to close, without having undertaken any offensive measure against the enemy. Your lordship is aware to what extent I have acted, under that impression, and how completely my views have been frustrated by the failure of our naval means in the very outset of my endeavours.

"With whatever sorrow I may think of the unfortunate occurrences to which I allude, I consider them as light and trivial when compared to the disastrous results which I am solemnly persuaded would have ensued, had any consideration of personal glory, or any unreflecting disregard of the safety of the province, or the honor of the army entrusted to my charge, induced me to pursue those offensive operations by land, (independent of the fleet) which it would appear, by your lordship's despatch, were expected of me. Such operations, my lord, have been attempted before, and on the same ground. The history of our country records their failure, and had they been undertaken again with double the force placed under my command, they would have issued in the discomfiture of his Majesty's arms, and in a defeat not more disastrous than inevitable.

"My lord, having attained the eminence on which I now stand, by unwearied exertions through the course of many years, to discharge faithfully my obligations to my king and country, and having always endeavoured to act a proper part, with firmness and constancy, I confess that the purport of your lordship's last communication has pro-

Chap. duced an agony of mind indescribable.—Placed in a comman[d]
XXIII. more unprecedented in extent than in difficulties—surrounded b[y]
barrassments of which no local information possessed by you[r]
1822. ship can give a full idea. since they arise fresh around me with
succeeding day ; and called upon to fulfil expectations incons[istent]
with the situation of the country, while, at the same time, I ha[ve to]
contend with ancient prejudices and false opinions long enterta[ined.]
I have firmly encountered all and conquered much. I have sh[runk]
from no exertion, personal or mental,—and now, though distant [from]
the scene where my conduct will be judged, I rest in the full co[nvic]tion that it will be viewed with fairness and candour, and will, [in the]
end, be found to have conduced to the best interests of our cou[ntry.]
" I have the honor, &c.

      (Signed)   " GEO. PREVOST.'
" To the right honorable the earl BATHURST."

That sir George Prevost, in giving orders to retire when he [did]
from before Plattsburgh, conscientiously believed he was doing [what]
was best for his country, though at the expense of his own popu[larity]
for the moment, abundant proof, it seems, could be adduced. [One]
fact that can be vouched for, that to a most intimate friend h[e de]clared, after the Plattsburgh affair, and before he was ordered h[ome,]
that on the night of the day when he recalled the troops fro[m the]
attack, and ordered a retreat, though foreseeing full well all the o[dium]
and temporary loss of reputation that would come upon him, in [con]sequence of it, he laid his head upon his pillow with the tra[nquil]
satisfaction that he had done what was right in sparing the u[seless]
effusion of blood.

Emigrants from the United Kingdom landed at Quebec—
  in 1821,............... 8,056
    1822,...............10,470

END OF THE SECOND VOLUME.
15th May, 1848.

www.ingramcontent.com/pod-product-compliance
Lightning Source LLC
Chambersburg PA
CBHW022124290426
44112CB00008B/796